CHRONIC ILLNESS AND DISABILITY

FAMILIES IN TROUBLE SERIES

**Series Editors: CATHERINE S. CHILMAN,
ELAM W. NUNNALLY, FRED M. COX**
all at University of Wisconsin—Milwaukee

Families in Trouble Series is an edited five-volume set designed to enhance the understanding and skills of human services professionals in such fields as social work, clinical psychology, education, health, counseling, and family therapy. Written by recognized scholars from several academic disciplines, this impressive series provides practice guidelines, state-of-the-art research, and implications for public policies from a family systems perspective. No other book or integrated series of books provides such an authoritative overview of information about the wide range of economic, employment, physical, behavioral, and relational problems and lifestyles that commonly affect today's families.

VOLUMES IN THIS SERIES:

Volume 1
Employment and Economic Problems

Volume 2
Chronic Illness and Disability

Volume 3
Troubled Relationships

Volume 4
**Mental Illness, Delinquency,
Addictions, and Neglect**

Volume 5
Variant Family Forms

CHRONIC ILLNESS AND DISABILITY

Families in Trouble Series, Volume 2

Edited by:
Catherine S. Chilman
Elam W. Nunnally
Fred M. Cox

WITHDRAW

SAGE PUBLICATIONS
The Publishers of Professional Social Science
Newbury Park   Beverly Hills   London   New Delhi

To our spouses, children, and grandchildren

For information address:

SAGE Publications, Inc.
2111 West Hillcrest Drive
Newbury Park, California 91320

SAGE Publications Inc.   SAGE Publications Ltd.
275 South Beverly Drive   28 Banner Street
Beverly Hills   London EC1Y 8QE
California 90212   England

SAGE PUBLICATIONS India Pvt. Ltd.
M-32 Market
Greater Kailash I
New Delhi 110 048 India

Printed in the United States of America

Library of Congress Cataloging-in-Publication Data

Families in trouble : knowledge and practice perspectives for
  professionals in the human services / edited by Catherine S.
  Chilman, Fred M. Cox, Elam W. Nunnally.
    p. cm.
  Includes bibliographies and indexes.
    Contents: v. 1. Employment and economic problems—v. 2. Chronic
illness and disability—v. 3. Troubled relationships—v.
4. Mental illness, delinquency, addictions, and neglect—v.
5. Variant family forms.
    ISBN 0-8039-2703-7 (v. 2) ISBN 0-8039-2704-5
(pbk.: v. 2)
    1. Problem families—United States.   2. Family social work—United
States.   3. Problem families—Counseling of—United States.
4. Problem families—Government policy—United States.   I. Chilman,
Catherine S.   II. Cox, Fred M.   III. Nunnally, Elam W.
HV699.F316   1988   88-6539
362.8′2′0973—dc19   CIP

FIRST PRINTING 1988

Contents

Introduction to the Series

CATHERINE S. CHILMAN, FRED M. COX,
and ELAM W. NUNNALLY

MAJOR PURPOSES AND CONCEPTS

The major purpose of this series of books is to enhance the understanding and skills of human services professionals in such fields as social work, education, health, counseling, clinical psychology, and family therapy so that they can more effectively assist families in trouble. There is no need to elaborate here that many of today's families are in serious trouble, as rising rates of divorce, unmarried parenthood, poverty, and family violence suggest. The stresses imposed by a rapidly changing society are creating severe strains for families and their members. There are also positive aspects of these changes, however, including improved health care and freedom from backbreaking toil, as well as increasing knowledge about family-related problems and ways to minimize them.

Thus, to reduce the negatives that are afflicting families and to enhance the positives, it is important to marshal the social and psychological knowledge and practice wisdom now available to enrich professional family-related practice, policies, and programs. The editors fully recognize that current knowledge is all to meager; much more needs to be developed. However, let us use the knowledge we do have while the search for more continues.

This series proposes to function as a basic knowledge, theory, and practice resource of the highest scholarly and professional quality. It is directed to practitioners and graduate students in the human service professions who work with troubled families. It emphasizes families in trouble, rather than families in general. As far as the editors can ascertain, no other book or integrated series of books combines an authoritative overview of information about the wide range of economic, employment, physical, behavioral, and relational problems and life styles that commonly affect today's families.[1]

This is especially true with respect to books that link up-to-date, research-based knowledge about common family-related problems to implications both for clinical practice and for policy and program development and implementation. For the most part, publications and curricula for the human services tend to be presented in discrete,

7

specialized units. In the family field, for instance, knowledge from the social and behavioral sciences is often presented in a separate course with its own texts that emphasize basic knowledge and theory, with little or no mention of the applications of this knowledge and theory to professional practice. Quite different courses and texts deal with clinical practice applications, often with little reference to the related knowledge and theory base. Another set of courses and texts deals with planning and policy strategies for programs to meet individual and family needs with little reference either to clinical practice techniques or to basic knowledge and theory foundations on which program and policy development should rest.

Thus, professionals tend to have serious difficulty forming clear links along the continuum of theory, knowledge, policies, programs, and clinical practice. Yet professional services cannot be adequately designed and delivered unless these links are made and applied, in an integrated way, to meeting the needs of families and their members.

FAMILY SYSTEMS PERSPECTIVE

A family systems perspective forms the fundamental conceptual scheme of this series. Families are seen as small, open systems, deeply affected by their internal, interpersonal dynamics and by the many aspects of the external environment with which they interact. From the internal dynamics perspective, everything that happens to one member of the family affects all members. The internal systems of families can vary in a number of ways, some of them dysfunctional. For example, the members of some families are so tightly and rigidly interconnected, or "fused," that members have virtually no sense of personal identity. Flexible changes of family patterns in order to meet changing conditions from within and from outside the family then become virtually impossible. Moreover, in such instances individual family members find they cannot extricate themselves from the poorly functioning family system.

In addition, some families form dysfunctional subsystems, such as a closed partnership between a father and son in competition with a closed mother-daughter partnership. Such alignments tend to undermine the parents' marriage and the development of sons and daughters as maturing individuals.

Some families with interpersonal problems, such as poor husband-wife relationships, deny their real difficulties and displace them onto another family member, such as a child, who may then become the problem-laden scapegoat for both parents.

There are many other variations on the internal systems theme, briefly sketched here. The chief point is that efforts aimed at treating individual members of families are often fruitless unless the operation of the whole family system is better understood and included in treatment plans, as well as in programs and policies. Moreover, individual treatment, without regard to family system dynamics, may increase rather than decrease the problems of the whole system and its members.

In seeking to understand family systems, it is also important to study the many "family actors"—older, middle, and younger generations and interactive members of the extended family such as grandparents, aunts, uncles, brothers, sisters, step-relations, former spouses, and close friends.

It is also essential to consider the development of families and their dynamics over the life span, with the recognition that family interactions, concerns, and tasks vary at different life cycle stages and crucial transition points such as marriage, child birth, launching children into schools and jobs, retirement, illness, and death.

Family structures and life styles vary, especially at this time in society when a variety of family forms is becoming more common, including single-parent, divorced, widowed, separated, reconstituted, gay or lesbian, extended, foster and adoptive, and two-career families; cohabiting, never-married couples who may also have children; childless couples; and, of course, the traditional two-parent nuclear family with one or more children. These various family forms each have their own particular strengths and vulnerabilities.

When families have particular problems such as unemployment, low income, chronic physical illness, death of a member, chemical dependency, mental illness, conflict with the law, and so on, their strengths are likely to be seriously undermined. The nature and extent of the stresses they experience will be affected by a number of factors, including family system characteristics and family developmental stage. It is crucially important, therefore, to consider family-related problems, such as those mentioned above, in a family-focused context rather than in the more usual framework that seeks to treat or plan for individuals without appropriate consideration and understanding of the complexities of family dynamics, both internal and external.

External factors affecting families are all to frequently overlooked or brushed aside by human service professionals, especially those in clinical practice. Viewing families ecologically, as open systems, leads to the recognition that many factors in the environment have a strong impact on them. These factors include the state of the economy, employment conditions, the availability of needed resources in the community, racism and other forms of discrimination, and so forth. When environmental conditions are adverse and community resources are inadequate, the stresses on families escalate, especially for families of relatively low income and low educational and occupational status. It then becomes the responsibility of professionals to help vulnerable families develop strategies to deal more effectively with these stresses. Professionals may also need to serve as advocates to assist families in obtaining available resources and to work with other local, state, and national groups to promote improved conditions and resources.

In light of the above, the proposed series includes overview chapters about existing and needed policies and programs that are directed toward more effective problem management in support of family well-being. It is hoped that this material will serve as a stimulus and information base for professionals in their larger community responsibilities.

CONTENT

With these purposes and concepts in mind, the editors offer a series of five books, each of which has the following underlying structure (a) research-based theory and knowledge about each topic, (b) suggested guidelines for methods of family-centered practice, and (c) implications for public programs and policy. At our invitation, recognized specialists from their respective fields have prepared chapters dealing with particular aspects of this overall plan. Specific problem areas that are often associated with trouble for families are covered in the five books: Volume 1, employment and income; Volume 2, physical illness and disabilities; Volume 3, disturbed family relationships; Volume 4, behavior that the community finds unacceptable; and Volume 5, participation in alternative family forms that are sometimes accompanied by difficulties for the families involved.

We recognize that not all problem topics are covered. Space constraints require that we select a set of subjects that seem to be most widespread and most apt to be related to serious troubles for families. We also do not cover all major methods of human service delivery. Our discussion is limited, for the most part, to methods of direct practice in the provision of social and psychological services. The reasons for this limitation are (a) the editors' expertise lies in the social-psychological area, (b) we believe these practice approaches to be of major importance in assisting families, and (c) the majority of human service professionals today are in direct practice.

Although we believe the methods of social planning, administration, and legislative advocacy, to name a few, also are essential to the human services enterprise, adequate coverage of these topics is beyond the scope of the present series.

UNDERLYING CONCEPTS

Definition of the Family

We define a family to mean two or more people in a committed relationship from which they derive a sense of identity as a family. This definition permits us to include many non-traditional family forms that are outside the traditional legal perspective, including families not related by blood, marriage, or adoption. This broad definition is essential if we are to recognize the full variety of family forms found in modern society.

"Families in Trouble" vs. "Troubled Families"

We begin with the premise that most, if not all, families are apt to encounter stresses at one time or another in their lives. Owing to these stresses they may, from time to time, be "in trouble." This concept is quite different from that which proposes that some families are inherently troubled, largely because of their own internal problems.

We build on the work of such systems theorists as Bertalanffy (1968), and Bateson (1972, 1979); family stress and coping theorists such as Hill (1949), Olson et al., (1983), and McCubbin et al., (1982); and such clinical theorists as Haley (1963, 1976), Minuchin (1974), Watzlawick, Weakland, and Fisch (1974) and Satir (1983). We amplify their concepts to develop a multi-faceted set of interrelated principles which are reflected, to one degree or another, in the various chapters.

In so doing, we weave together knowledge and theory from a number of the social, behavioral, and biological sciences and integrate them within a family systems framework. Although such a complex approach may seem overly ambitious, we believe it is important, especially if knowledge and theory about families are to be effectively applied to the fields of practice, programs, and policies.

Our basic theoretical position is that the reactions of family systems and their members to stressful experiences depends on the following major interacting factors:

(a) the nature, severity, and duration of the stress and its effects on each family member and the family structure;

(b) the perception of each member of the family system (which often includes the extended family) of what the stress is and what it means to each member in terms of that person's beliefs, values, and goals;

(c) the size and structure of the family (such as number, gender, and spacing of children); the marital status of the parents; the presence of other kin or friends in the household;

(d) the stage of family development and ages of each member;

(e) the psychological characteristics of each family member (including personality and cognitive factors);

(f) the physical characteristics of each family member (such as state of health and special physical assets and liabilities);

(g) the previous life experiences which each family member brings to the present stressor event. For instance, a series of losses of loved ones during childhood and adolescence can make a parent, as an adult, particularly sensitive to another severe illness or death;

(h) the characteristics of the family system, including the clarity or ambiguity of its boundaries, the rigidity or flexibility of behavioral patterns, the existence of sub-systems and their nature, the degree of fusion or distancing of relationships, interaction with external systems, and patterns of communication, plus social, psychological, and material resources available from within the family and its network;

(i) social, psychological, and material resources available to families from communities; this includes not only the existence of a wide variety of community services and resources that are potentially supportive of the well-being of families and their members but the recognition that families are apt to vary in their access to community resources depending on such factors as the degree of social stratification, racism, ethnocentrism, and power politics within the community.

In summary, the above formulation proposes that families are not inherently "stable" or "healthy" or conversely, "unstable," "troubled," or "sick," but that most families encounter external or internal stresses at different points in the life span of each member. These stresses vary from one family to another depending on many factors in the environment and within the family. Families also differ in their capacity to cope with these stresses; their coping capacities depend on the nature of these stresses, plus a complex of family system and structure variables together with the social, psychological, and physical characteristics of each member.

To differing degrees, human service professionals can be of important assistance to families and their members at times when stressful events threaten to overwhelm their coping capacities. This assistance may consist of direct treatment, resource mobilization, or efforts to improve public policies or programs, all central topics covered in this series. These efforts are most apt to be effective if the professional approaches her or his work objectively, rather than judgmentally, and with a high level of competence solidly based on the best available scientific knowledge and skills derived from that knowledge, also a major focus of this series.

Our choice of authors was made partly on the basis of their reputations for scholarly or clinical achievements and partly on the basis of their affinity to a systems approach to understanding families and their environments. All of our invited authors were requested to relate their contributions to a systems frame of reference. We have not excluded other theoretical views, however, and the reader will find articles which contain, for example, learning theory and behavioral concepts as well as systems thinking.

We chose a systems paradigm as the orientation for these volumes for several reasons. First, this paradigm readily permits one to view the interplay of individual, family group, and community or societal factors in understanding how troubles arise for families and how families cope. Second, the systems paradigm is hospitable to developmental analyses of families and their difficulties and strengths. Third, at this juncture some of the most fruitful research studies and most exciting clinical developments reported in the scholarly and clinical literature are systems oriented.

We have asked the authors of the various chapters to pay careful attention to the available research in their fields and to view this research in a critical fashion so that they can make distinctions between what knowledge has been clearly established, what has been only partially established, and what still exists largely in the area of clinical impressions and speculation. Although much more and better research, both basic and applied, is needed on most of the topics covered in this series, the needs of families are such that it is essential for human service professionals to proceed in the most effective way they can, on the basis of what knowledge and theory is available. It is also essential for researchers to continue with the many studies that are needed, for them to disseminate their results, and for practitioners to study the research in their fields as new information becomes available. The editors have made a serious attempt to assure that the present series brings together, in summarized and applicable form, the most pertinent, up-to-date research available on the various topics that are covered here.

TOPICS INCLUDED THROUGHOUT THE SERIES: RACISM, ETHNOCENTRISM AND SEXISM

As sketched above, each of the five books in the series deals with a set of issues that often cause trouble for families. Although the titles of each volume do not include the subjects of racism, ethnocentrism, and sexism, we recognize that these factors are of central importance and have a profound impact on the whole of our society as well as on many individual families and their members. Because these factors tend to have pervasive effects on numerous aspects of family lives, we incorporate a discussion of them as an integral part of many of the topics covered, including chapters on poverty, employment, interpersonal difficulties within families, variations in family forms, family-community conflict, and implications both for direct practice and public policies and programs.

NOTE

1. As of this writing (early 1987), there appears to be one partial exception to this statement. A recent two-volume text by McCubbin and Figley, *Stress and the Family* (1983), includes some of the topics that we have dealt with. However, the following important family-related subjects are not included in that book: poverty, long-term unemployment, alcoholism, marital and parent-child conflict, family violence, cohabitation, gay and lesbian life styles, non-marital pregnancy and parenthood, chronic illness or disability of a parent, delinquency and crime, and aging. Moreover, the material on treatment in these volumes is rather sketchy and that on programs and policy almost non-existent.

Preface

ILLNESS AND DISABILITY

Practitioners of medicine, psychology, social work, nursing, and marriage and family therapy, as well as those who are studying for professional careers in these fields, will find *Families with Physically Impaired Members* an invaluable aid in their work, as they deal with families troubled by illness and disability. As in the rest of this series, a family systems perspective is employed throughout the book, and recognized scholars in their particular fields have written the various chapters.

Several chapters discuss the impact of chronic and life-threatening illness on families. John Rolland provides a conceptual model as an aid to understanding. Joan Patterson looks at the family impact of chronic illnesses affecting children, while James Blackburn and Pauline Boss do so with respect to chronic illnesses affecting the aged. Robert Schilling and his colleagues examine the effects of developmental disabilities on families.

Other chapters are addressed to implications for treatment. Marilyn Bonjean discusses psychotherapy with families caring for mentally impaired members. Robert Schilling reviews methods of helping families deal with developmentally disabled members. William Doherty discusses treatment of families dealing with chronic physical illness.

Finally, Catherine Chilman examines public policies affecting families, including the processes of forming and changing public policy. Margaret Walkover discusses social policies and their impact on families with impaired members, with an emphasis on health policy in the private and public sectors.

This volume will be of considerable use to anyone dealing professionally with families facing the adversities of illness and disability. It takes a unique and welcome approach to viewing family health difficulties in a total family systems perspective, one that recognizes the rights as well as the responsibilities of each family member in relation to other family members and the larger community.

Acknowledgments

We extend our gratitude to a number of people whose help has been of enormous importance in the development of this five-volume series:

To the Johnson Foundation, which graciously extended the hospitality of its Wingspread Conference Center in Racine, Wisconsin, for a two-day planning meeting of most of our authors at the start of this book project.

To the Milwaukee Foundation of Milwaukee, Wisconsin, which generously provided funds to meet some of the costs of the above-named planning conference.

To Mary Ann Riggs, Word Processor Extraordinary, who, with unusual skill and pertinacity, typed many of the chapters and prepared the bibliographies in standardized formats.

To Carolyn Kott Washburne, expert technical editor, who polished the writing of each chapter promptly and efficiently.

To all of our authors who cooperated gallantly with this project and who tolerated the frequently heavy revisions suggested by the series editors who have consistently held to the ideal of a high-quality product that would be of important use to human service professionals, both as students and practitioners.

To families everywhere whose strengths and whose vulnerabilities have provided the basic inspiration for this series.

Catherine S. Chilman
Fred M. Cox
Elam W. Nunnally

A Conceptual Model of Chronic and Life-Threatening Illness and Its Impact on Families

JOHN S. ROLLAND

This chapter will offer a conceptual base for theory building, clinical practice, and research investigation in the area of chronic and life-threatening illness. This model should furnish a central reference point from which clinicians and researchers of different persuasions may forge their own trails.

For clinicians and researchers alike, the heart of all systems-oriented biopsychosocial inquiry is the focus on *interaction*. In the arena of physical illness, particularly chronic disease, one's focus of concern is the system created by the interaction of a disease with an individual, family, or other biopsychosocial system (Engel 1977, 1980). Engel conceptualized a continuum and hierarchy of natural systems that begins at the level of the smallest subatomic particle and extends sequentially through the levels of the individual, family, community, culture, nation, and total biosphere. This chapter will choose the level of family as its central point. This choice is made with the recognition that the family is a system interacting with the larger environment and that the impact of chronic illness on a family will be affected by its own economic and extended social network plus kinship resources, as well as by the quality and availability of services in this larger environment. From the perspective of clinical assessment and intervention, the family may provide the best lens through which to view these other systems.

From the family point of view, family systems theory must first include the illness system in its thinking. A graphic representation of the family/illness system created by the interface of a family facing chronic disease might look like this (Figure 1.1).

There are critical missing links in this preliminary description of the dynamic interaction between these two systems. First, there is a need for a schema that recasts the myriad biological diseases into psychosocial terms. Second, refinement and expansion of a general family systems model is needed to allow a more appropriate and comprehensive description of the interactive system created when chronic illness occurs in a family. Components of family functioning that emphasize belief systems and a longitudinal developmental perspective need elaboration.

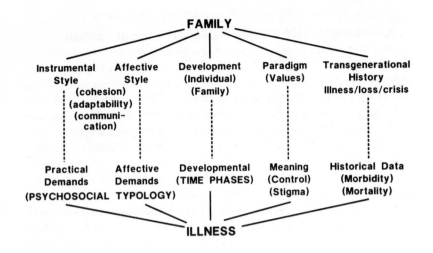

Figure 1.1. Interface of chronic illness and the family.

This chapter will offer a conceptual model and language that allows a more refined description and clinical assessment of certain salient aspects of the illness/family system. In the first section I will review the basics of a psychosocial typology of chronic and life-threatening illness (Rolland 1984, 1987). This typology will be used to represent medical diseases so that a more fluid dialogue can occur between the illness aspect and the family aspect of the illness/family system. In the second section, using the psychosocial typology as the background landscape, I will describe illness-oriented family dynamics that emphasize time and belief systems. In particular, I will discuss: the family "illness value system"; trans-generational aspects of illness, loss, and crisis; and the interface of disease with the individual and family life cycles. Integration of these two sections will provide an overall framework for assessing chronic illness in families. Finally, I will address some implications of this illness/family model for the interface of the family with the larger medical system and the community.

INTRODUCTION

In order to think in an interactive or systemic manner about the interface of the illness and the individual or the illness and the family, one needs a way of characterizing the illness itself. A schema to conceptualize chronic disease is required that remains relevant to the interactions of the psychosocial and biological worlds and provides a common metalanguage that transforms or reclassifies the usual biological language. Such a schema will facilitate coherent thinking about the system created at the interface of chronic illness with any other system. However, there are two major impediments to progress in this area. First, insufficient attention has been given to the areas of diversity and commonality inherent in different chronic illnesses. Second, the qualitative and quantitative differences in how various diseases manifest themselves over the course of the illness have been glossed over. Chronic illnesses need to be conceptualized in a manner that organizes these similarities and differences over the disease course so that the type and degree of demands relevant to psychosocial research and clinical practice are highlighted in a more useful way.

The great variability of chronic illnesses and their changing nature over time have presented a vexing problem to investigators who have attempted to identify the most salient psychosocial variables relevant to disease course or treatment compliance. Recent reviews of the psychosocial modifiers of stress emphasize a variety of methodological and conceptual weaknesses (Elliot & Eisdorfer, 1982; Kasl, 1982; Weiss et al., 1981). The difficulty originates when social scientists or psychotherapists accept a disease classification that is based on purely biological criteria that are clustered in ways to meet the needs of medicine. This nosology is more useful to establish a medical diagnosis and formulate a medical treatment plan, because in traditional medicine, the process of diagnosis and treatment planning is the primary concern. But one can argue that the problem of psychosocial research on physical illness suffers as much from a blind acceptance of this model of medicine as from its own shortcomings. A different classification scheme may provide a better link between the biological and psychosocial worlds, and, thereby, clarify the relationship between long-term illnesses and the family.

Historically, this specific-illness orientation has guided research and clinical investigations of the relationship between psychosocial factors and physical illness toward opposite ends of a continuum. Truths are sought either in each specific disease or in "illness" as a general, quasi-metaphorical concept. Findings with one disease are then indiscriminately generalized to cover all illnesses. Or, findings are held to be not generalizable and researchers study each illness in a narrow-focused way. Both of these extremes hamper the clinician. Lacking guidelines to balance unifying principles and useful distinctions, clinicians can become bewildered by the wide variety of chronic illnesses. They may apply a monolithic treatment approach to all chronic illnesses, or they may inappropriately transpose aspects of their clinical experience with psychiatric disorders. Extensive experience with a single kind of illness, such as terminal cancer, that requires intensive focus on issues of separation and loss may get transferred to a chronic illness, such as stroke, where other issues such as role reallocation predominate.

The psychosocial importance of different time phases of an illness is another dimension that is not well understood. A major reason for this in research has been the relative predominance of cross-sectional, in contrast to longitudinal, studies. Often studies include cases that vary widely in terms of the amount of time families have lived with a chronic illness (Atcherberg et al., 1977; Blumberg et al., 1954; Turk, 1964). Often separate investigations of the same disease produce conflicting results. Debates ensue without either side taking into account different time phases as a plausible explanation for conflictual results. Likewise, clinicians often become involved in the care of an individual or family coping with a chronic illness at different points in the "illness life cycle." Clinicians rarely follow the interaction of a family/illness process through the complete life history of a disease.

A few studies have explored short-range psychosocial effects on disease course. One study noted a synchronicity of emotional and behavioral factors with joint tenderness ratings in individuals with rheumatoid arthritis (Modolfsky & Chester, 1970). Others have studied diabetic and asthmatic exacerbations (Minuchin et al., 1975; Baker et al., 1975; Bradley, 1979; Hamburg et al., 1980; Matus & Bush, 1979). Minuchin, in his classic study of children with brittle diabetes, used the accepted medical correlation between a rise in blood, free fatty-acid levels and the development of diabetic exacerbations. He demonstrated a sustained rise of blood levels when the children were introduced into an interview where the parents were discussing a conflictual issue. Although these studies are important, their contributions concern microfluctuations rather than broad-scale phases of an illness (crisis, chronic, end stage, or terminal).

The importance of broad time phases of illness has surfaced periodically in the chronic illness literature. One example has been studies that examine the adaptive versus harmful role of denial, loosely defined as one's attempts at negating the existence of a problem, at different points of the disease course. For parents of a child with leukemia, denial may enable them adaptively to perform necessary duties during earlier phases of the illness but might lead to devastating consequences for the family if maintained during the terminal phase (Chodoff et al., 1964; Wolff et al., 1964). Likewise, denial may be functional for recovery on a coronary care unit after a myocardial infarction but harmful if this translates into ignoring medical advice vis-à-vis diet, exercise, and work stress over the long term (Croog et al., 1971; Hackett et al., 1968). These two examples illustrate how denial can at certain points in a long-term illness serve to reduce the potential for overwhelming affect and facilitate the accomplishment of other illness-related tasks. These studies highlight the importance of a longitudinal perspective (in this instance in relation to a particular defense mechanism—denial), but an overarching framework is not articulated.

There is a need for a model that provides a useful guide to both clinical practice and research, one that allows dynamic, open communication between these disciplines. The first section of this chapter proposes a typology of chronic or life-threatening illness. The problems of illness variability and time phases are addressed on two separate dimensions: (a) chronic illnesses are grouped according to key biological similarities and differences that dictate significantly distinct psychosocial demands for the ill individual and his or her family; and (b) the prime developmental time phases in the natural evolution of chronic disease are identified. I will complete this section by discussing some of the clinical, research, and health services delivery implications of this schema.

PSYCHOSOCIAL TYPOLOGY OF ILLNESS

Any typology of illness is by nature arbitrary. The goal of this typology is to facilitate the creation of categories for a wide array of chronic illnesses. This typology is designed not for traditional medical treatment or prognostic purposes but to examine the relationship between family or individual dynamics and chronic disease.

This typology conceptualizes broad distinctions of onset, course, outcome, and degree of incapacitation of illness. These categories are hypothesized to be the most significant at the interface of the illness and the individual or family for a broad range of diseases. Also, there is a correspondence between each of the categories—

onset, course, and outcome—and a particular temporal phase of chronic disease. While each variable is in actuality a continuum, it will be described here in a categorical manner by the selection of key anchor points along the continuum.

Onset

Illnesses can be divided into those that have either an acute or gradual onset. This division is not meant to differentiate types of biological development but to distinguish the kinds of symptomatic presentation that can be noted by the patient subjectively or by other individuals objectively. Strokes and myocardial infarction are examples of illnesses with sudden clinical presentation but arguably long periods of biological change that led to a marker event. Examples of gradual onset illnesses include arthritis, emphysema, and Parkinson's disease. For an illness with gradual onset, such as rheumatoid arthritis, the diagnosis serves as a somewhat arbitrary confirmation point after clinical symptoms have started.

A gradual crisis presents a different form of stressor to an individual or family than does a sudden crisis. The total amount of readjustment of family structure, roles, problem solving, and affective coping might be the same for both types of illness. However, for acute onset illnesses, such as stroke, these affective and instrumental changes are compressed into a short time. This will require of the family more rapid mobilization of crisis management skills, and some families are better equipped to cope with rapid change. Families able to tolerate highly charged affective states, exchange clearly defined roles flexibly, problem solve efficiently, and utilize outside resources will have an advantage in managing acute onset illnesses.

The rate of family change required to cope with gradual onset diseases, such as rheumatoid arthritis or Parkinson's disease, allows for a more protracted period of adjustment but perhaps generates more anxiety before a diagnosis is made. For acute onset diseases there is relatively greater strain on the family members to juggle their energies between protecting against further disintegration, damage, or loss through death and making progressive efforts that maximize mastery through restructuring or novel problem solving (Adams & Lindemann, 1974).

Course

The course of chronic diseases can take essentially three general forms: progressive, constant, or relapsing/episodic. By this definition a *progressive* course disease (e.g. cancers, Alzheimer's disease, juvenile onset diabetes, rheumatoid arthritis, and emphysema) is one that is continually or generally symptomatic and progresses in severity. The individual and family are faced with the effects of a perpetually symptomatic family member, where disability increases in a stepwise or progressive fashion. Periods of relief from the demands of the illness tend to be minimal. Continual adaptation and role change are implicit. Increasing strain on family caretakers is caused by both the risk of exhaustion and the continual addition of new caretaking tasks over time. Family flexibility, both in terms of internal role reorganization and willingness and/or ability to use outside resources, is at a premium.

It is profitable to distinguish further between illnesses that progress rapidly or slowly. The demands on the family coping with a rapidly progressive illness such as nonresponsive lung cancer or acute leukemia are different from the demands of slowly progressive illnesses such as rheumatoid arthritis, chronic obstructive pulmonary disease (e.g. emphysema, chronic bronchitis), or adult onset diabetes. The pace of adaptation required to cope with the continual changes and ever-new demands of a rapidly progressive disease mounts as the time course shortens. A slowly progressive illness may place a higher premium on stamina over a long period of time than on continual adaptation and change.

A *constant* course illness is one in which, typically, an initial event occurs after which the biological course stabilizes. Examples include: stroke, single-episode myocardial infarction, trauma with resulting amputation, or spinal cord injury with paralysis. Also typically, after an initial period of recovery the chronic phase is characterized by some clear-cut deficit such as paraplegia, amputation, speech loss, or cognitive impairment. Or there may be a residual functional limitation such as diminished physical stress tolerance or a restriction of previous activities. Recurrences can occur, but the individual or family is faced with a semipermanent change that is stable and predictable over a considerable time span. The potential for family and patient exhaustion exists without the strain of new role demands over time.

The third kind of course is characterized as *relapsing* or *episodic*. Illnesses such as ulcerative colitis, asthma, peptic ulcer, migraine headache, and multiple sclerosis are examples of this course. Forms of cancer in remission, such as resectable and chemotherapy-responsive kinds, might be included in this category. The distinguishing feature of this kind of disease course is the alternation of stable periods of varying length, characterized by a low level or absence of symptoms, with periods of flare-up or exacerbation. Often the family can carry on a "normal" routine. However, the specter of recurrence hangs over their heads.

Relapsing illnesses demand a somewhat different sort of family and patient adaptability. Relative to progressive or constant course illnesses, they may require the least ongoing caretaking or role reallocation. But the episodic nature of an illness may require a flexibility that permits movement back and forth between two forms of family organization. In a sense, the family is on call to erect a crisis structure to handle exacerbations of the illness. Strain on the family system is caused by both the frequency of transitions between crisis and noncrisis and the ongoing uncertainty of *when* a crisis will next occur. Also, the wide psychological discrepancy between periods of normalcy versus illness is a particularly taxing feature unique to relapsing chronic diseases.

Outcome

The extent to which a chronic illness is a likely cause of death and the degree to which it can shorten one's life span are critical distinguishing features with profound psychosocial impact. The most crucial factor is the *initial expectation* of whether a disease is a likely cause of death. On one end of the continuum are illnesses that do not typically affect the life span, such as lumbosacral disc disease, blindness, arthritis, spinal cord injury, or seizure disorders. At the other extreme are illnesses that are clearly progressive and usually fatal, such as metastic cancer, Acquired Immune Deficiency Syndrome (AIDS), and Huntington's chorea. In addition, there is an intermediate, more unpredictable category that includes both illnesses which shorten the life span, such as cystic fibrosis, juvenile onset diabetes, and cardiovascular disease, and those with the possibility of sudden death, such as hemophilia, recurrences of myocardial infarction, and stroke.

The major differences among these kinds of outcomes is the degree to which the family experiences anticipatory grief and its pervasive effects on family life. All chronic illnesses potentially involve the loss of bodily control, identity, and intimate relationships (Sourkes, 1982). With a life-threatening illness, the loss of control entails greater consequences—death and the permanent loss of relationships. The ill member fears life ending before living out his or her "life plan" and being alone in death. The family fears becoming survivors alone. For both there exists an undercurrent of anticipatory grief and separation that permeates all phases of adaptation. Families are often caught between a desire for intimacy and a pull to "let go" emotionally of the ill member.

The expectation of future loss can make it extremely difficult for a family to maintain a balanced perspective. A literal torrent of affect could potentially distract a family from the myriad of practical tasks and problem solving that maintain family integrity (Weiss, 1983). Also, the tendency to see the ill family member as practically "in the coffin" can set in motion maladaptive responses that divest the ill member of important responsibilities. The end result can be the structural and emotional isolation of the ill person from family life. This psychological alienation has been associated with poor medical outcomes in life-threatening illness (Davies et al., 1973; Derogatis et al., 1979; Schmale & Iker, 1971; Simonton et al., 1980).

With illnesses that may shorten life or cause sudden death, loss is less imminent or certain an outcome than for clearly fatal and non-fatal illnesses. Because of this, issues of mortality predominate less in day-to-day life. It is for this reason that this type of illness provides such a fertile ground for idiosyncratic family interpretations. The "it could happen" nature of these illnesses creates a nidus for both overprotection by the family and powerful secondary gains for the ill member. This is particularly relevant to childhood illnesses such as hemophilia, juvenile onset diabetes, and asthma (Minuchin et al., 1975, 1978).

Incapacitation

Incapacitation can result from impairment of cognition (e.g. Alzheimer's disease), sensation (e.g. blindness), movement (e.g. stroke with paralysis, multiple sclerosis), energy production, or disfigurement, or other medical causes of social stigma. Illnesses such as cardiovascular and pulmonary diseases impair the body's ability to produce raw energy. This can lower peak performance or the ability to sustain motor, sensory, or cognitive efforts. Illnesses such as leprosy, neurofibromatosis, or severe burns are cosmetically disabling to the extent that sufficient social stigma impairs one's ability for normal social interaction. AIDS is socially disabling because of the combined efforts of its perceived high risk of contagion, long asymptomatic incubation/carrier period, current status as incurable, and links with highly stigmatized groups in our society—homosexuals and intravenous drug users.

The different kinds of incapacitation imply sharp differences in the specific adjustments required of a family. For instance, the combined cognitive and motor deficits of a person with a stroke necessitate greater family role reallocation than a spinal-cord injured person who retains his or her cognitive faculties. Some chronic diseases such as hypertension, peptic ulcer, many endocrine disorders, or migraine headaches cause either no, mild, or only intermittent incapacitation. This is a highly significant factor moderating the degree of stress facing a family. For some illnesses, such as stroke or spinal cord injury, incapacitation is often worst at the time of onset and exerts its greatest influence at that time. Incapacitation at the beginning of an illness magnifies family coping issues related to onset, expected course, and outcome. For progressive diseases, such as multiple sclerosis, rheumatoid arthritis, or dementia, disability looms as an increasing problem in later phases of the illness. This allows a family more time to prepare for anticipated changes. In particular, it provides an opportunity for the ill member to participate in disease-related family planning.

As a caveat, several studies cite the importance of the family's expectations of a disabled member. An expectation that the ill member could continue to have responsible roles and autonomy was associated with both a better rehabilitation response and successful long-term integration into the family (Bishop & Epstein, 1980; Cleveland, 1980; Hyman, 1975; Litman, 1974; Slater et al., 1970; Sussman & Slater, 1971; Swanson & Maruta, 1980). Bishop and Epstein (1980) envisioned that, because of the sheer amount of role change required, the family would have the greatest difficulty in deciding realistic role expectations with both mildly disabling illnesses, which were most ambiguous in their demands, and the most severely incapacitating ones.

In sum, the net effect of incapacitation on a particular individual or family depends on the interaction of the type of incapacitation with the preillness role demands of the ill member and the family's structure, flexibility, and resources. However, it may be the presence or absence of *any* significant incapacitation that constitutes the principal dividing line relevant to a first attempt to construct a psychosocial typology of illness (Viney & Westbrook, 1981).

By combining the kinds of onset (acute vs. gradual), course (progressive vs. constant vs. relapsing/episodic), outcome (fatal vs. shortened life span vs. nonfatal), and incapacitation (present vs. absent) into a grid format, we generate a typology with 32 potential psychosocial types of illness. It is clear that certain types of disease (i.e. constant course fatal illnesses) are so rare or nonexistent that for practical purposes they can be eliminated. This grid is shown in Figure 1.2. The number of potential types can be further reduced by combining or eliminating particular factors. This would depend on the relative need for specificity in a particular situation.

The extent to which illnesses are predictable has not been formulated as a separate category in the typology. Rather, predictability should be seen as a kind of metacharacteristic that overlays and colors the other attributes: onset, course, outcome, and incapacitation.

		INCAPACITATING ACUTE	INCAPACITATING GRADUAL	NONINCAPACITATING ACUTE	NONINCAPACITATING GRADUAL
PROGRESSIVE	FATAL		Lung cancer with CNS metastases A.I.D.S. Bone marrow failure Amyotrophic lateral sclerosis	Acute leukemia Pancreatic cancer Metastatic breast cancer Malignant melanoma Lung cancer Liver cancer, etc.	Cystic fibrosis *
RELAPSING				Cancers in remission	
PROGRESSIVE	POSSIBLY FATAL / SHORTENED LIFE SPAN		Emphysema Alzheimer's disease Multi-infarct dementia Multiple sclerosis (late) Chronic alcoholism Huntington's chorea · Scleroderma		Juvenile diabetes * Malignant hypertension Insulin dependent adult onset diabetes
RELAPSING		Angina	Early multiple sclerosis Episodic alcoholism	Sickle cell disease * Hemophelia *	Systemic lupus erythematosis *
CONSTANT		Stroke Mod/severe myocardial infarction	P.K.U. and other inborn errors of metabolism	Mild myocardial infarction Cardiac Arrhythmia	Hemodialysis treated renal failure Hodgkins disease
PROGRESSIVE	NONFATAL		Parkinson's disease Rheumatoid arthritis Osteo-arthritis		Non-insulin dependent adult onset diabetes
RELAPSING		Lumbosacral disc disease		Kidney stones Gout Migraine Seasonal allergy Asthma Epilepsy	Peptic ulcer Ulcerative colitis Chronic bronchitis Other inflam. bowel diseases Psoriasis
CONSTANT		Congenital malformations Spinal cord injury Acute blindness Acute deafness Survived severe trauma & burns Post-hypoxic syndrome	Non-progressive mental retardation Cerebral palsy	Benign Arrhythmia Congenital heart disease	Malabsorption syndromes Hyper/Hypothroidism Pernicious anemia Controlled hypertension Controlled glaucoma

* early

Figure 1.2. Categorization of chronic illnesses by psychosocial type. From "Toward a Psychosocial Typology of Chronic and Life-Threatening Illness" by J. S. Rolland, 1984, *Family Systems Medicine*, Vol. 2, No. 3.

There are two distinct facets to the predictability of a chronic illness. Diseases can be more or less uncertain as to the actual *nature* of the onset, course, outcome, or incapacitation. And they can vary as to the *rate* at which changes will occur. Some diseases such as spinal cord injury can be accurately typed at the point of diagnosis and have a highly predictable course. Other illnesses such as stroke, myocardial infarction, hypertension, and lung cancer are rather unpredictable as to course and outcome. With these kinds of diseases the initial prediction of type may change.

For instance, if a second episode occurs, a stroke or myocardial infarction can be considered relapsing or progressive. Lung cancer can become incapacitating if brain metastases occur. Some cases of lung cancer progress rapidly, while others advance slowly with a long remission, or not at all ("spontaneous cure"). Some illnesses such as rheumatoid arthritis or migraine headaches tend to have predictable long-range courses but can be highly variable day to day. This kind of uncertainty can interfere more with daily than with long-term planning. The typology of illness cannot predict these changes, and in a particular case, if important changes occur during the course of the disease, an individual can switch from one illness type to another.

Several other important attributes that differentiate illnesses are excluded from this typology because they seem of lesser importance or are relevant to only a subgroup of disorders. When appropriate they should be considered in a thorough, systemically-oriented evaluation.

The complexity, frequency, and efficacy of a treatment regimen, the amount of home versus hospital-based care required by the disease, and the frequency and intensity of symptoms vary widely across illnesses and have important implications for individual and family adaptation including demands on family financial resources. Some treatment regimens require significant expenditures of time and/or energy (e.g. home kidney dialysis) or necessitate another person to carry them out (e.g., postural lung drainage for children with cystic fibrosis). Treatments least likely to be adhered to are those that have a high impact on one's lifestyle, are difficult to accomplish, and have minimal effects on the level of symptoms or prognosis (Strauss, 1975). While they reduce time-consuming dependence on medical centers, treatments that are home based place a greater onus on the patient or other members of the family. Therefore, the degree of family emotional support, role flexibility, effective problem solving, and communication in relation to these treatment factors will be crucial predictors of long-term treatment compliance.

It is important to consider the likelihood of disease-related crises (Strauss, 1975). Fears about these crises are often a major cause of an undercurrent of anxiety among family members. A clinician should assess the understanding of these members about the possibility, frequency, and lethality of a medical crisis. How congruent is their understanding with that of the medical team? Are their expectations catastrophic, or do they minimize real dangers? Are there clear warning signs that the patient or family members can recognize? Can a medical crisis be prevented or mitigated by the detection of early warning signs or the institution of prompt treatment? For example, when a patient or other family members heed the early warning signs of a diabetes insulin reaction or asthma attack, a full-blown crisis can usually be averted. How complex are the rescue operations? Do they require simple measures carried out at home (e.g., medication, bed rest), or do they necessitate outside assistance or hospitalization? How long can crises last before a family can resume "day-to-day" functioning?

It is essential to ask the members of a family about their planning for such crises. In particular, the extent and accuracy of their medical knowledge is of paramount importance. How clearly has leadership, role reallocation, emotional support, and use of resources outside the family been formulated? If an illness began with an acute crisis (e.g. stroke), then assessment of that event gives the clinician useful information as to how the members of that family handle *unexpected* crises. Evaluating the overall viability of the family's crisis planning is the key to this part of an assessment.

The knowledge or ignorance of family members about the possible role of genetic transmission of a disease is another illness variable of major psychosocial importance. It is important for future family planning and for the emotional adaptation of the family members for the clinician to explain whether a disease is (a) not genetically linked and therefore unlikely to recur, (b) definitely genetically transmitted, or (c) more likely to occur in a particular family but the predisposition can be offset by environmental/social factors (Rucquoi, 1983). For many diseases that "run in families" (e.g., heart disease, cancer) the role of genetics is acknowledged but, at present, not well understood. Other diseases, such as hemophilia or sickle cell disease, have clear modes of genetic transmission.

The genetics of illness is a complex field. There are many biological processes involved that influence whether (a) a disease requires the genetic contribution of one or both parents, (b) a person can be a carrier of a genetic trait without showing it, or (c) a disease is gender linked. Clinicians should evaluate the accuracy of the family's knowledge, the family's cross-generational experience with a particular illness, and mythologies among family members that have developed in connection with a genetic or possibly genetic illness. In particular, these kinds of diseases provide a powerful nidus for blame, guilt, and self-incrimination. For this type of disease, genetic counseling is an extremely useful adjunct to a comprehensive, psychosocial treatment plan (Hsia et al., 1979).

Finally, the age of illness onset in relation to child, adult, and family stages of development is a critical factor beyond the scope of this chapter.

Time Phases

To complete a matrix, the time phases of an illness need to be considered as a second dimension. Often one hears about "coping with cancer," "managing disability," or "dealing with life-threatening illness." These clichés can create a kind of tunnel vision that precludes sufficient attention to the phases of an illness. Each phase has its own psychosocial tasks which require significantly different strengths, attitudes, and changes from a family. To capture the core psychosocial themes in the natural history of chronic disease, three major phases can be described, crisis, chronic, and terminal. The relationship between a more detailed chronic disease time line and one grouped into broad time phases can be diagrammed as follows in Figure 1.3.

The *crisis* phase includes any symptomatic period before actual diagnosis when the individual or family has a sense something is wrong, but the exact nature and scope of the problem is not clear. It includes the initial period of readjustment and coping after the problem has been clarified through a diagnosis and initial treatment plan.

During this period there are a number of key tasks for the ill member and the other people in his or her family. Moos (1984) describes certain universal, practical, illness-related tasks. These include: (a) learning to deal with pain, incapacitation, or other illness-related symptoms; (b) learning to deal with the hospital environment and any disease-related treatment procedures, and (c) establishing and maintaining workable relationships with the health care team. In addition, there are critical tasks of a more general,

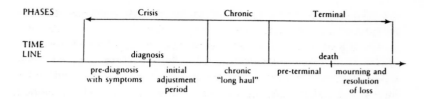

Figure 1.3. Categorization of chronic illnesses by psychosocial type. From "Toward a Psychosocial Typology of Chronic and Life-Threatening Illness" by J. S. Rolland, 1984, *Family Systems Medicine,* Vol. 2, No. 3.

sometimes existential nature. The family is a unit, and all of its members need to: (a) create a meaning for the illness event that maximizes a preservation of their sense of mastery over their lives and their competency; (b) grieve for the loss of the preillness family identity; (c) move toward a position of acceptance of permanent change while maintaining a sense of continuity between their past and future; (d) pull together to undergo short-term crisis reorganization; and (e) in the face of uncertainty develop a special system flexibility toward future goals.

These tasks are apt to fall heavily on parents who need to carry the major burden of an illness themselves, whether their youngsters are children or adolescents. Besides assuming major caretaking functions, parents need to help each of their children understand and try to come to terms with the illness in ways that are appropriate to each child's particular development and idiosyncratic needs.

The *chronic* phase of an illness can be long or short, but essentially it is the time span between the initial diagnosis and readjustment period and the third phase, when issues of death and terminal illness predominate. It is an era that can be marked by constancy, progression, or episodic change. In this sense, its meaningfulness cannot be grasped by simply knowing the biological behavior of an illness. Rather, it is more a psychosocial construct that has been referred to as the "long haul," or "day-to-day living with chronic illness" phase. Often the patient and other family members come to grips psychologically and/or organizationally with the permanent changes presented by a chronic illness and have devised an ongoing modus operandi. At one extreme, the chronic phase can last for decades as a stable, nonfatal, chronic illness. On the other hand, it may be nonexistent in an acute onset, rapidly progressive, fatal disorder where the crisis phase is contiguous with the terminal phase.

The ability of the members of the family to maintain the semblance of a normal life under the "abnormal" presence of chronic illness and heightened uncertainty is a key task of this period. For a fatal illness, it is a time of "living in limbo." For certain highly debilitating but not clearly fatal illnesses, such as a massive stroke or dementia, the family can become saddled with an exhausting problem "without end." Paradoxically, the hope of some families to resume a "normal" life cycle might only be realized through the death of their ill member. This is particularly true both for economically disadvantaged families dealing with illness that can drain scarce family resources and for enmeshed families that can become emotionally stuck in a cycle of overprotection that prohibits personal autonomy or use of outside resources. All of this highlights another crucial task of this phase: the maintenance of maximal autonomy for *all* family members in the face of a pull toward mutual dependency and caretaking.

The last phase is the *terminal* period. It includes the preterminal stage of an illness in which the inevitability of death becomes apparent and dominates family life. It encompasses the periods of mourning and resolution of loss. This phase includes the central issues surrounding separation, death, grief, resolution of mourning, and the eventual resumption of "normal" family life.

Critical transition periods link the three time phases. Carter and McGoldrick (1980) and Levinson (1978, 1986) have clarified the importance of transition periods in the family and adult life cycle. It is the same for the transitions between developmental phases in the course of disease. This is a time to reevaluate the appropriateness of the previous family life structure in the face of new, illness-related developmental demands. Unfinished business from the previous phase can complicate or block movement through the transitions. Families or individuals can become permanently frozen in an adaptive structure that has outlived its utility (Penn, 1983).

For example, the usefulness of pulling together in the crisis period can become in the chronic phase a maladaptive and stifling prison for all family members. Enmeshed families, because of their rigid and fused nature, would have difficulty negotiating this delicate transition. A family that is adept at handling the day-to-day practicalities of a long-term stable illness but limited in its skills in affective coping may encounter difficulty if the family member's disease becomes terminal. The relatively greater demand for affective coping skills in the terminal versus the chronic phase of an illness may create a crisis for a family navigating this transition.

The interaction of the time phases and the typology of illness provide a framework for a chronic disease, psychosocial developmental model. The time phases (crisis, chronic, and terminal) can be considered broad developmental periods in the natural history of chronic disease, with each phase having certain basic tasks independent of the type of illness. In addition to the phase-specific developmental tasks common to all psychosocial types of disease, each "type" of illness has specific supplementary tasks. This is analogous to the relationship between a particular individual's development and certain universal life tasks. The basic tasks of the three illness time phases and transitions recapitulate in many respects the unfolding of human development.

For example, the crisis phase is similar in certain fundamental ways to the era of childhood and adolescence. Piaget's (1952) research demonstrated that child development involves a prolonged period of learning to assimilate from and accommodate to the fundamentals of life. Parents often temper other developmental plans (e.g., career) to accommodate raising children. In an analogous way, the crisis phase is a period of socialization to the basics of living with chronic disease. During this phase other life plans are frequently put on hold by family members to accommodate the socialization-to-illness process. Themes of separation and individuation are central in the transition from adolescence to adulthood. Erikson (1963) pointed out that adolescents are granted a kind of moratorium or postponement period during which the identity of childhood gradually merges into that of adulthood. Eventually the adolescent must relinquish this moratorium to assume normal adult responsibilities.

In a similar way, the transition to the chronic phase of illness emphasizes the autonomy of each family member and the creation of a viable ongoing life structure for each, given the realities of the illness (life). In the transition to the chronic phase a moratorium on other developmental tasks that served to protect the initial period of socialization/adaptation to life with chronic disease is reevaluated. The separate developmental tasks of "living with chronic illness" and "living the other parts of one's life" must be brought together and forged into one coherent life structure. I will return to this concept of illness development later.

At this point we can combine the typology and phases of illness to

ONSET	COURSE	OUTCOME	INCAPACITATION
A = acute	P = progressive	F = fatal or shortened	Yes = (+)
G = gradual	C = constant	lifespan	No = (−)
	R = relapsing	NF = nonfatal	

ILLNESS TYPE	I CRISIS	II CHRONIC	III TERMINAL
A P F +			
A P F −			
A P NF +			
A P NF −			
A C F +			
A C F −			
A C NF +			
A C NF −			
A R F +			
A R F −			
A R NF +			
A R NF +			
G P F +			
G P F −			
G P NF +			
G P NF −			
G C F +			
G C F −			
G C NF +			
G C NF −			
G R F +			
G R F −			
G R NF +			
G R NF −			

Figure 1.4. Matrix of illness types and time phases.

construct a two-dimensional matrix (Figure 1.4) that permits the grouping and differentiation of illnesses according to important similarities and differences. It subdivides types of chronic illnesses into three time phases. This allows examination of a long-term illness in a more refined way.

By the addition of a family systems model to this matrix, we can create a three-dimensional representation of the broader illness/family system (Figure 1.5). Psychosocial illness types, time phases of illness, and components of family functioning constitute the three dimensions. This model offers a vehicle for flexible dialogue between the illness aspect and the family aspect of the illness/family system. In essence, this model allows speculation about the importance of strengths and weaknesses in various components of family functioning in relation to different types of diseases at different phases in the illness life cycle.

Clinical Implications

There are several important implications of this model for clinical practice. At their core, the components of the typology provide a means to grasp the character of a chronic illness in psychosocial terms. They provide a meaningful bridge for the clinician between the biological and psychosocial worlds. Perhaps the major contribution is the provision of a framework for assessment and clinical intervention with a family facing a chronic or life-threatening illness. The clinician can think with greater clarity and focus using this model. Attention to features of onset, course, outcome, and incapacitation provides markers that facilitate integration of an assessment. This will help focus a clinician's questioning of a family.

For instance, acute onset illnesses demand high levels of adapt-

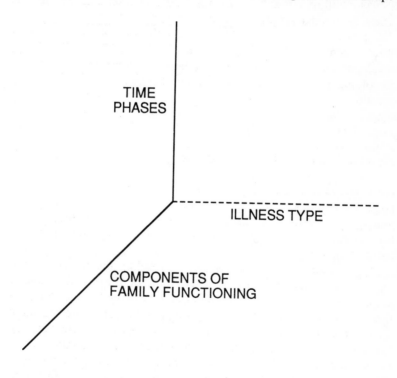

Figure 1.5. Three-dimensional model: Illness type, time phase, family functioning.

ability, problem-solving, role reallocation, and balanced cohesion. A high degree of family enmeshment might make a family less likely to be able to cope with these demands. A family with rigid boundaries might have difficulty allowing people outside the immediate family limit to provide assistance. A family in which considerable conflict and alienation preexisted the illness may lack the commitment to provide care for the ill member. A family which encounters simultaneous stresses, such as the illness or disability of another member, unemployment, or the birth of a child, may lack the psychic resources to effectively cope with the chronic illness of the patient. Forethought on issues such as these would cue a clinician toward a more appropriate family evaluation.

The concept of time phases provides a way for the clinician to think longitudinally and to reach a fuller understanding of chronic illness as an ongoing process with landmarks, transition points, and changing demands. An illness timeline delineates the psychosocial developmental stages of an illness, each phase with its own unique developmental tasks. Kaplan (1968) has emphasized the importance of solving phase-related tasks within the time limits set by the duration of each successive developmental phase of an illness. He suggests the failure to resolve issues in this sequential manner can jeopardize the total coping process of the family. Therefore, attention to time allows the clinician to assess a family's strengths and vulnerabilities in relation to the present and future phases of the illness.

Taken together the typology and time phases provide a context to integrate other aspects of a comprehensive assessment. This would involve evaluation of a range of universal and illness-specific family dynamics in relation to the psychosocial type and time phases of illness. This could include assessment of: the family's illness belief system; the meaning of the illness to each family member; the interface of the illness with individual and family development; the family's transgenerational history of coping with illness, loss, and crisis; the family's medical crisis planning; the family's capacity to perform home-based medical care; and the family's illness-oriented communication, problem solving, role reallocation, affective involvement, social support, and use of community resources.

The model clarifies treatment planning. First, awareness of the components of family functioning most relevant to particular types or phases of an illness guides goal setting. The act of sharing this information with the family members and deciding upon specific goals will provide a better sense of control and realistic hope to them. This knowledge educates them about warning signs that should alert them to seek family treatment, guiding families who often lack prior exposure to psychiatric care to call upon a family therapist at appropriate times for brief, goal-oriented treatment.

Clinical Applications: The Therapeutic Quadrangle

Using the psychosocial typology and time phases of illness as a reference point has important implications for health services delivery, both for the patient and family's relationship to health professionals and for the organization of services.

Haley (1976) observed that helping professionals need to be included in the conceptualization of any therapeutic treatment system with a family. The application of this idea in the medical world has led to various descriptions of "the Therapeutic Triangle in Medicine" (Doherty & Baird, 1983). This triangle includes the patient, the members of his or her family, and the physician (health care team). Doherty and Baird point out the illusory nature of thinking in dyadic terms about the patient/family and physician/patient relationships. They emphasize active participation of the physician in the former and of the family in the latter. A schematic representation of this set of relationships is shown in Figure 1.6.

The inclusion of the concept of psychosocial illness "types" into the scheme creates a four-member system composed of four interlocking triangles (Figure 1.7). It is easier to conceptualize the illness as a fourth member if one pictures each illness "type" as having a personality (which includes the kind of onset, course, outcome, degree of incapacitation, and predictability) and developmental life course (which includes the time phases of chronic illness).

Within this paradigm one might take the original therapeutic triangle diagrammed in Figure 1.6 (the patient, the family, and the health care team) and see how it is colored by different types of illnesses. For instance, consider the concept of locus of control in relation to disease (Wallston et al., 1976, 1978). This concept refers to how much the patient and other family members see outcomes as being influenced by their own efforts. Their beliefs about their potential to control biological processes can vary along a continuum from an internal to an external orientation. A certain minimal level of agreement concerning this kind of health belief is critical for the establishment of a viable therapeutic relationship between the patient, the rest of his or her family, and the health care team. The degree of consensus concerning locus of control can vary dramat-

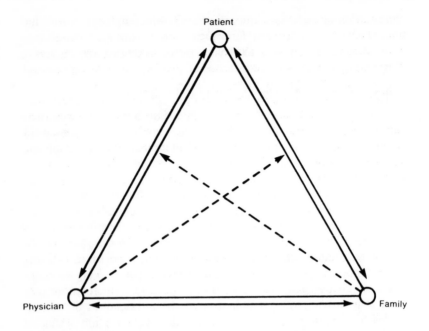

Figure 1.6. The therapeutic triangle in medicine. From *Family Therapy and Family Medicine: Toward the Primary Care of Families* by W. J. Doherty and M. A. Baird, 1983, New York: Guilford Press.

ically for this triad depending on the "type" of chronic disease. A particular family physician may have had a good working relationship with family members who had presented over the years illnesses that were not life-threatening or incapacitating. If the father suffers a serious heart attack, and there are differences in beliefs about control which surface in relation to this more life-threatening and incapacitating illness, the stability of the longstanding therapeutic triangle might be threatened. If the physician has checked his or her own beliefs and questioned the family members about theirs in relation to a life-threatening, incapacitating disease, a potential serious rift in this therapeutic system might be averted.

The therapeutic quadrangle also allows analysis of how a particular psychosocial type of illness interfaces with the health care team's relationship with the family and the patient independently.

In terms of the organization of services, the psychosocial typology and time phases of illness have implications for periodic reevaluation of the family in relation to the illness life cycle, with the time phases and transition points suggesting the timing of the evaluations. Strengths and weaknesses in various components of family functioning can thus be addressed, taking into account all relevant factors related to the "psychosocial type" of the illness.

The typology facilitates the development of various prevention-oriented psychoeducational or support groups for patients and their families. For example, groups could be designed to meet the needs of patients dealing with progressive, life-threatening diseases; relapsing disorders; acute onset, incapacitating illnesses; or the chronic phase of constant course diseases. Sometimes there are not enough families involved with any particular disease to form such groups. This is particularly relevant in more rural settings or for less common illnesses. Thinking about group-oriented services in terms of illness types helps to overcome these obstacles while maintaining the groups' thematic coherence. Also, packaging brief psychoeducational "modules," timed for critical phases of particular "types" of diseases, encourages families to accept and digest manageable portions of a long-term coping process. Each module could be tailored to the particular phase of the illness life cycle and family coping skills necessary to confront disease-related demands. This would provide a cost-effective, preventive service that could also aid in the detection of families at high risk for maladaptation to chronic illness.

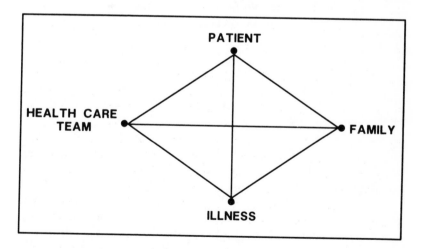

Figure 1.7. The therapeutic quadrangle.

FAMILY ASSESSMENT

Equipped with a psychosocial typology of illness, we can return to our original diagram (Figure 1.1), which depicts the interface of the family with chronic illness. In this section, I will discuss the family part of the larger family/illness system from two vantage points. First, based on the assumption that traditional family assessment models need recasting and selective expansion to better fit the larger family/illness system, this discussion will center on illness-oriented family dynamics that emphasize belief systems and the dimension of time. Second, these dynamics will be used to illustrate how one can apply the psychosocial typology and time phases of illness to family assessment more generally.

All family systems models incorporate concepts of organization (i.e., power, roles, hierarchy, boundary integrity), flexibility versus rigidity, affective closeness versus distance, and communication styles (e.g., Epstein, Bishop, & Levin, 1978; Lewis et al., 1977; Minuchin, 1974; Olson, Sprenkle, & Russell, 1979). All models assume families face three kinds of life tasks: basic (e.g. food and shelter), developmental, and hazardous (unexpected life events such as chronic illness); these models also assume that most of these tasks have both instrumental (practical) and expressive/affective parts (Parsons & Bales, 1955). Further, there is a burgeoning literature which describes family coping and adaptation to a wide variety of normative and unexpected life stresses (Hill, 1949; Burr, 1973; McCubbin, 1979; McCubbin et al., 1980; Hansen & Johnson, 1979; Figley & McCubbin, 1983; McCubbin & Figley, 1983).

Researchers and clinicians have documented key elements in successful family coping and adaptation to a specific type of stressor such as chronic illness (Moos, 1984). Most endorse the notion that chronic illnesses become incorporated into the family system and all its inherent processes. As such, they emphasize how diseases interface with both universal and illness-specific family dynamics such as communication, problem-solving, hierarchy, role reallocation, affective involvement, information gathering, social support, utilization of community resources, mastery of home-based medical care, medical crisis planning, and maintenance of self-esteem.

Although these important family-systems-oriented concepts have been generated on the subject of chronic illness, I believe a developmental framework and family paradigms may provide the best lens through which to view family dynamics and long-term illness. In this regard, the following three topics will be considered in more detail: (a) the family illness belief system; (b) the family transgenerational history of coping with illness, loss, and crisis; and (c) the interface of the illness with the individual and family life cycles. The interrelationship of the psychosocial typology and time phases of illness with each of these components of family functioning will be highlighted through condensed clinical examples. These vignettes are provided to suggest a broader, more comprehensive application of the typology to other major components of family functioning that will not be detailed in this chapter.

Illness Value System

Before addressing illness values, it is important to consider certain problems that all societies, families, and individuals must face as part of the fact of human existence. All of us as individuals or as part of larger systems adopt a value orientation, belief system, or philosophy that shapes our patterns of behavior toward these common problems. Beliefs lend coherence to cognitive and affective dimensions of family life, and temporal continuity to past, present, and future. Values provide a mode of approaching new and ambiguous situations. Depending on which system we are speaking of, this phenomenon can be labeled as values, culture, religion, belief system, world view, or family paradigm.

The anthropologist Florence Kluckhohn has described five universal problems and the range of possible value orientations toward each problem (Kluckhohn, 1960). A society's approach toward life is reflected in the particular constellation of value orientations it preferentially chooses. These universal problems (and possible value orientations) include: the character of innate human nature (good vs. neutral vs. evil); the relation between human and nature (subjugation-to-nature vs. harmony-with-nature vs. master-over-nature); the temporal focus of human life (past vs. present vs. future); the preferred pattern of human activity (being vs. becoming); and the nature of the relationship between humans (hierarchical/cross-generational vs. individualistic vs. collective). This discussion will highlight the value which concerns one's relationship to nature because it is a particularly important determinant of a family's style of coping and adaptation to chronic illness.

At the level of the family David Reiss has written eloquently about the family paradigm as an enduring structure of shared beliefs, convictions, and assumptions about the social world that evolve from the family's past experiences (Reiss, 1981). As a caveat, Reiss believes that families initiate their own culture/paradigm as an extension of their experiences with adversity and crisis. In this regard the family's legacy of dealing with illness and loss becomes paramount. Although individual family members can hold different beliefs, from a family systems perspective the values operative at the level of the whole family may be the most significant.

Given this prelude, one can examine two aspects of the family illness paradigm: (a) the specific values to which the family adheres, and (b) the congruence of the family value system, both internally with its various subsystems (e.g., spouse, parental, extended family, intergenerational family) and with external, larger systems (e.g., societal, ethnic, health system).

In her discourse on the relationship between human and nature, Kluckhohn described a continuum with a "sense of subjugation" at one end and "mastery over nature" at the other. This value is very similar to the concept of locus of control, which has been defined as the beliefs that individuals or families hold regarding the significance of their role in the ways in which given outcomes occur. Internal locus of control corresponds with a sense that one can affect the outcome of situations (mastery over nature). External locus of control refers to a belief that situations are governed by external factors beyond the individual or family's control (subjugation to nature) (Lefcourt, 1982; Dohrenwend, 1981). McCubbin and his colleagues helped elucidate this value in an instrument they designed to assess family coping strategies (McCubbin et al., 1981). Positive responses to statements such as "Knowing we have the power to solve major problems" or "Showing that we are strong" reflect an internal locus of control orientation. Affirmative answers to statements such as "Luck plays a big part in how well we are able to solve family problems," or "If we wait long enough, the problem will go away" highlight an external locus of control belief system.

Levenson (1973, 1974, 1975) argued that externally oriented beliefs could be better understood by distinguishing between those individuals who rely on fate or chance and those who believe in external control by "powerful others." This is an important distinction when considered in terms of health beliefs. Families that view illness in terms of chance will endorse statements such as "Luck plays a big part in determining how soon my family member will recover from an illness." Individuals who see health control in the hands of powerful others will see health professionals but not themselves as exerting control over their bodies (B.S. Wallston et al., 1976, 1978).

The family, as a unit or individual members, may adhere to a different set of values concerning control when dealing with a *biological* process as opposed to other day-to-day types of problem solving. Therefore, it is important to assess a family's basic value system first. Then, with increasing specificity, one can assess the family's notions about control for illnesses in general, chronic and life-threatening illness, and, finally, the specific disease facing the family. A family guided normally by an internal locus of control may switch to an external viewpoint when a member develops any chronic illness, or perhaps only in the case of a life-threatening disease. Such a change might occur in a family with a strong need to remain in accord with society's values, a particular ethnic background, or where the adult family members may have had specific experiences with life-threatening diseases in their family of origin. One can inquire as to whether family members have any particular beliefs surrounding specific types of illnesses. For example, regardless of the actual severity in a particular instance, cancer may be equated with "death" or "no control" because of medical statistics, cultural myth, or prior family history. For many certain types of heart diseases with a life expectancy similar to certain forms of cancer could be seen as more manageable because of prevailing beliefs. Imagine a family traditionally guided by a strong sense of personal control. If the paternal grandfather, the staunch patriarch of the family, dies because of a rapidly progressive and painful form of cancer, the family may develop an encapsulated exception to their views about control that is specific for cancer or generalized to include all life-threatening illnesses.

It is critical to distinguish whether family belief systems are internal, external via "chance," or external via "powerful others." This is a fundamental substrate to the family's health paradigm and strongly affects the nature of their relationship to biological processes, particularly to the illness in a biopsychosocial sense, and to the health care system. It is a predictor of certain health behaviors, particularly treatment compliance, and it suggests the family preferences about participating in the patient's treatment and healing. In my experience, families that view disease progression and outcome as a matter of chance tend to establish marginal relationships with health professionals largely because their belief system minimizes the importance of their own or a health professional's relationship to a disease process. Just as any psychotherapeutic relationship depends upon a shared mythology or belief system, a fit between the patient, his or her family, and the health care team in terms of these fundamental values is essential. Families that express feelings of being misunderstood by health professionals are often referring directly or indirectly to a lack of joining at this basic value level.

A family's beliefs about the etiology of an illness need to be assessed separately from their beliefs pertaining to control once an illness is present. One way to gather this information is to ask each family member for his or her explanation for the very existence of the disease. Responses usually reflect a combination of the current level of medical knowledge about the particular disease in concert with family mythology. This mythology might include punishment for prior misdeeds (e.g., an affair), blaming a particular family member or dyad ("Your drinking made me sick"), a sense of injustice ("Why am I being punished? I have been a good person"), blaming genetics (e.g., cancer runs on one side of the family), negligence by the patient or parents, or bad luck. Asking this question can function as an effective family Rorschach, bringing to light unresolved family conflict.

Further, families guided by a strong sense of potential control of a chronic disease frequently see etiology as more of a chance event. In my clinical experience, families with the strongest, at times extreme, beliefs about personal responsibility and those with the most severe dysfunctional patterns will be those most likely to attribute the cause of the illness to a psychosocial factor. For the former, an ethos of personal responsibility guides all facets of life including the etiology of an illness. For highly dysfunctional families, illnesses become ammunition in long-term power struggles characterized by unresolved conflicts and intense blaming.

Variations in a family's beliefs about mastery can occur depending on the time phase of the illness. For some illnesses the crisis phase involves a lot of outside-the-family involvement. For instance, the crisis phase after a stroke may begin with the patient's stay in an intensive care unit and continue during months of extended care at a rehabilitation facility. This kind of extensive and protracted care, occurring largely outside the family's direct control, may be particularly taxing for a family that prefers to tackle its own problems with a minimum of outside leadership. For this family the patient's return home may increase the workload but allow members to re-establish more fully their values concerning control. A family guided more by a preference for external control by experts will have greater difficulty when their family member returns home. For this family leaving the rehabilitation hospital means the loss of their locus of competency—the professionals. Health providers' cognizance about this basic difference in belief about control can guide a psychosocial treatment plan tailored to each family's needs.

The terminal phase of an illness is again a time when a family may feel least in control of the biological course of the disease and the decision-making regarding the overall care of their ill member. Family members with a strong need to sustain their centrality may need to assert themselves more vigorously with health providers. Effective decision-making regarding the extent of heroic medical efforts or whether a patient will die at home, in an institution, or with hospice care requires an effective family/health care team relationship that respects the basic beliefs of each person in the family.

The attitudes and behaviors of the medical team can have a major influence in either facilitating or hindering this process for a family. A medical team that maintains heroic efforts to control the terminal phase of an illness can convey confusing messages, as it can be extremely difficult for families to know how to interpret continued lifesaving efforts by the health care team. Is there still real hope which should be read by the family as a message to redouble their faith in and support of medical improvement? Or do the physicians feel bound to a technological imperative which requires them to exhaust *all* possibilities at their disposal, regardless of the odds of success? Often physicians feel committed to this course for ethical reasons (a "leave no stone unturned" philosophy) or because of fears concerning legal liability. Or perhaps is the medical team having its own difficulties letting go emotionally due to its own attachment to a patient?

Strong relationships with certain patients can be fueled by identification with losses, often unresolved ones, in their own lives. Health care professionals and institutions can collude in a pervasive societal wish to deny death as a natural process truly beyond technological control (Becker, 1973). Endless treatment can represent the medical team's inability to separate a general value placed on controlling disease from their beliefs about participation, separate from cure, in a patient's total care. Professionals need to examine closely their own motives for treatments geared toward cure rather than palliation, particularly when a patient may be entering a terminal phase. This needs to be done in concert with careful attention to family beliefs about control and participation and the dynamics of the total family system, including interpersonal agreement and disagreement within families as to the preferred course of action.

It is difficult to characterize an "ideal" family illness paradigm. On one hand, a major thesis of this volume is that there is always an interplay between disease and other levels of system. On the other hand, diseases and phases in the course of a given disease may vary considerably in their responsiveness to psychosocial factors versus their inherently inexorable nature. Distinctions need to be made between a family's beliefs about its overall participation in a long-term disease process, their beliefs about their ability to actually control the biological unfolding of an illness, and the flexibility with which a family can apply these beliefs. An optimal expression of family competence or mastery would seem to depend on their grasp of these distinctions. A family's belief in their participation in the total illness process can be thought of as independent of whether a disease is stable, improving, or in a terminal phase.

Sometimes mastery and the attempt to control biological process coincide. A family coping with a member who has cancer in remission may tailor its behavior to help him or her maintain health. This might include changes in family roles, communication, diet, exercise, and the balance between work and recreation. But suppose the ill family member loses his or her remission and vigorous efforts to reestablish a remission fail. As the family enters the terminal phase of the illness, participation as an expression of mastery must now be transposed to mean a successful process of letting go.

The difference between a family experiencing a loss with a sense of competency versus with profound failure is intimately connected to this flexible use of their belief system. It can be helpful if clinicians recognize that the death of a patient who has had a long, debilitating illness which has put heavy burdens on all concerned can be a matter of relief as well as sadness to some or all family members. Since a sense of relief over death goes against most conventions in our society, this can trigger massive guilt reactions that may get expressed tangentially through such symptoms as depression and negative family interactions. Clinicians will need considerable skill to help family members accept, with a minimum of guilt and defensiveness, the naturalness of the ambivalent feelings they may have for their deceased member.

Ethnicity, race, and religion are major determinants of a family's belief system concerning health and illness (McGoldrick, Pearce, &

Giordano, 1982; Zborowski, 1969). There also tend to be cultural differences among ethnic, racial, and religious groups about the definition of what constitutes a family, what the responsibility of a family is for the care of ill members, who in the family is chiefly responsible for this care (usually the wife/mother in traditional cultures), the role of the extended family in patient care, and so on. These overlapping factors warrant extensive discussion that goes well beyond the scope of this chapter. Health professionals should familiarize themselves with belief systems of various ethnic, racial, and religious groups in their community, particularly as these translate into different behavioral patterns in regard to illness. Deference to distinctions between professionals' cultural beliefs and those of the patient and his or her family may forge a working alliance that is basic to the treatment of a long-term illness. Disregard of these issues can lead families to wall themselves off from health providers and available community resources—a major cause of noncompliance and treatment failure. For instance, it is customary for Italians and Jews to describe physical symptoms freely and in detail. Individuals from Irish or Anglo-Saxon descent tend to deny or conceal ailments. One can speculate about the potential for misunderstanding and tension that could develop between Italian and Jewish health providers working with Irish or Anglo-Saxon patients and their families. A mutually frustrating cycle of health providers pursuing a distancing family could develop. At minimum dissatisfaction would be the end result. At worst a family might leave treatment and use their negative experience as a rationale to rigidify its alienation and isolation from adequate care.

Once a family has articulated the illness belief system of its members, a clinician should inquire about the degree of family congruence about these beliefs. Congruence means the degree of consensus or divergence among family members concerning a particular value such as health locus of control. This is vitally important, because it is a common, but unfortunate, error to regard "the family" as a monolithic unit that feels, thinks, believes, and behaves as an undifferentiated whole.

Before assessing the family's level of agreement, one should inquire as to the family's metarule, that is, its general policy concerning congruence. In other words, is the family rule "We must agree on all/some values," or are diversity and different viewpoints acceptable? Further, one should find out whether the family metarule about consensus is adhered to across its external boundary in relation to prevailing cultural or societal beliefs. In other words, can the family hold values that differ from the wider culture? The family's metarule has multiple determinants which include cultural norms that have a "period effect" or historical context. Were members socialized in an era which endorsed the family unit as a central value or in an era—the more recent one—which valued the individual autonomy of each member? The value system of the adults' families of origin must also be considered, including the role the kinship network continues to play in family life.

A family's metarule vis-à-vis congruence can have profound implications in terms of permissable options when a family faces chronic illness. If consensus is the rule, then individual differentiation implies deviance. If the metarule is "We can hold different viewpoints," then diversity is allowed. When working with illness-related values in a family where consensus is the rule, attention to the entire family is mandatory. One goal of treatment can be for clinicians to help families negotiate their differences and support the separate identity, needs, and goals of each member. In a family where diversity is permitted there may be greater latitude to work on certain disease-related psychosocial issues with the ill member alone or with particular members of the family without mobilizing family resistance.

Having established the family's metarule concerning consensus, it is important to look into the *actual* degree of congruence with regard to illness values, both within the family and between the family and medical system.

How congruent are the family's basic beliefs about control with their illness value system? A family that has a uniformly external view of control, that sees events in their lives as being determined by factors outside of themselves will generally adapt best if psychosocial interventions are tailored to that view. On the other hand, a family may generally adhere to an internal locus of control but have opposite beliefs concerning a particular disease. This requires the clinician to help family members clarify their understanding of the illness and to come to terms with what aspects of the situation can be affected by their efforts at personal control and what aspects cannot be. It is critical for the clinician to keep in mind that "beliefs about control" refers to a family's beliefs about the importance of their participation in and management of the total illness process rather than just their beliefs about a disease's curability.

It is also important for the clinician to analyze differences among family members in terms of illness values. Disparities in dyadic and triadic relationships involving the ill member are particularly significant. Consider a common situation in which there is a long-standing loyalty conflict for a man caught between his spouse and his mother. Both women vie for his devotion, while he is unable to define boundaries between his family of origin and his nuclear family. This dysfunctional triangular relationship may have smoldered for years in a precarious balance. Suppose the man develops a slowly progressive and debilitating illness such as multiple sclerosis. If the man and his mother share a strong sense of internal control while his spouse grew up in a family that saw chronic illness as a matter of fate, an unbalancing of this triangle is likely to occur. The smoldering mother/son coalition now reemerges in full force, fueled by shared basic beliefs concerning mastery, while the marital system is driven apart.

It is common for differences in beliefs or attitudes among family members to erupt at transition points in the treatment or disease course. For instance, in situations of severe disability or terminal illness, one member may want the patient to return home while another prefers that he or she remain hospitalized or be transferred to an extended care facility. Since the task of patient caretaking is usually assigned to the wife/mother, she is the one most apt to bear the chief burdens in this regard. If this same family also operates under the constraint of traditional role assignments where the wife/mother defers to her spouse as the family decision maker, she may not make her true feelings known and may, as the "family martyr," take on the home nursing tasks without overt disagreement at the time critical decisions are made with health professionals. Clinicians can be misled by a family that values the presentation of this kind of united front. A careful and perceptive assessment by a clinician can help avert the long-term consequences to such a family of role-overload, resentment, and deteriorating family relationships. This has important implications for the well-being of each family member as well as for marital, parent/child, and extended family relationships.

It is essential to assess the fit between the belief systems of the family and the health care team, and the same questions asked of the family are relevant to the medical team. What is the attitude of the health care team as to their and the family's ability to influence the course/outcome of the disease? How does the health team see the balance between their versus the family's participation in the treatment and control of the disease? If basic differences in beliefs about health locus of control issues exist, it is critical to assess how these differences are to be reconciled. Because of the tendency of most health facilities to disempower individuals and thereby foster dependence, utmost sensitivity to family values is needed to create a true therapeutic system. In my clinical experience a significant proportion of the breakdown in relationships between "noncompliant" or marginal patients and their health care providers is related to lack of congruence at this basic level.

Health providers should always assess how a family's illness beliefs might influence their overall illness behavior within a community (Mechanic, 1978; Kleinman, 1975). How a particular family behaves across its external boundary is influenced by many family and larger system factors (e.g., social, economic, and political). To create a context for understanding, one must know the availability of and access to community resources relevant to the management of long-term illnesses. This includes a range of primary and tertiary medical, rehabilitation, respite, transportation, housing, institutional, and financial entitlement services. It also includes potential psychosocial support from friends, neighbors, self-help groups, and religious, ethnic/cultural, or other group affiliations. On the family side, one must inquire about a family's prior experience using any of the above resources. Have these experiences been affirming or alienating? To what extent is the family adequately informed about potential outside sources of help? Ignorance may reflect family isolation from the community due to such things as geographical distance in a rural setting, lack of education (e.g., literacy), a language barrier, poverty, race, and ethnic or religious distinctions from the wider culture. On the other side, a family's willingness to use outside resources may be limited by ethnic/cultural values, certain family dynamics, and their own illness paradigms.

For example, families that are rigidly enmeshed tend to view the outside world as dangerous and threatening to their fragile sense of autonomy, and individual autonomy is sacrificed to keep the family system intact. Their beliefs about control are defined within a framework of family exclusiveness that minimizes the role of outsiders. The occurrence of a chronic illness presents a powerful dilemma for these families because the illness may necessitate frequent excursions beyond the family borders or require the inclusion of outside professionals in disease management. Any hope of establishing a viable family/health care team relationship depends upon exquisite sensitivity to this interplay of dysfunctional family dynamics and to their belief system.

For any family coping with long-term illness, health care providers need to be mindful of the myriad issues that determine whether an effective alliance can be forged across the boundaries between the family and larger community systems. Family beliefs, values, attitudes, and rules that govern transactions across its boundary need to be assessed within the context of the access and availability of community resources. Further, the use of outside resources is important for all family members, not just the patient. Rigidly maintained family boundaries may prevent family members from using resources in the larger community that can promote the well-being of each member and lighten the burdens imposed on the family by the chronic illness of one of its members.

Transgenerational History of Illness, Loss, and Crisis

Systems-oriented theoreticians have emphasized that a family's present behavior cannot be adequately comprehended apart from its history (Boszormenyi-Nagy & Spark, 1973; Bowen, 1978; Carter & McGoldrick, 1980; Framo, 1976; McGoldrick & Walsh, 1983; Paul & Grosser, 1965). They see historical questioning as a way to track key events and transitions to gain an understanding of a family's organizational shifts and coping strategies *as a system* in response to past stressors. This is not a cause and effect model but reflects a belief that such an historical search may help explain the family's current style of coping and adaptation. An historical, systemic perspective involves more than simply deciphering how a family organized itself around past stressors; it also means tracking the evolution of family adaptation over time. In this respect patterns of adaptation, replication, and discontinuity; shifts in relationships (i.e., alliances, triangles, cutoffs); and sense of competence are important considerations. McGoldrick and Walsh (1983) describe how these patterns are transmitted across generations as family myths, taboos, catastrophic expectations, and belief systems. By gathering this information, a clinician can create a basic family genogram (McGoldrick & Gerson, 1985)

A chronic-illness-oriented genogram involves the same basic tracking process but focuses on how a family organized itself as an evolving system specifically around previous illnesses and unexpected crises in both the current and previous generations. A central goal is to bring to light the adults' "learned differences around illness" (Penn, 1983).

The typology of illness and time phases are useful concepts in this part of the family evaluation. Although a family may have certain standard ways of coping with any illness, there may be critical differences in their style and in their success at adapting to different "types" of diseases. A family may disregard the differences in demands related to different illnesses and thus may show a disparity in their level of coping with one disease versus another. If the clinician inquires separately about the same and similar illnesses versus different types (e.g., relapsing versus progressive, life-threatening versus non-life-threatening), he or she will make better use of historical data. For instance, a family may have consistently organized itself successfully around non-life-threatening illnesses but reeled under the weight of the paternal grandmother's metastic cancer. This family might be particularly vulnerable if another life-threatening illness were to occur. A different family may have had experience only with non-life-threatening illnesses and be ignorant of how to cope with the uncertainties of life-threatening ones. Cognizance of these facts will draw attention to areas of strength and vulnerability for a family facing cancer.

A recent family consultation highlights the importance of tracking prior family illnesses.

Joe, his wife Ann, and their three teenage children presented for a family evaluation 10 months after Joe's diagnosis with moderate-severe asthma. Joe, age 44, had been successfully employed for many years as a spray painter. Apparently exposure to a new chemical in the paint triggered the onset of asthmatic attacks that necessitated hospitalization and disability in terms of his occupation. Although somewhat improved, he continued to have persistent and moderate respiratory symptoms. Initially his physicians had discussed with him that improvement would occur but remained noncommittal as to the level of chronicity. His continued breathing difficulties contributed to increased symptoms of depression, uncharacteristic temperamental outbursts, alcohol abuse, and family discord.

As part of the initial assessment, I inquired as to their prior experience coping with chronic disease. This was the nuclear family's first encounter with chronic illness. In terms of their families of origin, they had limited experience. Ann's father had died seven years earlier of a sudden and unexpected heart attack, and Joe's brother had died in an accidental drowning, but neither had had experience with disease as an ongoing process. Joe had assumed that improvement meant "cure."

For both Ann and Joe illness meant either death or recovery. The physician/family system were not attuned to the hidden risks for this family going through the transition from the crisis phase to the chronic phase of his asthma, the juncture where the permanency of the disease needed to be addressed.

Tracking a family's coping capabilities in the crisis, chronic, and terminal phases of previous chronic illnesses will highlight complications in adaptation related to different points in the "illness life cycle." A family may have adapted well in the crisis phase of living with the paternal grandfather's spinal cord injury but failed to navigate the transition to a family organization consistent with long-haul adaptation. An enmeshed family with a tendency toward rigid over-closeness may have become frozen in a crisis structure and been unable to deal appropriately with maximizing individual and collective autonomy in the chronic phase. Another family with a member with chronic kidney failure may have functioned very well in handling the practicalities of home dialysis. However, in the terminal phase their limitations around affective expression may have left a legacy of unresolved grief. A history of time-phase-specific difficulties can alert a clinician to potential vulnerable periods for a family over the course of the current chronic illness. A family seen in treatment illustrates the interplay of problems coping with a current illness, problems that are fueled by unresolved issues related to a particular type and/or phase of disease in one's family of origin.

Mary, her husband Bill, and their son Jim presented for treatment 4 months after Mary had been involved in a life-threatening, head-on auto collision. The driver of the other vehicle was at fault; Mary had sustained a serious concussion. Also, for several months there was some concern by the medical team that she might have suffered a cerebral hemorrhage. Ultimately it was clarified that this had not occurred. During this time Mary became increasingly depressed and, despite strong reassurance, continued to believe she had a life-threatening condition and would die from a brain hemorrhage.

During the initial evaluation she revealed that she was experiencing vivid dreams of meeting her deceased father. Apparently her father, with whom she had been extremely close, had died from a cerebral hemorrhage after a 4-year history of debilitating brain tumor. His illness had been marked by progressive and uncontrolled epileptic seizures. Mary was 14 at the time and was the "baby" in the family, her two siblings being more than 10 years her senior. The family had shielded her from his illness, which culminated in her mother deciding to not have her attend either the wake or the funeral of her father. This event galvanized her position as the "child in need of protection," a dynamic that carried over into her marriage.

Despite her hurt, anger and lack of acceptance of her father's death, Mary had avoided dealing with her feelings toward her mother for over 20 years. Other family history revealed that her mother's brother had died from a sudden stroke, and a cousin had died after being struck on the head by a street lamp. Further, her maternal grandfather had died when her mother was 7 years old, and her mother had to endure an open casket wake at home. This traumatic experience was a major factor in her mother's attempt to protect the identified patient from the same kind of memory.

Mary's own life-threatening head injury had triggered a catastrophic reaction and dramatic resurfacing of previous losses involving similar types of illness and injury. Therapy focused on a series of tasks and rituals that involved her initiating conversations with her mother and visits to her father's gravesite.

The family's history of coping with crises in general, especially unanticipated ones, should be explored. Illnesses with acute onset (i.e., heart attack), moderate-severe sudden incapacitation (i.e., stroke), or rapid relapse (i.e., ulcerative colitis, diabetic insulin reaction, disc disease) demand in various ways rapid crisis mobilization skills. In these situations the family needs to reorganize quickly and efficiently, shifting from its usual organization to a crisis structure. Other illnesses can create a crisis because of the continual demand for family stamina (i.e., spinal cord injury, rheumatoid arthritis, emphysema). The family history of coping with moderate-severe ongoing stressors is a good predictor of adjustment to these types of illness.

For any significant chronic illness in either adult's family of origin, a clinician should try to get a picture of how those families organized themselves to handle the range of disease-related affective and practical tasks. Also it is important for a clinician to find out what role each played in handling these emotional or practical tasks. Whether the parents (as children) were given too much responsibility (parentified) or shielded from involvement is of particular importance. What did they learn from those experiences that influences how they think about the current illness? Whether they emerge with a strong sense of competence or failure is essential information. In one particular case, involving a family with three generations of hemophilia transmitted through the mother's side, the father had been shielded from the knowledge that his older brother who died in adolescence had had a terminal form of kidney disease. Also, this man had not been allowed to attend his brother's funeral. As a result of that trauma, he made a strong commitment to openness about disease-related issues with his two sons with hemophilia and his daughters who were genetic carriers.

By collecting the above information about each adult's family of origin, one can anticipate areas of conflict and consensus. Penn (1983) and Walker (1983) have described the frequency with which unresolved issues related to illness and loss can remain dormant in a marriage and suddenly reemerge, triggered by a chronic illness in the current nuclear family. Penn (1983) describes how particular coalitions that emerge in the context of a chronic illness are isomorphs of those that existed in each adult's family of origin. The following vignette is a prototypical example.

> If a mother has been the long-time rescuer of her mother from a tyrannical husband, and then in her own family bears a son with hemophilia, she will become his rescuer, often against his father. In this manner she continues to rescue her mother but, oddly enough, now from her husband rather than from her own father. . . . In this family with a hemophiliac son the father's father had been ill for a long period and had received all the mother's attention. In her present family, this father, though outwardly objecting to the coalition between his wife and son, honored that relationship, as if he hoped it would make up for the one he had once forfeited with his own mother. The coalition in the nuclear family looks open and adaptational (mother and son) but is fueled by coalitions from the past (mother with her mother, and father with his mother) (Penn 1983).

The reenactment of previous system configurations around illness can occur largely as an unconscious, automatic process. Further, the dysfunctional complementarity one sees in these families can emerge *de novo* specifically within the context of a chronic disease. On detailed inquiry couples will frequently reveal that a tacit understanding existed that if an illness occurred, they would reorganize to reenact "unfinished business" from their families of origin. Typically the role chosen represents a repetition or opposite of a role played by themselves or the same-sex parent in their family of origin. This process resembles the unfolding of a genetic template that gets switched on only under very particular biological conditions. It highlights the need for a clinician to maintain some distinction between functional family process with and without chronic disease. For families that present in this manner, placing a primary therapeutic emphasis on the resolution of family of origin issues might be the best approach to prevent or rectify an unhealthy triangle.

Families such as those just described with encapsulated illness "time bombs" need to be distinguished from families that show more pervasive and long-standing dysfunctional patterns. For the latter, illnesses will tend to become imbedded within a web of existing, fused family transactions. Just as parents can enact a detouring triangle through an ill child to avert unresolved marital conflict (Minuchin et al., 1975, 1978), so too the therapist can collude with a family's resistance by overfocusing on the disease itself. Distinctions between the family's illness versus nonillness patterns are, to a large degree, semantic when the illness serves to rigidify preexisting family dysfunction. In the traditional sense of "psychosomatic," a severely dysfunctional family displays a greater level of baseline reactivity such that when an illness enters their system, this reactivity gets expressed somatically through a poor medical course and/ or treatment noncompliance. These families lack the foundation of a functional nonillness system that can serve as the metaphorical equivalent of "healthy ego" in tackling family of origin patterns around disease. The initial focus of therapeutic intervention may need to be targeted more on the horizontal axis (nuclear family) rather than on the vertical intergenerational axis. The prognosis for this kind of family is more guarded.

A third group of symptomatic families facing chronic disease are those without significant intra- or intergenerational family dysfunctional patterns. Any family may falter in the face of multiple superimposed disease and nondisease stressors that have an impact in a relatively short time. Progressive, incapacitating diseases or the occurence of illness in several family members are typical scenarios. A pragmatic approach that focuses on expanded or creative use of supports and resources outside the family is most productive.

Interface of the Illness, the Individual, and the Family Life Cycles

To place the unfolding of chronic diseases into a developmental context, it is crucial to understand the intertwining of three evolutionary threads, the illness, the individual, and the family life cycles. This is a highly complex process that remains largely unexplored. In order to think in an interactive or systemic manner about the interface of these three developmental lines, one first needs a common language and set of concepts that can be applied to each and permit a trialogue. There are two necessary steps to lay the foundation for such a model. First, one needs a language that permits diseases to be characterized in psychosocial and longitudinal terms, with each illness having a particular "personality" and expected developmental life course. The psychosocial typology and time phases of illness offer such a language. Second, because an illnes *is* part of an individual, it is essential to think simultaneously about the interaction of individual and family development. Individual and family life cycle theoretical models need to be linked by culling out from each key overarching concepts. At present, the developmental relationship between these different levels of system remains mostly unaddressed.

A central concept for both family and individual development is that of the *life cycle*. The notion of cycle suggests an underlying order of the life course where individual, family, or illness uniqueness occurs within a context of a basic sequence or unfolding. A second key concept is that of the human *life structure*. Although Levinson's (1978) original description of the life structure was within the context of his study of individual male adult development, life structure as a generic concept can be applied to the family as a unit. By life structure he means the underlying pattern or design of a person's/family's life at any given point in the life cycle. Its primary components are a person's/family's reciprocal relationships with various "others" in the broader ecosystem (e.g., person, group, institution, culture, object, or place). The life structure forms a boundary between the individual/family and the environment, and it both governs and mediates the transactions between them.

Illness, the individual, and family development have in common the notion of eras marked by the alternation of life-structure-building/maintaining and life-structure-changing (transitional) periods linking developmental eras. The primary goal of a structure-building/maintaining period is to form a life structure and enrich life within it based on the key choices an individual/family made during the preceding transition period. The delineation of separate eras derives from a set of developmental tasks that are associated with each period. Transition periods are potentially the most vulnerable because previous individual, family, and illness life structures are reappraised in the face of new developmental tasks that may require discontinuous change rather than minor alterations (Hoffman, 1980).

Levinson (1978) has provided a pioneering effort in describing four major eras in individual life structure development: childhood and adolescence, and early, middle, and late adulthood. Each era lasts approximately 20 years. Duvall (1977) and Carter and McGoldrick (1980) have divided the family life cycle into eight and six stages respectively. Both Duvall (1977) and Carter and McGoldrick (1980) describe the following family life cycle stages: (a) the unattached young adult, (b) the newly married couple, (c) the family with young children, (d) the family with adolescents, (e) the family launching children and moving on, and (f) the family in later life.

A primary distinction between Levinson's and the family life cycle models needs to be mentioned. In family life cycle models marker events (e.g., marriage, birth of first child, last child leaving home) herald the transition from one stage to the next. Levinson's research elucidated a sequence of age-specific periods, 5 to 7 years in length, during which certain developmental tasks for adult males are addressed independent of marker events. In this model marker events will both color the character of a developmental period and, in turn, be colored by their timing in the individual life cycle.

The concept of centripetal versus centrifugal family styles and phases in the family life cycle is particularly useful to the task of integrating illness, individual, and family development (Beavers, 1982, 1983). Recent work of Combrinck-Graham (1985) elaborates the application of this concept to the family life cycle. She describes a family life spiral model, where she envisions the entire three-generational family system oscillating through time between periods of family closeness (centripetal) and periods of family disengagement (centrifugal). These periods coincide with oscillations between family developmental tasks that require intense bonding or normal enmeshment, such as early child rearing, and tasks that emphasize personal identity and autonomy, such as adolescence. Typically, an individual will experience three oscillations in a lifetime: one's own childhood and adolescence, the birth and adolescence of one's children, and the birth and development of one's grandchildren.

In a literal sense centripetal and centrifugal describe a tendency to move respectively toward and away from a center. In life cycle terms, they connote a fit between developmental tasks and the relative need for internally directed personal and family group cohesive energy to accomplish those tasks. During a centripetal period both the individual member's and family unit's life structures emphasize

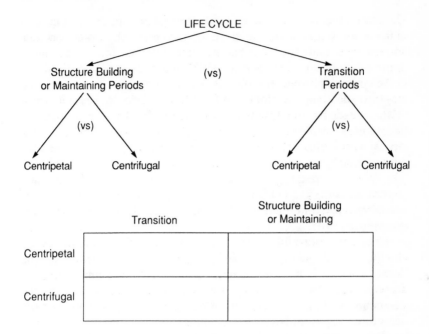

Figure 1.8. Periods in the family/individual life cycle.

internal family life. External boundaries around the family are tightened while personal boundaries between members are somewhat diffused to enhance family teamwork. In the transition to a centrifugal period, the family life structure shifts to accommodate goals that emphasize the individual family member's exchange with the extrafamilial environment. The external family boundary is loosened while nonpathological distance between some family members increases.

From this brief overview of life cycle models we can cull out several key concepts that provide a foundation for discussion of chronic disease. We can consider the life cycle to contain alternating transition and life-structure-building/maintaining periods. Further, particular transition or life-structure-building/maintaining periods can be characterized as either centripetal or centrifugal in nature. This set of relationships can be diagrammed in the following way (Figure 1.8). The following discussion will use these as its central reference point.

The notion of centripetal and centrifugal modes is useful in linking the illness life cycle to the individual and family life cycles. One can think about this interface from the vantage point of chronic illnesses in general or from the more fine-tuned perspective of specific illness types or phases in the unfolding of chronic disease.

In general, chronic disease exerts a centripetal pull on the family system. In family developmental models centripetal periods begin with the addition of a new family member (infant), which propels the family into a prolonged period of the socialization of children. In an analogous way the occurrence of chronic illness in a family resembles the addition of a new member, which sets in motion for the family a centripetal process of socialization to illness. Symptoms, loss of function, the demands of shifting illness-related practical and affective roles, and the fear of loss through death all serve to refocus a family inward.

If the onset of an illness coincides with a centrifugal period for the family, it can derail the family from its natural momentum. If a young adult becomes ill, he or she may need to return to the family of origin for disease-related caretaking. Each family member's extrafamilial autonomy and individuation are at risk. The young adult's initial life structure away from home is threatened either temporarily or permanently. Both parents may have to relinquish budding interests outside the family. Family dynamics as well as disease severity and duration will influence whether the family's reversion to a centripetal life structure is a temporary detour within their general movement outward or a permanent involutional shift. A moderately fused or enmeshed family frequently faces the transition to a more autonomous period with trepidation. A chronic illness provides a sanctioned reason to return to the "safety" of the prior centripetal period. For some family members, the giving up of the building of a new life structure that is already in progress can be more devastating than when the family is still in a more centripetal period where future plans may be at a more preliminary stage, less formulated, or less clearly decided upon. An analogy would be the difference between a couple discovering that they do not have enough money to build a house versus being forced to abandon their building project with the foundation already completed.

Disease onset that coincides with a centripetal period in the family life cycle (e.g., early child rearing) can have several important consequences. At minimum, it can foster a prolongation of this period. At worst, the family can become permanently stuck at this phase of development. In this instance, the inward pull of the illness and the phase of the life cycle coincide. The risk here is their tendency to amplify one another. For families that function in a marginal way before an illness begins, this kind of mutual reinforcement can trigger a runaway process leading to overt family dysfunction. Minuchin, Rosman, and Baker's (1975, 1978) research of "psychosomatic" families has documented this process in several common childhood illnesses.

When a parent develops a chronic disease during this centripetal child-rearing phase of development, a family's ability to stay on course is severely taxed. In essence, the impact of the illness is like the addition of a new infant member. This new member is like a child with "special needs" competing with the real children for potentially scarce family resources. For psychosocially milder diseases efficient role reallocation may suffice. A recent case illustrates this point.

> Tom and his wife Sally presented for treatment 6 months after Tom had sustained a severe burn injury to both hands that required skin grafting. A year of recuperation was necessary before he would be able to return to his job, which required physical labor and full use of his hands. Prior to this injury his wife had been at home full time raising their two children, aged 3 and 5. In this case, although Tom was temporarily handicapped in terms of his career, he was physically fit to assume the role of househusband. Initially, both Tom and Sally remained at home using his disability income to "get by." When Sally expressed an interest in finding a job to release financial pressures, Tom resisted, and manageable marital strain caused by his injury flared into dysfunctional conflict.
>
> Although sufficient resources were available in the system to accommodate the illness and ongoing child rearing tasks, their definition of marriage lacked the necessary role flexibility to master the problem. Treatment focused on rethinking Tom's masculine and monolithic definition of "family provider," a definition that had, in fact, emerged in full force during this centripetal phase of the family life cycle.

If the disease affecting a parent is more debilitating (e.g., traumatic brain injury, cervical spinal cord injury), its impact on the child-rearing family is twofold. A "new" family member is added, a parent is "lost," and the semblance of a single-parent family with an added child is created. For acute onset illness both events can occur simultaneously. In this circumstance, family resources may be inadequate to meet the combined child rearing and caretaking demands. This situation is ripe for the emergence of a parentified child or the reenlistment into active parenting of a grandparent. While these forms of family adaptation are not inherently dysfunctional, a clinician needs to assess these structural realignments in terms of their rigidity and impact on each person. Are certain individuals assigned permanent caretaking roles, or are the roles flexible and shared? Are caretaking roles viewed flexibly from a developmental vantage point? For an adolescent caretaker this means the family being mindful of his or her approaching developmental transition to an independent life separate from the family. For grandparent caretakers it means sensitivity to their increasing physical limitations or the need to assist their own spouse.

If we look at chronic diseases in a more refined way through the lens of the typology and time phases of illness, it is readily apparent that the degree of centripetal/centrifugal pull varies enormously. This variability has important effects on the family life cycle independent of family dynamics. The tendency for a disease to interact centripetally with a family grows as the level of incapacitation or risk of death due to the illness increases. Progressive diseases over time are inherently more centripetal in terms of their effect on families than constant course illnesses. The ongoing addition of new demands as an illness progresses keeps a family's energy focused inward. After a modus operandi has been forged, a constant course disease (excluding those with severe incapacitation) permits a family to enter or resume a more centrifugal phase of the life cycle. The added centripetal pull exerted by a progressive disease increases the risk of reversing normal family disengagement or freezing a family into a permanent state of fusion.

Mr. L., aged 54, had become increasingly depressed as a result of severe and progressive complications of the adult-onset diabetes that had emerged over the past 5 years. These complications included a leg amputation and renal failure that recently required instituting home dialysis four times daily. For 20 years Mr. L. had had an uncomplicated constant course, allowing him to lead a full active life. He was an excellent athlete and engaged in a number of recreational group sports. Short- and long-term family planning had never focused around his illness. This optimistic attitude was reinforced by the fact that two people in Mrs. L's family of origin had had diabetes without complications. Their only child, a son aged 26, had uneventfully left home after high school and had recently married. Mr. and Mrs. L. had a stable marriage, where both maintained many independent interests. In short, the family had moved smoothly through the transition to a more centrifugal phase of the family's life cycle.

His disease's transformation to a progressive course, coupled with the incapacitating and life-shortening nature of his complications, had reversed the normal process of family disengagement. His wife took a second job, which necessitated her quitting her hobbies and civic involvements. Their son moved back home to help his mother take care of his father and the house. Mr. L., disabled from work and his athletic social network, felt a burden to everyone and blocked in his own midlife development.

The essential goal of family treatment in developmental terms centered around reversing some of the system's centripetal overreaction back to a more realistic balance. For Mr. L. this meant reworking his life structure to accommodate his real limitations while maximizing a return to his basically independent style. For Mrs. L. and her son this meant developing realistic expectations for Mr. L. and reestablishing key aspects of their autonomy within an illness/family system.

Relapsing illnesses alternate between periods of drawing a family inward and periods of release from the immediate demands of disease. However, the on-call state of preparedness dictated by many such illnesses keeps some part of the family in a centripetal mode despite medically asymptomatic periods. Again, this may hinder the natural flow between phases of the family life cycle.

One way to think about the time phases of illness is that they represent to the family a progression from a centripetal crisis phase to a more centrifugal chronic phase. The terminal phase, if it occurs, forces most families back into a more centripetal mode. In other words, the so-called illness life structure, developed by a family to accommodate each phase in the illness life cycle, is colored by each time phase's inherent centripetal/centrifugal nature. For example, in a family where the onset of the illness has coincided with a centrifugal phase of development, the transition to the chronic phase permits a family to resume more of its original inertia.

One cannot overemphasize the need for clinicians to be mindful of the timing of the onset of a chronic illness with individual/family transition and life-structure-building/maintaining periods of development.

All *transitions* inherently involve the basic processes of termination and initiation. Arrivals, departures, and losses are common life events, during which there is an undercurrent of preoccupation with death and finiteness (Levinson, 1978). Chronic and life-threatening illness precipitates the loss of the preillness identity of the family. It forces the family into a transition in which one of the family's main tasks is to accommodate the anticipation of further loss and possibly untimely death. When the onset of a chronic illness coincides with a transition in the individual or family life cycle, one might expect that issues related to previous, current, and anticipated loss will be magnified.

Transition periods are often characterized by upheaval, rethinking of prior commitments, and openness to change. As a result, there exists at those times a greater risk for the illness to become unnecessarily embedded in family life or inappropriately ignored when planning for the next developmental period. During a transition period the very process of loosening prior commitments creates a context for family rules regarding loyalty through sacrifice and caretaking to take over. Feelings of indecision about one's future can be "resolved" by excessive focus on a family member's physical problems. This can be a major precursor of family dysfunction in the context of chronic disease. If a clinician adopts a longitudinal developmental perspective, he or she will stay attuned to future transitions and their overlap with each other.

An example can highlight the importance of the illness in relation to future developmental transitions. Imagine a family in which the father, a carpenter and primary financial provider, develops multiple sclerosis. At first his level of impairment is mild and stabilized. This allows him to continue part-time work. Because their children are all teenagers, his wife is able to undertake part-time work to help maintain financial stability. The oldest son, aged 15, seems relatively unaffected. Two years later the father experiences a rapid progression of his illness, leaving him totally disabled. His son, now 17, has dreams of going away to college and getting educated for a career in science. The specter of financial hardship and the perceived need for a "man in the family" creates a serious dilemma of choice for the son and the family. In this case there is a fundamental clash between the developmental issues of separation and individuation and the ongoing demands of progressive chronic disability on the family.

This vignette demonstrates the potential clash between simultaneous transition periods: the illness transition to a more incapacitating and progressive course, the adolescent son's transition to early adulthood, and the family's transition from the stage of "living with teenagers" to that of "launching young adults." Also, this example illustrates the significance of the type of illness. An illness that was less incapacitating or relapsing (as opposed to a progressive or constant course disease) might interfere less with this young man's separation from his family of origin. If his father had an intermittently incapacitating illness, such as disc disease, the son might have moved out but tailored his choices to remain close by and thus available during acute flare-ups.

The onset of a chronic illness may cause a different kind of disruption if it coincides with a *life-structure-building/maintaining period* in individual or family development. These periods are characterized by living out a certain life structure, an outgrowth of the rethinking, formulation, and change of the preceding transition period. The cohesive bonds of the individual/family are oriented toward protecting the current life structure. Thus, diseases with only a mild level of psychosocial severity (e.g. nonfatal, none/mild incapacitation, nonprogressive) may require of the individual/family some revision of their life structure but not a radical restructuring that would necessitate a more basic return to a transitional phase of development. A chronic illness with a critical threshold of psychosocial severity will demand the reestablishment of a transitional form of life at a time when individual/family inertia is to preserve the momentum of a stable period. An individual's or family's level of adaptability is a prime factor determining the successful navigation of this kind of crisis. In this context the concept of family adaptability is referred to in its broadest sense—the ability of a family to transform its entire life structure to a prolonged transitional state.

For instance, in our previous example, the father's multiple sclerosis rapidly progressed while the oldest son was in a transition period in his own development. The nature of the strain in developmental terms would be quite different if his father's disease progression had occurred when this young man was 26, had already left home, had finished college and secured a first job, and had married and had his first child. In the latter scenario the oldest son's life structure would be in a centripetal, structure-maintaining period within his newly formed nuclear family. To fully accommodate to the needs of his family of origin could require a monumental shift of his developmental priorities. When this illness crisis coincided with a developmental transition period (age 17), although a dilemma of choice existed, the son was available and less fettered by commitments in progress. At age 26, he would have made developmental choices and would be in the process of living them out. Not only would he have made commitments, but also they would be centripetal in nature—focused on his newly formed family. To serve the demands of an illness transition, the son might have needed to shift his previously stable life structure back to a transitional state. And the shift would happen "out of phase" with the flow of his individual and nuclear family's development. One precarious way to resolve this dilemma of divided loyalties might be the merging of the two households, thereby creating a single, superlarge centripetal family system.

This discussion raises several key clinical points. From a systems viewpoint, at the time of a chronic illness diagnosis it is important to know the phase of the family life cycle and the stage of individual development of all family members, not just the ill member. This is important information for several reasons. First, chronic disease in one family member can profoundly affect developmental goals of another member. For instance, a disabled infant can be a serious roadblock to a mother's mastery of child rearing, or a life-threatening illness in a young adult can interfere with the spouse's task of beginning the phase of parenthood. Second, family members frequently do not adapt equally to chronic illness. Each family member's ability to adapt and the rate at which he or she does so is directly related to each individual's own developmental stage and his or her role in the family (Ireys & Burr, 1984). The oldest son in the previous example illustrates this point.

Clinicians and researchers generally agree that there exists a normative and nonnormative timing of chronic illness in the life cycle. Coping with chronic illness and death are considered normally anticipated tasks in late adulthood. Illnesses and losses that occur earlier, however, are "out of phase" and tend to be developmentally more disruptive (Herz, 1980; Neugarten, 1976). As untimely events chronic diseases can severely disrupt the usual sense of continuity and rhythm of the life cycle. Levinson's research (1978) showed that the timing in the life cycle of an unexpected event, such as a chronic illness, will shape the form of adaptation and the event's influence on subsequent development.

This discussion suggests that the notion of "out of phase" illnesses can be conceptualized in a more refined way. First, as described earlier, diseases have a centripetal influence on most families. In this sense, they are naturally "out of phase" with families in transition to a more centrifugal period.

Second, the onset of chronic disease tends to create a period of transition, the length or intensity of which depends upon the psychosocial type and phase of the illness. This forced transition is particularly "out of phase" if it coincides with a life-structure-building/ maintaining period in the individual's or family's life cycle. Third, if the particular illness is progressive, relapsing, increasingly incapacitating, and/or life-threatening, then the phases in the unfolding of the disease will be punctuated by numerous transitions. Under these conditions a family will need to more frequently alter their illness life structure to accommodate to the shifting and often increasing demands of the disease. This level of demand and uncertainty keeps the illness in the forefront of a family's consciousness, constantly impinging upon their attempts to get back "in phase" developmentally.

Finally, the transition from the crisis to the chronic phase of the illness life cycle is often the key juncture in which the intensity of the family's socialization to living with chronic disease can be relaxed. In this sense, it offers a "window of opportunity" for the family to correct its developmental course.

Some investigators feel that chronic diseases that occur in the child rearing period can be most devastating because of their potential impact on family financial and child rearing responsibilities (Herz, 1980). Again, the actual impact will depend on the "type" of illness and the preillness roles and resources of each family member. Families governed by rigid, gender-defined roles as to who should be the primary financial provider and caretaker of children will potentially have the greatest problems with adjustment. This kind of family needs to be coached toward a more flexible view about interchanging clearly defined roles.

In the face of chronic disease, an overarching goal is for a family to deal with the developmental demands presented by the illness without family members sacrificing their own or the family's development as a system. Therefore, it is vital to ask about what life plans the family or individual members had to cancel, postpone, or alter as a result of the diagnosis. It is useful to know whose plans are most and least affected. And by asking a family when and under what conditions they will resume plans put on hold or address future developmental tasks, a clinician can anticipate developmental crises related to "independence from" versus "subjugation to" the chronic illness. He or she can also help family members resume their life plans, at least to some extent, by helping them resolve feelings of guilt, over-responsibility, and hopelessness and find resources internal and external to the family so as to give them more freedom, both to pursue their own goals *and* provide needed care for the ill member.

CONCLUSION

This discussion has been an attempt to clarify conceptual thinking about the system created at the interface of chronic illness with the family. Several problems were identified as major impediments to progress in this field. These difficulties suggested the need for: (a) a categorization scheme that organizes similarities and differences between diseases in a manner useful to psychosocial rather than medical inquiry; (b) greater attention to the variation of illnesses over their time course; and (c) expansion of a general family systems model to include illness-related dynamics that emphasize belief systems and the dimension of time.

A three-dimensional model emerged in the process of addressing these needs. On the first dimension psychosocial "types" of illnesses are created based on combinations of four components: onset, course, outcome, and degree of incapacitation. The second dimension distinguishes three phases in the life history of chronic disease: crisis, chronic, and terminal. The third dimension includes various universal and illness-specific components of family functioning. Particular attention was given to the family illness value system; the family's transgenerational history of illness, loss, and crisis; and to the interface of the individual and family life cycles with chronic disease.

This three-dimensional model provides a way to better appreciate the illness/family system. It facilitates interactional thinking about the relationships between the illness type, the time phase of the illness, and family functioning. Finally, this model furnishes a central reference point to understand the broader context of the illness/family system.

Chronic Illness in Children and the Impact on Families

JOAN M. PATTERSON

INTRODUCTION

In the words of Robert Massie (1985), a 25-year-old with hemophilia, "The most important thing to remember about a chronic illness is that it is exactly that: chronic. It never goes away. It pervades every moment and aspect of life, often from birth until death. The chronic illness becomes molded into the child's identity—I am a hemophiliac." This pervasive, relentless impact strikes not only the chronically ill child but his or her family as well. For many chronically ill children, life depends on the ability of their families to exert a lifetime of daily effort on their behalf (Travis, 1976).

While each specific chronic disorder has its own unique pathophysiology and medical treatment needs, these illnesses as a group share many commonalities in terms of their impact on families. Chronically ill children and their families are confronted with a set of unrelenting demands—financial strain, the daily burden of care, the search for and dependence on a host of medical and other services, uncertainty about the future, marital and sibling tension, and so on—all of which place them at greater risk for problems at every stage of the life cycle. The medical literature on chronic illness in childhood is generally disease specific, reflecting an approach which has led to advances in early identification and treatment. This, in turn, has prolonged and improved the quality of life for these children. This purely biomedical approach, however, has focused little attention on the psychosocial impact and how families are able or not able to manage living with and caring for a chronically ill child. Yet the nature of the family, as much or more than the nature of the disorder, appears to be associated with how well the child does (Pless & Perrin, 1985). According to Zucman (1982), the child's illness is not the "provocateur" of family difficulty but the "revealer" of it.

In this chapter chronic childhood illnesses are examined from a generic perspective as opposed to disease specific. A systemic approach is taken, examining the reciprocal impacts of the illness of the family as well as how characteristics and changes in the family system influence the course of the illness over time.

THE NATURE OF CHRONIC ILLNESS IN CHILDREN

What do we mean by "chronic" illness? Perrin (1985) provides a general definition of chronic illness as "a condition that interferes with daily functioning for more than 3 months in a year, causes hospitalization of more than 1 month in a year, or (at time of diagnosis) is likely to do either of these" (p. 2). This is in contrast to acute illness, which begins abruptly and usually lasts for a period of days or possibly weeks but then is over and the prior healthy state of the child returns. For families the implications of having a child with a chronic illness versus an acute illness are many.

Most serious acute illnesses are managed by a physician, often in a hospital setting. Family members may be informed about treatment, but usually both the family and the physician accept that the locus of responsibility for the treatment lies with the physician. In most cases the outcome is positive: the illness goes away and the child is healthy again.

In contrast, the child with chronic illness never returns to perfect health and must spend his or her entire life coping with limitations which often are progressively debilitating. Most of the time the child lives at home, and his or her family is tasked with the responsibility of providing the care and treatment. This notion of the family being responsible for providing treatment requires a major shift in orientation, not only for the family, but for the whole medical profession. Technological advances in medicine have been based on an acute disease model where medical scientists took charge and discovered causes (often singular, e.g., an infectious agent) and subsequent cures for illnesses. The doctor treated; the patient got well. With chronic illness the child and family must cope with the residuals of what can't be cured—pain, debilitation, progressive loss of bodily functions, and so on. In addition, the family may need to follow through with complex, time-consuming regimens of care to reduce complications and prolong life. Many families struggle with accepting this responsibility for care and try to shift it to the medical system. This attitude can lead to recurrent exacerbations of the illness, requiring hospitalizations where the acute illness model becomes activated. Recurrent ketoacidosis in a child with diabetes would be an example. In many ways the medical system seems best suited to respond to these crises, and it struggles with its own deficiencies in what to offer families who are coping with a chronically ill child (Burish & Bradley, 1983).

Prevalence

Chronic physical illness confronts an estimated 10 to 15% of all children under 18 years of age and their families (Pless & Perrin, 1985). It is further estimated that about 10% of these have *severe* conditions (1% of the total childhood population). With an estimated 62 million children under age 18 in the United States, about 7.5 million have a chronic health condition, with about one million of these being severe disorders (Hobbs, Perrin, & Ireys, 1985).

For the most part the incidence of new cases of chronic childhood illness is not changing; that is, the number of new cases as a percentage of the population has remained stable over several decades. What has changed dramatically, however, is the increase in the survival rate for many conditions. With advances in medical technology children who are born with illnesses such as cystic fibrosis or hemophilia or acquire conditions such as leukemia or end stage renal disease are living into adolescence and adulthood. Thus the prevalence of chronic illness in children has increased dramatically in recent decades (Gortmaker & Sappenfield, 1984). The consequence of this increased longevity has, in many ways, increased the hardships for these children and their families, given the protracted burden of care and the ambiguity about the future inherent in chronic childhood illness.

Unlike adults, where the types of chronic illnesses are few in number but are prevalent (e.g., hypertension and diabetes), each of the hundreds of different conditions in children is relatively rare. The estimated prevalences for 18 chronic childhood illnesses are presented in Table 2.1. Except for a few common disorders such as mild asthma, the prevalence of any single condition is less than 1 per 100 children. For families these low prevalence rates have implications. Medical services for diagnosis and treatment may be harder to locate since many primary care physicians are not skilled in treating rare conditions. Thus, early identification, referral, and long-term management become issues for families. In addition, information about the illness may be hard to obtain. Regional medical centers are the primary source for medical treatment, which may require frequent travel or, possibly, relocation to be near service providers. A child and his or her family are unlikely to know or meet others coping with the same illness, and they may feel different, isolated, and not understood. Families with chronically ill children face these and many other hardships which will be discussed below.

Table 2.1
Estimated Prevalence of Select Chronic Illnesses in Children
Ages Birth to 20 Years in the United States, 1980

Chronic Illness	Prevalence Estimate per 1000
Asthma (moderate to severe)	10.00
Congenital heart disease	7.00
Seizure disorder	3.50
Cerebral palsy	2.50
Central nervous system injury (paralysis)	2.10
Arthritis	2.20
Diabetus mellitus	1.80
Cleft lip/palate	1.50
Down's syndrome	1.10
Blindness	.60
Spina bifida	.40
Sickle cell anemia	.28
Cystic fibrosis	.20
Hemophilia	.15
Leukemia	.11
Deafness	.10
Chronic renal failure	.08
Muscular dystrophy	.06

Adapted from "Chronic childhood disorders: Prevalence and impact" by S. L. Gortmaker and W. Sappenfield, 1984, *Pediatric Clinics of North America 31*, pp. 3–18.

What Causes Chronic Illness?

The simplest distinction regarding etiology is between genetic and environmental factors. Genetic factors include chromosomal defects (e.g., Down's syndrome) and single gene disorders (Hobbs et al., 1985). With most gene disorders parents do not have the condition but are carriers of a recessive gene causing it. Some conditions result from the pairing of a recessive gene from each parent (e.g., sickle cell anemia), whereas with sex-linked recessive disorders, only one parent needs to have the recessive gene to transmit it to the opposite sex child (e.g., hemophilia). Knowledge of these genetic factors often produces guilt in parents (or leads to blame) and may become a factor in their subsequent ability to adapt.

Environmental factors can be an issue in chronic disorders (a) during pregnancy (intrauterine), (b) at the time of delivery (perinatal), or (c) at any age after the child is born. Intrauterine exposure to hazardous factors such as radiation, toxic drugs, or infections is associated with retardation and malformations (e.g., German measles leading to congenital heart defect). Traumatic or infectious events at the time of delivery such as a knotted umbilical cord causing deprivation of oxygen to the fetus may cause damage to the central nervous system and subsequent retardation. Exposure to accidents such as a spinal cord injury leading to quadriplegia or environmental exposure to toxic agents at any point in life are associated with many chronic conditions.

Most chronic illnesses probably arise from a combination of both genetic and environmental factors (Hobbs et al., 1985). It would appear that often there is a genetic susceptibility, and with the necessary environmental exposure the condition emerges. For example, in some cases juvenile diabetes has its onset following an acute viral infection in children who have a genetic predisposition for it. In addition, the course of many chronic illnesses is shaped by environmental factors as in the case of asthma, where exacerbations occur following exposure to toxic or infectious agents.

Knowledge of what causes chronic disease is important because of our desire to prevent it. At the time of diagnosis, family members often focus strongly on what caused it as a way to alleviate the anxiety they feel. The definition the family members arrive at regarding cause can be very important in how they ultimately cope with the condition. Generally, stress theorists have argued that when family members believe that the cause is internal—something they did wrong, such as using alcohol or drugs during pregnancy—there is greater disruption to the family system and more difficulty coping (Hill, 1958). Conversely, when the cause for the chronic illness is viewed as coming from outside the family and as something beyond their control (e.g., fate), this stressor may serve to bring the family together; hence, better adaptation would be expected. Since most chronic illnesses seem to be caused by multiple factors, some of which are yet unknown, it is important to help families arrive at a definition of cause which alleviates their sense of guilt and blame.

Prevention of chronic illness can occur at the primary, secondary, or tertiary level, and all three have important implications for families (Hobbs et al., 1985). *Primary prevention* avoids the onset of the disease. For example, a couple may decide not to conceive children based on the knowledge that they carry the recessive genes for transmission of cystic fibrosis. The problem here, of course, is that parents often do not know they carry the recessive gene until a child is born. Avoiding exposure to toxic substances such as alcohol or drugs during pregnancy is another example of primary prevention.

Secondary prevention takes place after conception of an affected fetus and may involve efforts to terminate the pregnancy; in some rare cases it is possible to do fetal surgery to correct the condition (e.g., hydrocephalus). Clearly, in these cases families are confronted with difficult moral/ethical decisions. Because of advanced medical technology, the decision on how aggressive to be in prolonging the life of a defective fetus is one with which families and the whole medical profession now struggle. The necessity to make such agonizing decisions may result in marital conflict for some couples.

Tertiary prevention is focused on minimizing the undesirable or unnecessary consequences of chronic illness. With most chronic illnesses there are recommendations for home treatment to slow the progression of the illness, to reduce medical complications, and to prolong life. Families vary in their ability to follow through with such recommendations depending on factors such as the complexity of the treatment, the resources they can acquire, and the amount of time involved in hours and years. In addition, tertiary prevention is aimed at minimizing the psychological and social consequences for the child and his or her family. It is here that knowledge about the reciprocal impacts of illness on family and family on illness become crucial.

KNOWLEDGE ABOUT FAMILIES AND CHRONICALLY ILL CHILDREN

These reciprocal impacts are not yet well understood. Our knowledge of chronic childhood illness and families is gleaned from several approaches. One approach is the personal, descriptive accounts written by parents and afflicted children, such as Deford's (1983) description of the impact of his daughter's cystic fibrosis on their family; Featherstone's (1980) account of family life with her handicapped child; and Smith's (1986) reflections on the meaning and impact of living with cystic fibrosis. Subjective, qualitative reports from clinicians (nurses, physicians, psychologists, social workers, and other health professionals) who work with chronically ill children and their families comprise the largest body of literature in this area. Sometimes these reports are based on a single case, but more often they represent the distillation of experience in working with many children who either all have the same illness or who have had any kind of chronic illness.

In addition to these qualitative approaches, there are a smaller number of quantitative studies reported in the literature using objective measures of individual or family variables to describe the psychosocial impact of the chronic illness. These objective measures involve self-report questionnaires as well as observer assessments of patients and family members. Most of these descriptive studies are retrospective or cross-sectional; very few have systematically followed patients or families in an effort to understand the different factors and processes which shape adaptation over time. Finally, there are a few experimental or quasi-experimental studies involving different kinds of psychosocial interventions. Minuchin, Rosman, and Baker's (1978) work involving family therapy interventions with dysfunctional families of chronically ill children is one of the few examples.

Select findings from studies using all of the above approaches will be reported below. In reviewing this literature, some themes and commonalities emerge. First, there is a host of chronic hardships and demands which are reported to be associated with the diagnosis of a chronic childhood illness. Second, the capabilities of the child, parents, siblings, the family, and the community have been identified which mediate these demands. In addition, there appear to be different ways of viewing this situation; that is, different meanings are attributed to the chronic illness and its hardships as well as to the family's capabilities which shape their response. The outcomes of family efforts to adapt to living with the chronic illness also are reported.

These four major conceptual domains—demands, capabilities, meanings, and outcomes—are the major constructs of a family stress theoretical model, The Family Adjustment and Adaptation Response—FARR (McCubbin & Patterson, 1982, 1983a, 1983b; Patterson, in press). In an effort to provide some coherence for the studies reported in this chapter and possibly set the stage for a more theoretical approach to future investigations, chronic childhood illness and its impact on families will be examined using this FAAR Model.

THE FAMILY ADJUSTMENT AND ADAPTATION RESPONSE MODEL

The Family Adjustment and Adaptation Response Model is presented in Figure 2.1. The family, like all social systems, attempts to maintain balanced functioning or homeostasis by using its *capabilities* to meet its *demands*. The *meanings* the family ascribes to what is happening to them (demands) and to what they have for dealing with it (capabilities) are a critical factor in achieving balanced functioning. The outcome of the family's efforts to achieve balanced functioning is conceptualized in terms of *family adjustment* or *family adaptation,* both ranging on a continuum from good to poor. Good outcomes are reflected in (a) positive physical and mental health of individual members, (b) optimal role functioning of individual members, and (c) maintenance of a family unit which can accomplish its life cycle tasks.

There are two phases in the FAAR Model, adjustment and adaptation, separated by family crisis. The adjustment phase is intended to denote a relatively stable period during which families resist major change and attempt to meet demands with existing capabilities. The patterns of family interaction are predictable and stable. A *crisis,* or state of disequilibrium, emerges in the family system when demands exceed existing capabilities and this imbalance persists. During the adaptation phase families attempt to restore homeostasis by (a) acquiring new resources and coping behaviors, (b) reducing the demands they must deal with, and/or (c) changing the way they view their situation.

Over time, families go through repeated cycles of adjustment/ crisis/adaptation (see Figure 2.2). Some cycles are triggered by normal developmental changes (e.g., a child becoming an adolescent) which produce normative crises or transitions followed by periods of stability. In other instances the nature of a major stressor, such as the diagnosis of chronic illness in a child, creates a demand/capability imbalance and hence a crisis for the family. Sometimes a family is more vulnerable to recurrent crisis because their overall adjustment is poor, as reflected in symptomatic members or conflicted patterns of family interaction. One might expect that families with a chronically ill child would be more vulnerable to recurrent crises by virtue of the multiple, chronic hardships always facing them (Christensen & DeBlassie, 1980). Any additional change (stressor) would push them beyond the threshold of balanced functioning. Conversely, one could argue that because families develop capabilities to meet the demands they face, families with chronically ill children should be stronger and more resilient. Both scenarios may, in fact, exist. Some stress investigators (Hetherington, 1984) have found that in families with a high level of demands, especially chronic strain, the variance on most outcome measures increases, suggesting that families move to the extremes of doing very well or doing very poorly. Adaptation is a continuous process with many cycles through crisis. Since crisis is

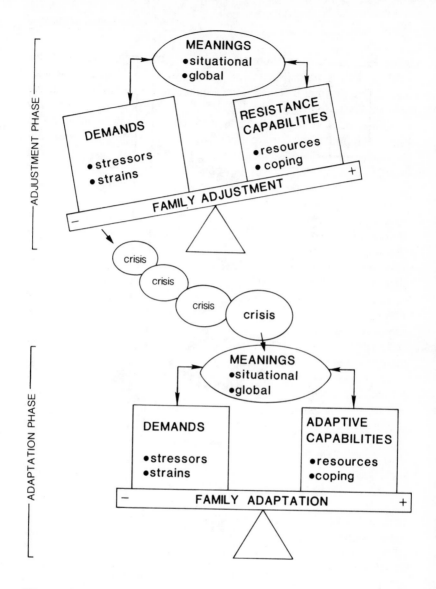

Figure 2.1. The Family Adjustment and Adaptation Response (FAAR) Model.

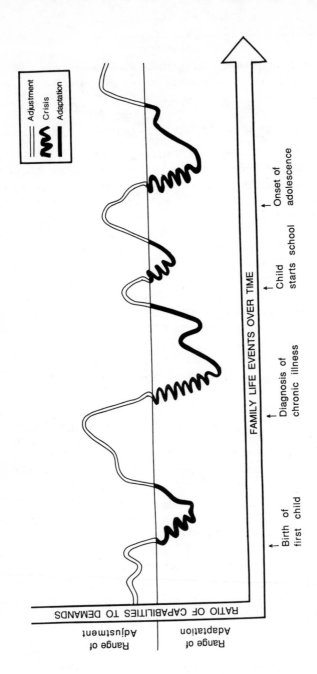

Figure 2.2. Cycles of family adjustment crisis adaptation over time.

both a danger and an opportunity, the disequilibrium of crisis affords the family an opportunity for resilience, recovery, and better adaptation (Drotar, 1981).

Systemic Nature of Family Change Over Time

Over time, as some stressors or strains are resolved, new demands emerge. Similarly, new capabilities are acquired, while others may become depleted. In the process of managing demands with capabilities, patterns of individual and family behavior emerge and become stabilized. These behavioral outcomes are, in a sense, indicators of adaptation and can be classified as adaptive or maladaptive. Recursively, these outcomes are information which becomes feedback to the family system (see Figures 2.3a and 2.3b). The relatively stable maladaptive symptoms or patterns of behavior (e.g., depression and marital conflict) are feedback that becomes part of the pileup of demands. Conversely, adaptive behavioral outcomes (e.g., self-efficacy and family cooperation) are also feedback to the system that becomes part of the family's capabilities.

In the absence of longitudinal studies it is not always possible to know which of the family's demands are symptoms (individual or family) of poor adaptation to the chronic illness or which ones existed prior to the diagnosis. Hence, we must be careful in assuming linear, cause-effect relationships, i.e., the illness "caused" marital breakdown, or marital conflict "caused" exacerbation of the chronic illness. Most descriptive and empirical findings are really punctuations in a process involving feedback across many levels of system— the family system, the individual, organ systems, and so on. For example, hyperglycemia in a diabetic child may contribute to his or her emotional liability and thus to a greater incidence of conflict with siblings or parents. Conversely, parental conflict may contribute to internalized tension on the part of the diabetic child and a neuroendocrine response leading to hyperglycemia. In the literature review to follow the reader should keep in mind that the distinctions between demands, capabilities, meanings, and outcomes are arbitrary punctuations and that, as just described, these constructs interact with each other over time.

DEMANDS IN FAMILIES WITH CHRONICALLY ILL CHILDREN

Demands include *stressors* (an event producing change) and *strains* (ongoing tension from unresolved stressors or from tension

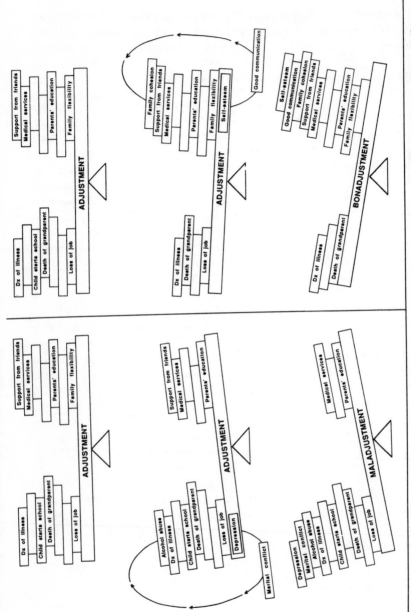

Figure 2.3a. Bad outcomes are feedback that increase family demands.

Figure 2.3b. Good outcomes are feedback that contribute to family capabilities.

80

associated with role performance). These demands include the normative tasks associated with individual development (e.g., establishing an identity at adolescence) and family development (e.g., birth of the first child). Demands also include nonnormative events such as the diagnosis of chronic illness in a child member (a stressor event), which produces a host of hardships for the family, many of which can never be resolved and hence create chronic strain. Families are never dealing with a single demand; rather, these stressors and strains accumulate, creating a pileup of demands which interact with each other and change over time. The literature on chronically ill children and their families is replete with identification of these demands producing stress.

Developmental Demands of the Illness, Child, and Family

While the idea of change over time is an obvious one, for families with chronically ill children it poses a unique set of developmental stressors and strains. The illness itself has a developmental course starting with the age of the child and family at illness onset and extending to the prognosis for life expectancy. In addition, the illness demands interact with the normative developmental tasks of the chronically ill child, not only at the time of diagnosis but at each successive stage of development in the child's life.

Age at Onset

The child's age when the illness begins is an important factor which affects family adaptation (Newbrough et al., 1985). Many of the chronic conditions of childhood have their onset at birth, and so the child never knows life without it. It becomes part of the child's identity from the beginning. In some ways, it may be easier for a child to adjust to never having certain functional abilities than to suddenly lose abilities later. For example, a child with spina bifida from birth will adapt differently than a child who suddenly becomes a paraplegic in adolescence due to an injury. Parents, however, will probably grieve the loss of perfect health for their child at whatever age the diagnosis is made.

The course of the child's physical, psychological, and social development will forever be altered by the chronic condition. Since development proceeds sequentially, and relative success at mastering the tasks of one stage is a prerequisite for facing the challenges of the next stage, one could hypothesize that the earlier the onset, the greater the adverse impact on development.

In addition to the child's age, the age of parents at the time of illness onset is also a factor in adaptation. Teenage parents who have a chronically ill child are at greater risk because their own developmental needs are still very prominent, and they are less likely to have the maturity and resources to cope with the added demands of the child (Sutkin, 1984). For older parents (e.g., those over 35 years), there is greater risk for having a child with certain kinds of chronic disorders (e.g., Down's syndrome), and older parents may lack the stamina for the extra burden of care required. They are also more aware of their own mortality and may worry about who will care for their child when they are gone.

The age of the family at onset may also affect adaptation. When a couple has a child with a chronic illness early in their marriage, it may place too much stress on a new family system which has barely stabilized. Or if the family is at a major transition phase and is already in disequilibrium, such as launching the oldest child, the added stress from the new diagnosis may make family adaptation more difficult.

Life Expectancy

Will the child's life span be shortened due to the illness? And, if so, how much? Some chronic disorders, such as mild mental retardation and blindness, have no direct impact on the length of life. Many chronic illnesses used to result in immediate or early death. However, medical advances have produced treatments which now prolong the lives of many chronically ill children. The discovery of insulin for treating children with diabetes is one example. Children with cystic fibrosis who used to die in early childhood now live into young adulthood, sometimes having children of their own. Such technological advances keep alive the hope that new and improved treatments and, ultimately, cures will be found for more chronic disorders. In some ways, this awareness increases the ambiguity families feel about how long their child will live and about how to plan for the future. Thus, this increased longevity is not without cost, both in terms of dollars and in terms of the extended burden of care on families.

Developmental Tasks of the Chronically Ill Child

For chronically ill children, the normative psychosocial (Erikson, 1963) and cognitive (Piaget, 1952) tasks of development (see Table 2.2) interact with the illness hardships repeatedly throughout the child's life. In many ways the illness takes on new meanings as the

Table 2.2
Tasks Associated with Stages of Cognitive and Psychosocial Development in Children

Age of Child	Cognitive Stages	Psychosocial Stages
Infancy (birth–1 year)	**Sensorimotor** • repetition of cause-effect sequences • object permanence	**Trust vs. mistrust** • attachment with caregiver • experiencing consistent, safe environment
Toddlerhood (1–3 years)	**Preoperational** • symbolic, magical imagery • egocentric or singular focused logic • acquisition of language	**Autonomy vs. shame & doubt** • sense of self-control • bowel and bladder control • parallel play with peers • testing of social limits
Preschool (3–6 years)	**Preoperational** • classifying objects • ability to plan • increased verbal skills • ability to contrast & compare	**Initiative vs. guilt** • initiate & explore • learn rules & expectations • beginning of conscience • interactive, cooperative play with peers • sex role imitation
School age (7–11 years)	**Concrete operations** • logical thinking with ability to serialize, reverse, and conserve mental images • decentered, self-other, and part-whole thinking • generalized rules and principles	**Industry vs. inferiority** • sustained effort to master tasks and produce • skill acquisition • greater peer involvement and need for peer approval • concern about "fairness"
Adolescence (12–18 years)	**Formal operations** • abstract & probabilistic thinking • deductive reasoning • ability to apply knowledge to solve problems • ability to evaluate one's own thinking	**Identity vs. role confusion** • sense of and confidence in one's personality • making career choices • social maturity and comfort with same and opposite sex • clear sexual identity • establishing beliefs and values • greater independence from parents

child and family are confronted again and again with discovering how best to meet the child's needs given the limits of the illness (Wikler et al., 1981). With chronic conditions which are progressively debilitating, the chronically ill child's capacity for independence decreases as normative development calls for increasing levels of independence. The convergence of the illness course and the developmental course places families in a bind. The challenge of finding the right fit between what is normative for children at a given age and what the child's illness will permit is stressful for both parents and child. The limitations of many chronic illnesses shape development from infancy through youth and adolescence, making accomplishment of these tasks difficult and sometimes impossible.

Infancy

Chronic physical illness in infancy is likely to interrupt a consistent, dependable, safe environment. Parents may be afraid of their sick infant, may find him or her repulsive if visibly deformed, and may consciously or unconsciously reject the baby (Roberts, 1984). The grief parents feel when they learn the diagnosis, their fear about early death, or their guilt about possibly having caused it can result in withdrawal from emotional involvement and sometimes in inconsistent physical care (Perrin & Gerrity, 1984).

Chronically ill infants who are acutely sick at birth often must remain hospitalized or be rehospitalized during the first year. These separations from parents interfere with bonding and attachment to the primary caregiver which is critical for the development of trust (Klaus & Kennell, 1982). The infant may experience pain and discomfort from the illness or treatment, and the intensive care nursery may be overstimulating as there are usually multiple caregivers. Thus the child's early environment may be experienced as chaotic, inconsistent, and unsafe.

Some conditions involve physical defects which interfere with feeding (e.g., cleft palate), or there may be neurologic deficits which retard the infant's social responsiveness. In both cases parents may become discouraged and attachment may be compromised. Just as the infant needs to attach to a parent to develop trust, so, too, the parent needs to attach to the infant to develop the sense of parental competence necessary for an ongoing nurturing relationship (Sutkin, 1984).

If there is motor or sensory impairment and the infant is unable to explore his or her environment, cognitive development may be slowed. At this early stage the infant's only conception of illness can be a generalized sense of pain and discomfort when present and possibly anxiety and fear if there have been separations from parents because of hospitalizations and inconsistent care (Magrab, 1985).

Toddlerhood

Developing a sense of autonomy and self-control through active exploration of the environment is the task of healthy toddlers. For the chronically ill toddler this active exploration may be restricted because of motor or sensory deficits, because of lethargy and malaise, or because acute exacerbations of the illness require hospitalizations. Perhaps the child's efforts to make personal choices about eating may need to be monitored by parents (e.g., diabetic diet). Or the task of toilet training, so important for the development of self-control, may be affected by the illness (e.g., the foul smelling stools of children with cystic fibrosis).

Parents may find it difficult to allow the child autonomy to explore for fear of injury (e.g., hemophilia) or exposure to environmental hazards (e.g., asthma). They may be overly protective, have a hard time setting limits, and encourage passivity because of their own sorrow or guilt about the child's illness. Such restrictions in environmental exploration will diminish the opportunity to learn self-expression and self-control and may slow the development of cognitive and verbal skills. Social interactions with peers may be restricted because the child is too sick or because stigma associated with the visibility of the illness may lead to teasing, ridicule, or rejection.

Illness, pain, and treatment for the illness or disability are often viewed by the toddler as punishment for bad behavior (Magrab, 1985). Death may also be viewed as punishment and is often confused with sleep. The child at this age thinks magically and tends to believe parents could cure the illness if they wanted to. If the child is hospitalized during this age, the separation from parents creates anxiety and fear of abandonment.

Preschool

The preschool child is now able to plan and carry out activities and in doing so may "go too far" and feel guilt about the outcome (Sutkin, 1984). Again, the realities of their physical and mental limitations may restrict chronically ill children's active exploration of the environment. They may be discouraged from pursuing goal-directed activities because of these limits (Perrin & Gerrity, 1984). When their own physical and mental limits are not restricting them, protective parents may be. A balance between encouragement and limit-setting characterized by consistency is optimal for the child's development at this stage. Many parents of chronically ill children find this difficult and become frustrated about knowing how restrictive or permissive to be with their child. This is especially true when the diagnosis occurs at this age and parents relax their expectations for age-appropriate behavior.

During this stage sex role definition begins. Frequent, regular contact with the same-sex parent can help foster gender identification and positive self-worth. In many instances chronically ill children are cared for exclusively by the mother; thus, for a son contact with his father may be limited or nonexistent. Then, too, a child's sense of his or her sexual identity is strongly affected by interactions with and acceptance by the opposite sex parent as well. For instance, a girl benefits from frequent positive interactions with her father as well as her mother.

The preschoolers' preoperational thinking is concrete, linking events that are contiguous in time or place. For instance, they may explain the cause of their illness as due to "eating too much candy" (diabetes) or "breathing too fast" (asthma). Frequently their preoccupation with winning approval and being good leads to beliefs that cures for their illnesses can occur by "following the rules" (Perrin & Gerrity, 1984).

School age

Acquiring a sense of industry by producing things through skill development and sustained effort is a central task of middle childhood. The cognitive, motor, or sensory limits of some chronic conditions may interfere with mastery of age-related tasks and contribute to lack of confidence, low self-esteem, and a sense of inferiority. School is a central place for the school-age child to learn new skills and master tasks. Bouts of sickness or hospitalizations may lead to school absences, making success at school even harder. Teachers who do not understand the chronic illness may be afraid of the child, may minimize actively working with the child, may be overprotective, or may have unrealistically low expectations for performance. Underachievement may result, compromising the child's sense of competence and mastery. Magrab (1985) cites several studies which have found significantly lower academic achievement among selected groups of chronically ill children with normal cognitive ability. While there are public laws mandating appropriate educational services for handicapped children, these laws generally do not extend to meeting the needs of chronically ill children (Hobbs et al., 1985).

Involvement with and acceptance by the peer group is important to the school-age child's social development. Children with a chronic illness worry about their differentness. When possible, they may try to hide it, or they may withdraw socially, fearing rejection. Healthy school-age children, struggling with their own need for peer approval, are often intolerant of differentness and can be very cruel in taunting and teasing a child who looks different or must do things differently (e.g., eat certain foods, take medications, avoid certain activities). Or they may avoid the chronically ill child out of fear that the illness is contagious (Whitt, 1984). One risk at this age is for sympathetic parents to pull the child back into the family so he or she won't have to experience rejection or failure at the mastery of tasks (Sutkin, 1984). In these cases the child has an even harder time discovering his or her potential as well as learning how to separate more from the family and become involved with peers and adults outside the family in preparation for even more independence during adolescence.

With concrete operational thought school-age children can differentiate between self and the world. They often view illness as the result of germs or contamination (Cerreto & Travis, 1984) and believe that they will be cured by following the doctor's orders. In many ways they feel powerless relative to their symptoms, which is difficult given their need for mastery of their environment. They may deal with this powerlessness by asking a lot of questions about their illness as a way to gain control (Perrin & Gerrity, 1984). At this age death is viewed as permanent although not necessarily the end of physical existence.

Adolescence

Adolescents, who normatively undergo major physiological, psychological, and social changes, have the task of discovering their identity and separating from their parents. In some instances normal physiological change is slowed by the disease process, as in the case of hemodialysis patients who have had the disease since childhood (Magrab, 1985). Or physiological changes may directly interact with symptoms of the illness, as in the case of increasing hormones and changes in neuroregulators leading to increases in blood sugar levels in diabetics (Holmes, 1986). For other chronically ill adolescents there may be some form of body disfigurement from the illness or handicap or from the treatment. In all of these instances normal adolescent concern about body image is aggravated, and this affects identity formation.

For the chronically ill adolescent identity means not only discovering one's personality, values, beliefs, and career choices, but integrating the reality of his or her illness and its limitations into this identity. Because the body is undergoing rapid physiological changes, generating new sensations and feelings of uncertainty, concerns about physical attractiveness, sexuality, and reproductive competence are especially troubling for the chronically ill adolescent. For some, visible deformity or deficit may interfere with sexual expression, as in the case of a paraplegic or a diabetic with secondary impotence. There is some evidence that chronically ill girls may be at greater risk for pregnancy because of their desire to disavow their illness and prove their normalcy (Holmes, 1986). Mentally subnormal teens may be subjected to sexual exploitation by others. Sex education, often inadequate for normal teens, is even more inadequate for the chronically ill who often are perceived as asexual persons (Coupey & Cohen, 1984).

Adolescents, functioning at the level of formal operations (if there are no cognitive deficits), can think abstractly, and thus their illness takes on new meaning. They are now aware of their own ability to affect symptoms and outcomes. They also understand the permanence of the illness and can think about the future and early death or increased incapacitation. Allen et al. (1984) found that with increased cognitive development adolescents with diabetes became more anxious about their future, especially social relationships, careers, adult lifestyle, and medical complications. In addition, this new cognitive awareness may trigger a kind of denial about the condition. The result is often noncompliance with prescribed treatment and sometimes high risk taking as a way to challenge their own mortality. Exacerbations and acute episodes of illness are not uncommon during this stage, and a sense of hopelessness about limitations in performing adult roles (getting a job, finding a marriage partner, having children, and so on) or early death may lead to depression and withdrawal.

Searching for independence, adolescents strive to make their own decisions and to gain a sense of mastery and control. However, the realities of the illness or in some instances overprotective parents preclude a sense of control. Anger, rebellion, and hostility are common. Again, noncompliance as a way of taking control of the illness may occur.

The expectation that adolescents should be establishing independence from the family is a painful issue for chronically ill adolescents and their parents. With many chronic conditions the adolescent can never achieve independence but is forever dependent on others for care and treatment. Where and by whom should this care be given? For parents this may mean their child will never leave home and that the burden of care will never end. Even for those adolescents who are able to leave home and pursue adult roles, there is still the worry about how well they will take care of themselves. In fact, shifting the responsibility for self-care at an appropriate age is a difficult transition for some families, which prolongs the dependency and reduces the likelihood of leaving home.

For many of the chronic diseases such as cystic fibrosis, hemophilia, leukemia, chronic renal failure, and so on, it is only in recent decades that children have survived to adolescence. But even adolescents who have lived with their chronic condition from birth rebel at accepting their limitations given their greater cognitive understanding coupled with their search for identity and independence. This struggle appears to be most difficult for the adolescents with more marginal conditions where symptoms are not visible and where they can achieve independence and perform most adult social roles. With more severe conditions a kind of passive resignation to lifelong dependence may have occurred. When the illness or handicap begins in adolescence and interrupts what had been normal developmental progression, the crisis for the adolescent and family is particularly acute, often requiring a longer period of reorganization to restore equilibrium to the system.

Other Demands Experienced by the Chronically Ill Child

Illness Symptoms

Pain, suffering, and discomfort are inherent in most chronic conditions. There may be physical pain, (e.g., juvenile arthritis joint pain) as well as psychological pain due to restrictions, limitations, perceived differentness, and so on (Steinhauer et al., 1974). Many chronically ill children have never known a day without bodily discomfort. This pain may be aggravated by health care providers who are insensitive and only concerned about treatment. Besides pain, physiologic changes may cause irritability (e.g., high blood sugar in diabetics) or fatigue and weakness (Bruhn, 1977). Malaise and long hours spent in bed lead to boredom and frustration for many children. Some symptoms, such as flatulence in the child with cystic fibrosis (Mattsson, 1972), cause embarrassment, and the child and family may respond by becoming socially isolated.

For some conditions symptoms flare up and recede, often in unpredictable ways. Fluctuations in blood sugar for the diabetic child, wheezing and hyperventilation in the asthmatic, or accidents and bleeding in the hemophiliac can require rapid interventions, lead to trips to the emergency room, and/or hospitalizations. This unpredictability keeps the family on edge, producing tension and often overreactivity to even benign change.

For many chronic conditions there is progressive deterioration with increasing pain, symptoms, incapacitation, and, often, impending early death. Intervention may become more aggressive in an effort to prolong life, but eventually the reality of helplessness to alter the disease course must be faced by the child, the family, and the medical system.

Treatment

For many conditions the treatment causes more pain and discomfort than the disease. Many of these treatments must be carried out at home and require knowledge, skill, expense, and time from family members. Doing pain-producing therapies on one's child can cause psychological distress for parents, especially when they know that a young child cannot understand why and may view it as punishment. For example, bronchial drainage treatment for children with cystic fibrosis involves pounding on the chest and back with cupped hands to loosen mucous. In some instances treatment has iatrogenic effects (i.e., adverse effects caused by the treatment itself), leading families to struggle with decisions about whether to proceed with invasive treatments that have uncertain outcomes (Grave, 1976).

As children become older they often can begin doing some of their own treatment or therapy. Every time they do this, however, it is a reminder that they are persons with chronic conditions with all the associated implications and meanings, e.g., different, shortened life span, increasing incapacitation, loss of autonomy, and so on. Compliance with treatment regimens is a real Catch-22 for the chronically ill person; while it may prolong life and improve the quality of life, it is also a constant reminder of being less than normal (Klusa et al., 1983). From this perspective it is not surprising that several investigators have found that young persons with less severe or marginal (to normal) conditions have the greatest struggle in this regard. If the condition is not visible, the chronically ill child may attempt to mask it by being like other youngsters—same food, same activity, same risk taking, and so on.

Losses

There are many potential physical, psychological, and social losses associated with different chronic illnesses (Grave, 1976). Most chronic illnesses involve the loss of one or more bodily functions such as sight, hearing, mobility, cognitive ability, and so on. This loss may happen all at once at the time of diagnosis or injury, or there may be more gradual deterioration as the illness progresses. Sometimes this functional loss is perceived as a loss of control over one's body, as in the case of recurrent pneumonia for the child with cystic fibrosis, hyper- or hypoglycemia for the diabetic, wheezing and hyperventilation for the asthmatic, and so on. Implicit in these physiological losses is the loss of the opportunity to accomplish normal developmental tasks and, often concomitantly, a loss of a sense of mastery, competence, and self-esteem. There is often a loss of age-appropriate autonomy and the actual or perceived loss of the ability and opportunity to live independently.

Also for the child with chronic illness there is the potential for loss of many kinds of attachments. In infancy the primary attachment to a nurturant parent may be threatened by physical separations (i.e., hospitalizations) or by barriers due to deformity (e.g., inability to suck due to cleft palate). Sometimes the barrier is a psychological one when, for example, a parent rejects the child because of differentness or fear that the child will die soon. Conversely, sometimes a parent becomes overly attached to the chronically ill child in an effort to protect or compensate for deficits, or believing this will prolong life. Overinvolvement with one parent, usually the primary caretaker, is often at the exclusion of the other parent, usually the father, and, hence, there is a lost relationship. Moreover, as the overly involved child matures, he or she may resist extreme dependency and either strike out angrily at the too-needed parent or passively withdraw from the relationship. Either behavior can be deeply disturbing to the parent who may feel much of his or her life has been given to the child.

Many of the child's normal social experiences are lost due to illness episodes, malaise, hospitalizations, missed school, and so on. Nonparticipation precludes attachments to peers or even siblings. Even when the child is physically present, attachments may be threatened by the child's perceived differentness such that he or she is rejected by peers or, conversely, social stigma leads to the child's withdrawal. The latter response may be exacerbated by overly involved parents who want to protect their child from the pain of social rejection.

The ultimate deprivation for many children with chronic illness is the loss of a normal life span, the loss of fulfilling fantasies about the way life should be, and the expectation that death will come at an early age. For the child the full impact of this comes with the development of formal operational thought, around 13 years, when the youngster can think abstractly about the future.

For most chronically ill children, the losses enumerated here are interactive and cumulative. Progressive physical and functional losses provide a feedback loop to psychological loss. For example, increasing loss of the ability to perform the activities of daily living may lead to greater social isolation and greater psychological loss as self-esteem, confidence, and hope diminish.

Demands Experienced by Parents of Chronically Ill Children

In addition to the demands experienced by the chronically ill child, his or her parents also experience many stressors and strains. One way to classify these demands is in terms of the cognitive, emotional, and behavioral domains affected (Sargent & Baker, 1983).

Cognitive Demands

The parents often must learn and master knowledge and information about the disease and how to manage it. Often complex skills for home care must be learned. Sometimes parents are provided with conflicting information from physicians and other health care providers, which they must reconcile. In many cases the diagnosis may be difficult to make because many conditions are rare, and physicians may have had little or no experience with a given illness. Hence, parents often struggle to find competent, reliable medical resources. This latter search can be exacerbated by the parents' emotional reactions when they deny and are not yet willing to accept an accurate diagnosis (Hobbs et al., 1985).

Emotional Demands

The emotional problems experienced by parents of chronically ill children have received considerable attention in the literature. The loss associated with having a less-than-perfect child leads to recurrent sorrow and grief (Solnit & Stark, 1961). Parents may experience guilt if they believe they caused the illness, e.g., by defective genes or inadequate prenatal care. Similarly, one parent may blame the other for similar reasons, creating intense marital conflict, distancing, and, sometimes, separation and divorce. Parents are apt to worry about their own life-giving capability and about whether they should have more children, especially if the child is the firstborn (Zucman, 1982). When parents are unable to express their emotional pain, they may become symptomatic, and their collusion of silence makes the child's adjustment more difficult (Burton, 1973).

Parents often empathize with their child's pain, wishing they could suffer for the child but often feeling helpless to do anything about it. This latter reaction is associated more with fathers (Shapiro, 1983), who traditionally function more in the instrumental role where they expect to solve problems (e.g., make the child well). For both parents this sense of helplessness may contribute to the loss of perceived competence and self-esteem. Parents worry about dangers and risks to their child and struggle with what kinds of limits to impose and how much supervision to provide (Schaffer, 1964).

Behavioral Demands

The tasks associated with caring for a chronically ill child often consume an inordinate amount of parents' time and physical energy (Foster & Berger, 1985). This intense and chronic demand for care is aggravated by the difficulty of finding respite care. There are few, if any, community child care resources which have the ability and willingness to care for children with chronic conditions. Relatives, too, often are afraid to care for children who look or act differently or appear fragile and vulnerable. Parents find that time and energy for self, spouse, and other children are often sacrificed. Mothers are reported to feel this burden of care most acutely because many, following the traditional role for women, assume the major part of the care.

The work lives of parents must often be rearranged to accommodate the needs of a chronically ill child (Satterwhite, 1978). One parent, usually the mother, may terminate employment or even a career to stay home and care for the child, especially when there are no alternate sources of care. A corollary to this loss of one parent's income is that the other wage-earning parent may have to work more hours to earn enough to support the family, especially given the added financial burden imposed by the needs of the chronically ill child. Parents may decide to turn down job promotions requiring relocation because they choose to stay close to a specialized treatment center for their child. In this and many other ways parents' plans and dreams for managing their work and family roles must be altered.

Demands on the Marital Relationship

The demands of caring for their ill child frequently create or exacerbate conflict in the marital relationship. Lack of consensus about how to manage the child (White et al., 1984), other family demands, goals for the future, and so on, may create tension and conflict which become chronic and unresolved. Less time together and more segregated roles (e.g., father earning income, mother caring for the child) create distance in time and space and, hence, make resolution more difficult (Sabbeth, 1984). This potential for conflict is congruent with reports of increased dissatisfaction with the marriage, less role consensus, more role tension, and increased marital distress (Crain et al., 1966; Koski & Kumento, 1977; White et al., 1984).

Demands Experienced by Siblings of Chronically Ill Children

When a brother or sister has a chronic illness, siblings are faced with a unique set of demands and experience changes in their own developmental trajectory (Grave, 1976). Siblings may experience a range of emotional reactions such as fear of getting sick, a sense of guilt for not being the sick one, guilt for having somehow caused the illness (e.g., by wishing bad things), embarrassment and shame about their brother or sister, or resentment and envy because they don't get as much attention (Sabbeth, 1984). These emotional reactions vary depending on the developmental stage of the sibling and on how the parents are coping with the family's demands.

Many siblings are expected to contribute in a significant way to meeting the family's needs. Sometimes the expectations exceed their child status, and they become parentified. A parental child may be expected to share responsibility for care of the chronically ill child, attend to maintenance tasks of the family (cooking, cleaning, and so on), contribute to family income, or sacrifice personal wants and needs. Children sometimes become the sounding board for their parents' emotional trauma, particularly when parents can't talk to each other or when there is a single parent.

Because the chronically ill child has so many needs, there may be less time, energy, money, and attention for the normal sibling. At the same time there may be a covert expectation that the normal sibling should compensate for all the things the chronically ill child will never accomplish and, hence, the expectation to be better than average in physical activity, school performance, social relationships, and so on. In some cases siblings may be asked to provide part of their bodies (e.g., bone marrow, kidney) to a chronically ill brother or sister (Grave, 1976).

Demands Experienced by the Family System

In addition to the demands experienced by individual family members, there are demands which have an impact on the whole family as a systemic unit. The internal structure of the family, that is, their roles, rules, and routines—must often be changed to accommodate the needs of the chronically ill child (Wishner & O'Brien, 1978). For example, eating habits (e.g., type of food and time of meals) are often changed in families with diabetics; pets may have to be given up if there is an asthmatic child; sleeping arrangements may be changed because of nighttime therapy (e.g., mist tent for a child with cystic fibrosis). The family's mobility and freedom for recreational pursuits may be restricted (Bruhn, 1977). Rules for the chronically ill child are usually different than for other children, sometimes more strict to prevent harm (e.g., for a hemophiliac) and sometimes more permissive because parents want to compensate for things the child misses. These double standards are often hard to explain to other children in the family.

There is usually a very large financial burden associated with the care of a chronically ill child—surgeries, drugs, equipment, supplies, doctor bills, travel, special schools, and so on. Meeting these financial demands creates worry and tension not only for parents but often for the whole family (White et al., 1984). Parents may seek additional jobs or work longer hours to pay the bills. The financial burden is exacerbated when one parent, usually the mother, is needed to care for the child and hence cannot work for pay outside the home.

Lower income families have a particularly difficult time managing a child with chronic illness. They struggle just to cope with the basic needs for food, clothing, and so on, and have a harder time attending to the psychological needs of family members. Furthermore, caregivers accord poor families less respect, and these parents often do not know how to assert their rights (Zucman, 1982). The marital relationship for poor couples is usually stressed more because of the multiple pressures in their lives. Farber (1959) has described the diagnosis of chronic illness as a tragedy for poor families compared to a situation requiring role reorganization for other families.

Often a disproportionate share of the family's resources—time, energy, money, and so on—are devoted to the needs of the chronically ill child. This, plus fatigue and the strong negative emotions which are recurrently felt by family members, makes the family task of maintaining morale and motivation more difficult (Burr, 1985). Trying to attend simultaneously to multiple family needs in the face of the uncertain course of the illness is a challenge to family equilibrium. For example, a pileup of family stressors and strains is associated with poorer health status in children with cystic fibrosis (Patterson & McCubbin, 1983b) and asthma (Zlatich et al., 1982). A history of chronic, stress-creating family problems makes management of the illness harder (Gath et al., 1980). In many ways chronic illness lowers the family's threshold of tolerance for other problems. Johnson (1980), in her review of psychosocial factors in chronic illness, reports a higher incidence of family conflict. This challenge to the maintenance of the family as a unit sometimes does not work out, and the unit dissolves. An unstable family composition usually makes managing the chronic illness more difficult (White et al., 1984).

Demands Which Emerge from the Community

Some of the demands these families face are at the interface between them and the community. The family's external boundaries become more permeable (Roberts, 1984) as the family's privacy is invaded by the constant need for service—physicians, nurses, therapists, social workers, psychologists, special teachers, and so on (Strauss et al., 1984). All these professionals probe into many domains of family life with the intent of helping, but at the same time they are often judging and trying to change the family. Sometimes professional helpers are insensitive to the emotional demands on these families, and this may be related to the professional's unwillingness to process his or her own emotional reactions (Zucman, 1982).

Ironically, even as the family feels invaded, it also feels isolated—from normal social interaction. The family may feel judged and unaccepted by others (Roberts, 1984). Schools sometimes try to avoid having to deal with the special needs of these children, and friends, relatives, and others, fearing the illness and not knowing how to respond appropriately, avoid the family. These same fears contribute to the lack of respite care for the chronically ill child and, hence, further isolate the family and make it difficult for parents to have time alone together (Levine & Ebert, 1983).

Finally, cultural norms for child and adolescent social interaction are often not consistent with the needs of a chronically ill child. Some forms of play are too vigorous or dangerous, diets which include "junk" food may be prohibitive, and peer group norms to experiment with alcohol and other substances are particularly taboo for an adolescent with a chronic illness.

CAPABILITIES IN FAMILIES WITH CHRONICALLY ILL CHILDREN

In the FAAR Model a *capability* is defined as a potentiality the family has available to it for meeting demands. There are two types: *resources,* which are what the family *has,* and *coping behaviors,* which are what the family *does* to manage demands.

Resources

Resources are traits, characteristics, or competencies of individual family members, the family system, or the community which can be used to manage demands. Resources may be tangible, such as money, or intangible, such as self-esteem. Most resources are not inherent in a person or a system but are acquired over time, usually in response to demands. While not as extensively documented as demands, some resources have been identified that help families manage life with a chronically ill child. Again, it is not clear from most studies whether the resources existed in the family before the diagnosis of chronic illness or were developed in response to the new demands.

Personal Resources

Self-esteem is an important resource for children with chronic illness (Hauser et al., in press). It contributes to a sense of mastery and self-efficacy, feelings which are often associated with better adherence to treatment regimens (Simonds et al., 1981). Anderson et al. (1981), for example, found that diabetic children with a positive self-concept maintained better control of their diabetes.

Similarly, parental self-esteem, feelings of adequacy, and pride in being able to manage (Mattsson, 1972) contribute to their chronically ill child's well-being. Grey et al. (1980) found that in families with a diabetic child, parental self-esteem was a key factor predicting better outcomes through its association with better family functioning and child self-esteem. Parents' intelligence, education, health, and financial state are also important (Murphy, 1982).

Family System Resources

The identification of family system resources which contribute to better adaptation to chronic illness is a relatively new area of research. Several investigators have found that family organization is an important resource in adaptation to chronic illness (Hauser et al., in press; Patterson, 1985; Sargent, 1983). Organization includes clarity of rules and expectations (Shouval et al., 1982), family routines for daily tasks (Newbrough et al., 1985), and clear role allocation. Etzwiler and Sines (1962) found that a segregated role structure, with mothers in charge of care and treatment of the child and fathers helping when the child was hard to control, was the preferred structure in the diabetic families they studied. Clear generational boundaries (Koski & Kumento, 1977) with a parental hierarchy (Foster & Berger, 1985) that works together to make decisions and establish and maintain child discipline (Horan et al., 1986; Sargent & Baker, 1983) are critical factors in the family's organizational structure. Flexibility of family organization is also important as family needs and circumstances change (Bruhn, 1977). Cooperation and shared responsibility for the many tasks involved are associated with better outcomes (Hanson & Henggeler, 1984). An active family recreation orientation where an atmosphere of normalcy is maintained also facilitates adaptation (Dushenko, 1981; Patterson & McCubbin, 1985).

Cohesion, the bonds of emotional unity in the family, is another resource which may emerge or become stronger as the family learns to live with the demands of the illness (Anderson et al., 1981; Cederblad et al., 1982; Drotar, 1981). Emotional support from family members contributes to better adherence with treatment regimens (Borrow et al., 1985) especially when coupled with firm parental control (Zlatich et al., 1982). Marrero et al. (1981) found that family support was more important than peer support for good diabetic management with adolescents. The importance of the father's support (in addition to the mother's) has been emphasized in more recent studies (Boyle et al., 1976; Patterson & McCubbin, 1985; Shouval et al., 1982). However, the amount and way support is offered may need to change over the course of the illness. Steinhausen et al. (1977) found that high maternal support at the time of diagnosis, followed by a decrease over time, was associated with better outcomes in diabetics. However, Sargent et al. (1985) found that for 7- to 16-year-old diabetics, parental and sibling support was more important three years after diagnosis than in the first year. These findings, although contradictory, suggest that there is an important balance between family support and encouraging autonomy and independence so that the child takes age-appropriate responsibility for his or her illness (Anderson et al., 1981; Sargent, 1983). This parallels the normal task of families to find a balance of cohesion which is neither enmeshment nor disengagement (Olson et al., 1979).

A qualitative marital relationship characterized by mutual support, intimacy, satisfaction, and shared goals is a key resource in effective family functioning associated with better adaptation to the chronic illness demands (Foster & Berger, 1985; Sargent, 1983). The marital relationship is enhanced by couples who take time for themselves even in the face of many demands (Christensen & DeBlassie, 1980; Patterson & McCubbin, 1983a).

Problem-solving ability and conflict-resolution skills are other important resources (Borrow et al., 1985) for these families who have multiple, competing demands to deal with. Such skills help maintain a lower level of conflict which contributes to better outcomes (Johnson, 1980; Simonds et al., 1981). Hauser et al. (1986) found that mothers and their diabetic children engaged in communication styles which enabled problem resolution more than did a comparison group of acutely ill children and their mothers, suggesting that families develop this resource in response to the illness. Orr et al. (1984) found siblings of diabetic adolescents to be an important resource for obtaining problem-solving support.

A communication style that allows for the open expression of feelings is especially adaptive in these families who experience powerful, often conflicting emotions (Borrow et al., 1985; Boyle et al., 1976; Patterson, 1985). Schaffer (1964) found that families that encourage and tolerate expressiveness of positive and negative affect develop more adaptive interaction patterns.

Community Resources

Adequate, competent medical care has improved the life expectancy of chronically ill children and is one of the most critical resources these families must acquire (Steinhauer et al., 1974). Health care providers who listen, are sensitive to the emotional reactions of the family, and modulate providing information and offering support are especially valued (Blumenthal, 1969; Drotar et al., 1975). Health care providers who take a more wholistic view of the family may be more effective. Stein and Jessop (1984) randomized home care (versus clinic care) to half of their sample of 219 chronically ill children and found it improved child and parent psychological adjustment and improved family functioning. They suggest that home care may alter physician expectations, reduce negative judgments, and be more validating of the family. Zucman (1982) suggests that health care professionals who are attuned to their own emotional reactions are better able to help families become aware of their feelings. In addition, she challenges providers with empowering families so they can care for themselves versus making them overly dependent on the health care system. She reports a study in which handicapped children whose parents received more help did well at first but three years later were doing poorly compared to children whose parents sought less help.

Support from others who are coping with the same or a similar illness is a resource which helps families adapt. This may be found through support groups (Holmes, 1986; Mattsson, 1972) or, for older children, by having friends with the same illness (Borrow et al., 1985). The latter is less probable for children with rare conditions. Grandparents and other kin who offer loyalty and support in a way that empowers the family are another important resource (Zucman, 1982).

Coping

In the FAAR Model a *coping behavior* is defined as a specific effort by an individual or a family which is directed at maintaining or restoring the balance between demands and resources. As such, coping may function to (a) reduce the number or intensity of demands, (b) increase or maintain the family's resources, (c) alter the meaning of a situation to make it more manageable, and/or (d) manage the tension associated with unresolved strain.

Many chronic illness hardships cannot be eliminated. Thus these families may choose to reduce other potential demands they have control over, such as deciding not to have more children. Resolving relationship conflicts which produce strain may also become the target of coping efforts as a way to reduce demands.

In their study of parental coping in families where a child had cystic fibrosis, McCubbin et al. (1983) found that the coping patterns of (a) maintaining family cooperation and unity (a family resource) and (b) maintaining the parents' psychological well-being (a personal resource) were associated with better health outcomes in the child. These authors and others suggest that families who attend to multiple system needs (i.e., the family, parents, ill child) do better (Levine & Ebert, 1983). When parents develop and maintain cooperativeness and shared responsibility and when they work to maintain an atmosphere of normalcy by getting out and doing things as a family, children do better (Patterson, 1985). Developing a support network of understanding friends and relatives (community resource) who listen is an important strategy for reducing chronic stress (Levine & Ebert, 1983).

Coping strategies that alter the meaning of the chronic illness situation through reappraisal have received the most attention in the literature. Believing in the child's and the family's capabilities—"we can beat this"—is a typical example (Hauser et al., 1986). Believing that things could be worse or trying to normalize their circumstances (Bruhn, 1977) are appraisal strategies for reducing demands. "Living day to day" is a way to modulate the rate at which demands must be dealt with (Murphy, 1982; Levine & Ebert, 1983). Cowen et al. (1985) found that parents of children with cystic fibrosis minimized the normal developmental stresses of childhood more than parents of nonsick children in an effort to reduce the pileup of demands. Simmons et al. (1985) found that adolescents with cystic fibrosis were able to maintain good self-concepts by minimizing the illness demands, although this form of denial was associated with behavioral disturbances. Venters (1981) described among parents of children with cystic fibrosis a cognitive coping strategy of "endowing the situation with meaning" as a way to accept the demands.

Some have described the variation in coping efforts at different stages of adaptation to the illness—diagnosis, living with it, and terminal stage (Drotar et al., 1975; Power & Orto, 1980; Shapiro, 1983; Steinhauer et al., 1974). Primarily these authors focus on a grieving process which usually involves some of the following stages: shock, denial, anger, depression, blame, reorganization, and acceptance. When parents are asynchronous in going through these stages or in their coping efforts, misunderstanding and increased conflict are likely to emerge (Sabbeth, 1984).

Denial, especially when prolonged, is generally considered a maladaptive coping mechanism. In the case of chronic illness, however, there is a form of denial which appears to be efficacious for families. A certain amount of denial contributes to the maintenance of hope—believing that the child will get better, that a cure will be found, and so on. This kind of denial enables the family to invest in the child and to adhere to treatment regimens. Christensen and DeBlassie (1980) say that families accept reality selectively, perhaps choosing to see the child as normal. Health care providers need to be careful about judging or trying to prevent this kind of denial.

THE ROLE OF MEANINGS IN ADAPTING TO CHRONIC ILLNESS

Individual family members appraise their situation both in terms of the demands confronting them as well as their capabilities for dealing with them. Both can be increased or diminished by the appraisal process. These individual appraisals may be shared among family members so that there is congruence or shared meanings. Conversely, individual appraisals may be discrepant. Generally, congruence or shared meanings is considered more adaptive for families because it facilitates a coordinated response.

Meanings that Contribute to Demands

Some families catastrophize the illness and many of the other events they experience. They view the situation as hopeless, beyond their control. Frydman (1980) found that parents who over- or underestimated the severity of their child's symptoms of leukemia or cystic fibrosis also had more psychiatric symptoms. In some cases they believed responsibility lies with the health care system to find a cure (Wishner & O'Brien, 1978). When they view the situation this way, families generally do not take appropriate responsibility for the child's care.

Voysey (1972) created a 2 X 2 typology based on the family's beliefs about whether they were responsible for causing the illness (yes-no) and whether they had any power or control over outcomes (yes-no). The family's subjective view influenced its style of coping. Parents who felt both responsibility and power (yes-yes) experienced the most guilt and tried to overcompensate for the child's condition. Parents who felt responsible for causing the illness but felt no power to control it avoided others because they had no culturally acceptable explanation.

Sometimes there is ambiguity about how to define the child's status because of the illness. Should the child be considered sick or normal? Ironically, children with less severe or less visible disease often pose more of a problem in adaptation. Parents and others experience dissonance because the child looks normal but is actually ill. Bruhn et al. (1971) found that children whose hemophilia was moderate, compared to mild or severe, had more feelings of ambiguity about themselves and whether they fit into their families and had generally poorer psychological well-being. McAnarney et al (1974) found that children with less severe juvenile arthritis experienced more psychological adjustment problems, which the researchers attributed to the greater ambiguity about the child's health status and to the fact that peers and adults make more allowances when the illness is severe and visible.

Jessop and Stein (1985) found in a sample of diverse chronic illnesses that when the illness was less visible, there was more uncertainty, ambiguity, and denial. And among this group, those whose illness course was changing had the biggest problems. This added source of uncertainty about the course of the illness created an additional demand, making it difficult to plan for the future or even be ready to respond to the exacerbation of symptoms. Ferrari et al. (1983) found more negative outcomes for epileptic children in their sample compared to diabetics or controls, which they attributed to the unpredictability of epileptic seizures.

Meanings that Contribute to Capabilities

Family members hold meanings or beliefs that function as resources for them. When parents have confidence in their own abilities to manage (Borrow et al., 1985) and have a realistic attitude about the treatment regimen (Koski & Kumento, 1977), the child and family do better. Some parents believe that having a chronically ill child made them stronger (Zucman, 1982) or helped their other children develop more patience, tolerance, and empathy.

There are frequently reports that religious beliefs were strengthened by having a chronically ill child and that these beliefs in the supernatural enable families to manage (Murphy, 1982; Shapiro, 1983). In many ways what families seem to develop is a sense of coherence about life (Antonovsky, 1979), recognizing that there are some things they can control and other things that they must entrust to others or to something beyond their control.

OUTCOMES OF ADAPTATION

Over time the family is continually engaged in a process of managing their pileup of demands with their capabilities. Good adaptation is achieved when there is a minimal discrepancy between demands and capabilities such that individual family member needs are met and the family system's tasks are accomplished. Each system attempts to "fit" into its context, individual into family and family into community. As stated earlier, the relatively stable patterns of individual or family behavior which emerge in this process of balancing demands and capabilities are indicators of adaptation and can be viewed on a continuum from bad to good. The maladaptive outcomes become feedback, increasing the pileup of demands; bonadaptive outcomes become feedback, increasing the family's capabilities (see Figure 2.3).

When we study a family with a chronically ill child at any cross section in time, we seldom know *when* the observed patterns of behavior emerged; that is, calling them "outcomes" is an arbitrary punctuation the observer imposes. With this caution in mind, some of the more frequently cited maladaptive and bonadaptive patterns and symptoms will be summarized.

Maladaptive Outcomes that Contribute to Family Demands

Individual Maladaptive Outcomes

Keeping in mind that nearly all of these findings are equivocal, with one study often contradicting the results of another, chronically ill children are reported to show more than usual degrees of depression (Murphy, 1982; Orr et al., 1983), alienation and social isolation (Johnson, 1980), excessive school absence (Orr et al., 1983), lower school achievement (Gath et al., 1980), and developmental delays (Ferrari et al., 1983). Behavior problems such as hostility and agression (Tavormina et al., 1976), excessive risk taking, or fearfulness and overdependence (Mattsson, 1972) have also been reported. These behavior patterns and symptoms are usually associated with poorer health status in the child (e.g., poor diabetes control), but again, the direction of effects is unclear. Did the poor health "cause" the symptoms, or did the symptoms "cause" the poor health? Strunk et al. (1985) found that family dysfunction and patient-parent conflict were factors that discriminated asthmatics who died from those who lived.

Depression, anxiety, fatigue, and somatic symptoms are frequently reported for parents (Schaffer, 1964). Mothers with chronically ill children often show a number of adverse symptoms (Tavormina et al., 1981; Zucman, 1982). Levine and Ebert (1983) found that mothers assumed most of the stress of the children's illnesses and thus protected fathers and, theoretically at least, the marriage. Strong repressed emotions may contribute to these symptoms (Mattsson, 1972) as well as to a diminished sense of mastery (Breslau, 1983).

Siblings may get sick as a way to get attention (Bruhn, 1977) or exhibit behavior problems, especially if they feel overburdened, which is more likely to occur in single-parent families (Zucman, 1982). Siblings may become socially withdrawn, irritable, and emotionally disturbed (Vance et al., 1980) especially when the patient's illness is clearly visible (Ferrari, 1984; Lavigne & Ryan, 1979). Breslau (1983) found an interaction effect between age and gender for siblings of handicapped children. Male siblings who were younger than the handicapped child and female sibs who were older than the disabled child were more aggressive and more depressed. Frey (1984) notes that siblings of chronically ill adolescents often experience difficulty with launching, either leaving home abruptly as a way to escape or finding it impossible to leave because it will upset the family balance.

Family Patterns of Interaction as Maladaptive Outcomes

Different maladaptive patterns of parental responses to their chronically ill child have been described, such as: (a) overprotectiveness and overindulgence (Orr et al., 1983; Wishner & O'Brien, 1978), (b) rejection and indifference, and (c) perfectionism and control (Anderson & Auslander, 1980).

As sketched above another family pattern frequently described is when the mother becomes overly involved with the chronically ill child (parent-child coalition) and the father is pushed out. Often this emerges gradually because of the intense caretaking needs of the child and because of the financial demands leading the father to work more away from home. Physicians can exacerbate this coalition when only one parent participates in clinic visits and is provided medical information (Williamson, 1985). This pattern seems to be associated with more marital conflict and, often, separation and divorce.

Minuchin et al. (1975, 1978) have described a set of family patterns which seem to be associated with psychosomatic symptoms in chronically ill children: (a) enmeshment (excessive emotional involvement of family members with each other), (b) rigidity, (c) overprotectiveness, (d) lack of conflict resolution, and (e) involvement of the sick child in unresolved parental conflict. Schaffer (1964), studying families that had a child with cerebral palsy, found that 43% of them were judged to be overprotective and enmeshed, a situation that he attributed to repressed negative feelings and overcompensation.

There are conflicting findings about whether the incidence of divorce is higher in families with chronically ill children (Lansky et al., 1978; Masters et al., 1983; Murphy, 1982). In an small study Roesel and Lawlis (1983) found that divorce was more likely for parents of genetically handicapped children if the child was firstborn and male and the parents were young. Sabbeth and Leventhal (1984), in a review of 34 studies of marital adjustment when a child had chronic illness, concluded that divorce rates were not higher than average although there was more reported marital distress. They suggested that some conflict and squabbles may be adaptive as a way of managing tension and difficult emotions and issues. Probably the demands of chronic illness are one among many factors which may exacerbate marital conflict.

Adaptive Outcomes That Become Part of Family Capabilities

In a limited number of small studies investigators have found that children with chronic illness tend to show no differences in overall adjustment when compared with normal peers (Drotar et al., 1981; Gath et al., 1980). The degree to which parents are able to adjust to the demands of the chronic illness seems to facilitate adjustment of the chronically ill child and siblings (Foster & Berger, 1985; Masters et al., 1983). Ferrari (1984) found this was especially true for mothers of diabetics and autistic children in that the mother's perceived social support and adjustment predicted the children's overall adjustment; the same finding was not obtained for fathers, who tended to be less involved in the care of the child. In this same study Ferrari found that siblings of the ill and handicapped children were more socially competent than the siblings of normal controls. This is one of the few studies pointing to the positive outcomes of living with a chronically ill family member.

Ritchie (1980) found that families with an epileptic child tended to be more efficient problem-solving units than control families in that they minimized disagreements (a way to reduce demands) and had a greater tendency toward group consensus (a resource). Cowen et al. (1985) also found more uniformity of thought regarding family functioning for parents of children with cystic fibrosis compared to controls. A shared view of the situation may enhance adaptation.

CONCLUSION

It is clear from this review of the literature that we know much more about the hardships and demands in families of chronically ill children and how they develop problems than we know about how they successfully adapt. Yet identification of the resources, coping strategies, and positive meanings some of these families develop would provide targets for intervention. This focus on *successful* adaptation is clearly needed in future research.

In addition, future studies could be strengthened by attention to the following factors:

1. Longitudinal studies should be undertaken so that the complex, recursive interactions between the family and chronic illness could more adequately be studied. For example, the relationship between chronic illness and developmental tasks could be studied by following children through major transitions.
2. While small samples may be adequate for description and hypothesis generation, large sample sizes are needed to adequately test hypotheses and avoid Type II errors.
3. Designs should include comparison groups (e.g., another illness group or a healthy group) appropriate to the research question so that illness-specific findings can be adequately interpreted.
4. Sampling procedures should avoid nonrepresentative samples (e.g. predominantly middle-class, service-seeking families). Through sampling or statistical control there should be attention to (a) family structure (single parent, stepfamilies, and so on), (b) race and ethnicity, (c) age and developmental stage of the chronically ill child, and (d) severity of the chronic condition.
5. Greater attention should be paid to the methods for obtaining data. Multiple methods (self-report, direct observation, interaction coding, and so on) need to be employed. Mothers should not be the sole informant about the child and family, and when self-report instruments are used, they should have demonstrated reliability and validity.
6. Finally, future studies could be strengthened by using relevant theoretical models to guide the formulation of research questions and the conceptualization of variables to be studied. The FAAR Model used in this chapter to organize research findings would be one such model. It would facilitate the identification of critical factors in the community, within the family, and in individual family members which are used to balance the multiple demands experienced when a child member has a chronic illness and which allow these families to achieve good adaptation.

Chronic Health Problems of the Elderly

3

JAMES BLACKBURN

The purpose of this chapter is twofold: to discuss the most frequent chronic health problems affecting the elderly and to address the consequences of these health problems for the family system.

Health decline in advancing age is usually the result of chronic rather than acute health problems (Butler & Newacheck, 1981). More than 80% of the noninstitutionalized older population in 1984 reported the presence of at least one chronic health condition, and many older people have multiple chronic health conditions. However, as various researchers have noted (see, for example, Butler and Newacheck, 1981), the presence of a chronic health condition is not necessarily associated with functional limitations or disability. Therefore, the impact a particular chronic health condition has on daily functioning varies considerably among individuals and thus need for assistance also varies.

PREVALENT CHRONIC HEALTH PROBLEMS

The most prevalent chronic health disorders that lead to impaired functioning and mortality among the elderly are heart disease, cancer, stroke, arthritis, loss of vision and hearing, different types of dementia, and depression, which is the most common affective disorder in this age group. Heart disease is the principal cause of death among the elderly (Kart, 1985). In addition, heart disease accounts for a great deal of morbidity, disability, and inactivity in older people.

Heart Disease

The dominant causes or forms of heart disease are ischemia and hypertension (Bracklehurst & Hanley, 1981). Ischemic heart disease includes those conditions in which there is a deficiency of blood to the heart because the cardiac vessels that supply it narrow or constrict. Coronary heart disease is also known as ischemic heart disease. It should also be pointed out that in virtually all its aspects, heart disease is no different in old age than in youth (Bracklehurst & Hanley, 1981).

A significant number of elderly individuals have hypertension, or high blood pressure, which may lead to heart disease. As many as one in four older people has high blood pressure, defined as a diastolic pressure greater than 100mm Hg (Steinberg, 1976). In fact, studies of large groups of individuals indicate that both systolic and diastolic blood pressure continue to rise throughout adult life to old age. The most prevalent causes of hypertension in older people are arteriosclerotic changes. Such changes decrease the arteries' efficiency, so the heart has to work correspondingly harder to maintain blood flow to vital organs, with impaired circulation to the brain, heart, and kidneys being especially damaging. Morbidity and mortality can result as a consequence of hypertension and consequent heart failure, stroke, and kidney failure. Just as is true in youth, blood pressure can be controlled with the use of drug therapy, although as Bracklehurst and Hanley (1981) indicate, current geriatric opinion is in general antagonistic to antihypertensive therapy in old age, largely because of the possible side effects of treatment. However, if drug therapy is indicated, elderly people require a cautious approach. Exton-Smith and Overstall (1979) recommend aiming for a gradual reduction in blood pressure over several weeks to avoid possible heart failure.

Cancer

Cancer is the second leading cause of death and morbidity in the United States. The incidence of cancer also increases with age such that the death rate among those 65 years of age and over is 50 times that among those aged 25 to 44 and about four times that among those aged 45 to 64. In part, these facts reflect two important understandings that have been developed about the etiology of cancer (Wright et al., 1976).

First, most forms of cancer have a long latent period, and initiating factors start during young adulthood. Second, increasing age and the accompanying physiologic changes make the individual more susceptible to the actions of carcinogens. It should also be pointed out that in 1984 the death rate from cancer for older women was about 56% of that for men. The lungs, gastrointestinal tract, and genital and urinary organs are primary sites for men. The gastrointestinal tract, breasts, lungs, and cervix are primary sites for women.

Finally, older people should be encouraged to have periodic preventive medical examinations. Physicians should take corrective and preventive measures with regard to any predisposing factors or pre-malignant conditions. Older persons, their families, and their physicians should not misattribute such factors or conditions to old age.

Stroke

Just as heart tissue can be denied adequate blood supply, changes in blood vessels that serve brain tissue, cerebral infarction, or cerebral hemorrhage can reduce the supply of blood carried to the brain and result in a malfunction or death of brain cells. Such impaired brain tissue circulation is referred to as cerebrovascular disease. Also, when the brain is completely denied blood, a cerebrovascular accident, or stroke, results. The severity of the accident is determined by the particular area affected as well as by the total amount of brain tissue involved. Currently cerebrovascular disease is the third leading cause of death and morbidity in the United States among older people.

Cerebral thrombosis, a major cause of stroke in the elderly, occurs when a formed clot becomes lodged in an already narrowed artery. There may be no transient symptoms before the stroke occurs, or the stroke may develop over hours or even days. If a stroke occurs, varying degrees of damage may result. Exton-Smith and Overstall (1979) list disorders of motor function, disturbances of sensation, visual disturbances, aphasia, apraxia, and mental symptoms, among others, as possible clinical features of a stroke. Rehabilitation efforts should begin immediately, and family members and health care workers should be sensitive to the needs of the stroke patient. The family and physician need to realize that any gain in independent living can greatly strengthen an older person's sense of self-respect and dignity.

Arthritis

Arthritis is a generic term that refers to the inflammation of or degenerative change in a joint. This condition represents the number one crippler of not just the elderly but of all age groups in the United States.

Osteoarthritis, commonly known as "degenerative joint disease," is a degenerative joint change that takes places with aging. Its cause is not definitely known. With this condition there is a gradual wearing away of joint cartilage, and the resulting exposure of rough underlying bone ends can cause pain and stiffness. Bony outgrowths known as osteophytes may appear at the margin of the affected bone. Chronic osteoarthritis can also damage the internal ligaments, resulting in abnormal movements of the bones and joint instability or disorganization.

Although osteoarthritis affects more people, rheumatoid arthritis is more serious and carries the greatest potential for pain, disfigurement, and crippling. The disease is not typically a condition of old age per se, but like other chronic health problems, most people carry it into old age. Therefore, rheumatoid arthritis is a chronic, systemic, inflammatory disease of connective tissue that is two to three times more common among elderly women than elderly men. Persistent and progressive joint involvement leading to disorganized joints and great pain and discomfort represent the most common characteristics. Symptoms include fatigue, weight loss, fever, joint pain, redness, swelling and stiffness, and deformity (Kart, 1985). The disease is characterized by acute episodes and remissions. Within 10 to 15 years, most rheumatoid arthritis victims will develop a moderate to severe decline in functional capacity.

The cause of rheumatoid arthritis is also not fully understood. However, it is now viewed as an autoimmune disease that results from the production of antibodies that work against the body's own tissue. The autoantibody known as rheumatoid factor (RF) is present in 85% of rheumatoid arthritis patients. The multiple factors that probably lead to the development of their condition include possible previous exposure to an infectious agent and genetic factors that program a given immune response.

Also associated with the aging process is a gradual loss of bone that reduces skeletal mass without disrupting the proportions of minerals and organic materials (Shock, 1961). This general loss of bone, known as osteoporosis, has been recognized for many years. The quantitative decrease in bone mass can result in diminished height, backache, and a reduction in the structural strength of bones that makes them more susceptible to fracture. In fact, it is now believed that many falls and associated hip fractures of old age actually represent an osteoporatic femoral neck that broke under its weight-bearing tasks. Radiographic evidence actually indicates that approximately three out of four of those elderly individuals, mostly women, who suffer from a broken hip express evidence of osteoporatic involvement of the femoral neck. So significant is the mortality and disability associated with hip fracture among the elderly that osteoporosis is listed as the 12th leading cause of death among the elderly in the United States.

Therefore, bone and muscle changes can greatly alter an elderly individual's lifestyle by making simple tasks of daily living almost impossible. In fact, if an elderly person becomes bedridden and immobilized as a result of these changes, complications can result that can lead to death.

Loss of Vision and Hearing

Many persons maintain nearly normal sight well into old age. However, surveys of the incidence of blindness and problems of visual acuity show that these problems are often associated with old age. Degenerative changes that become more frequent with age contribute to the poorer visual acuity experienced by older people (Anderson & Palmore, 1974). In addition, presbyopia is a degenerative change that occurs in the aging eye. With this condition the lens loses its ability to focus, a change that leads to farsightedness. Thus, there is a marked tendency for older persons to hold things at a distance in order to see them.

This degenerative process also causes the lens of the eye to undergo a yellowing effect. This change is significant, because it becomes more difficult for an elderly person to discern certain color intensities, especially blues, greens, and violet, which are filtered out. Yellow, red, and orange are generally seen more easily.

Cataracts, the most common disability of the aged eye, represent an opacity of the normally transparent lens of the eye. The opaqueness of the lens interferes with the passage of rays of light to the retina, so that a person may need to hold objects extremely close in order to see them and may need brighter and brighter light in which to read. Surgical removal, however, provides safe and effective treatment for cataracts.

Glaucoma is the most serious eye disease affecting the aged. If left untreated, it will result in total blindness. The disease generally develops somewhere between the ages of 40 and 65 in response to increased pressure within the eyeball, pressure that can lead to irreparable damage to the optic nerve. One of the earliest indications of glaucoma is a gradual loss of peripheral vision, which may cause the elderly person to bump into things or not see passing cars in the adjacent lane of a highway.

Before chronic glaucoma develops to such an extent, an elderly person will express other warning signs, including severe headache, nausea, blurred vision, dull eye pain, tearing of the eyes, and the appearance of halos around objects of light.

Macular degeneration is another common visual disorder that develops in old age. This condition involves a degeneration of the macular area of the retina, the area which ordinarily permits a person to discriminate detail such as fine print. The loss of this discriminating ability entails a loss of central vision, which may begin in the early 50s.

It should also be pointed out that age-related visual impairment may produce alterations in behavior as well as in reduced feelings of self-esteem as the visually impaired older person begins to suffer from communication problems. Special efforts can and should be made to help make independent living possible for visually impaired older adults.

Although most older people retain hearing sufficient for normal living, the elderly individual is three times more likely to display a significant loss of hearing than is a younger person. Impaired hearing associated with aging is known as presbycusis (Welford, 1980). It is noted first in the higher sound frequencies and becomes evident in most individuals by the age of 50. At first the loss of ability to perceive higher frequencies does not involve normal speech patterns. However, as the condition progresses, conversation does become affected. Presbycusis is most frequently the result of changes in important structures of the inner ear, most commonly the loss of hair cells in the organ of Corti.

Hearing loss can also result from interrupted conduction. Factors that can lead to hearing loss of a conductive nature include genetic conditions, exposure to environmental noise, the use of certain drugs, and chronic ear infections.

Depression

Psychopathological conditions are also present in the elderly. According to Pfeiffer (1977), approximately 15% of the elderly population in the United States suffers from significant or moderate psychopathological conditions although such estimates must always be viewed with caution, as the epidemiology of psychopathological conditions is beset by conceptual and methodological difficulties. Despite these difficulties, however, it is clear that many older people do have mental health problems and needs. Depression appears to be the most common functional psychiatric disorder in the later years.

Depression can vary in duration and degree; it may be triggered by the loss of a loved one or by the onset of physical disease.

Depressive symptoms may be obvious and apparent or occult and hidden. Usual indicators of depression are feelings of helplessness, sadness, lack of vitality, frequent feelings of guilt, loneliness, boredom, sexual disinterest, and impotence. Insomnia, early morning fatigue, and marked loss of appetite may also be seen, and sleep is often disturbed with the more depressed elderly individual. It is currently often difficult or impossible to identify the exact cause of a particular depression (Zung & Green, 1973).

The psychosocial triggers and/or causes of depression, when they are present, can be external or internal. External or exogenous depressions are explained by outside events in one's life. Internal or endogenous depressions are apparently not caused by immediate outside occurrences but may be related to early developmental deprivations and losses. They may also be caused by the inner process known as a "life review" in which older persons examine past actions. Yet it is often not possible to differentiate clearly between these types of depression.

Busse and Pfeiffer (1973) have also emphasized decreased self-regard as much more important than guilt in the causation of depression in older people. However, I believe this is overstated. Older people are still capable of actions that produce guilt. Old age does not erase vindictiveness, anger, or greed, and older persons also must deal with their guilt from the past, particularly during the life review process. Even recognizing that reduced self-regard is an important ingredient in depression does not deny the fact that the more guilty are more vulnerable. A prolonged depressive reaction following the death of someone close is often related to problems with the deceased person earlier in life. Thus, the grief is exacerbated by guilt.

Severe depressive reactions are often found associated with physical diseases, especially with diseases that leave people incapacitated or in pain (Dovenmuehle & Verwoerdt, 1963). Unfortunately, the presence of physical or organic disorders tends to discourage practitioners from treating the depressions that accompany or are added to them. In addition, family members may agree with nontreatment, believing that treatment would be too much for the person to handle. Another prominent cause of depression among older people is drug use. Drugs such as tranquilizers, antihypertensive medications, the antiarhythmic heart drugs can cause a whole range of depressions.

Dementia

Dementia is a phenomenon that many lay people and, unfortunately, too many medical personnel refer to by the inaccurate term "senility." All too often, for lack of a thorough evaluation, reversible disorders are also subsumed under this category and termed untreatable. However, it was only about 45 years ago that reversible and nonreversible chronic disorders began to receive differential diagnosis and treatment. It is now becoming clear that one must look for reversibility in *all* disorders, even those like dementia, which had been considered irreversible. But even when this is not the case, a careful plan of treatment should be initiated to make the older person as comfortable and functional as possible.

In some older persons with dementia, brain impairments may represent the only behavior disturbance observed, with the rest of the personality and behavior remaining unchanged. These cases are uncomplicated in the sense that the person attempts to make suitable adjustments and has insight into what has happened to his or her intellectual abilities, especially in the early stages. Such a person can function fairly well with little assistance. Even when impairment has progressed to a more severe stage, the person can often live at home with proper supports.

When there are accompanying emotional symptoms, the situation becomes more complex. Associated behavioral reactions fall into several categories: first are the reactions caused by the deficit itself; second are emotional reactions and adaptations to the deficit; and third are the reactions termed "release phenomena." The latter appear as latent personality traits and tendencies as a result of brain damage. It is now generally agreed that not only the organic disorder but also the individual's basic personality, his or her inherited or constitutional traits, and the environmental situation affect the kind and severity of symptoms that appear. People react to threats to their intellectual capacities in highly individualized ways, and this is most true in the beginning phases of decline (Butler & Lewis, 1982).

A leveling effect in personality takes place as impairment increases, and in the final stages people may become completely mute or inattentive. However, advanced dementia is not necessarily the irreversible condition it first appears to be and may respond to treatment. For example, direct instruction and supplying orientation aids (i.e., signs, colors, and so on) may improve orientation.

Memory changes are the most obvious and noticeable symptoms

of dementia, since memory so intimately affects interpersonal relationships with family and friends (Butler & Lewis, 1982). An added factor in memory loss is the possibility of emotional influence on recall abilities. This may lead to depression and preoccupation with problems that may not be noticed yet can interfere with learning and memory.

An additional factor associated with memory loss is disorientation, which is a more easily and accurately tested symptom. Disorientation about time is the first major indicator of confusion to occur as a result of dementia. In the final phase the person also loses the ability to remember who he or she is. Among the elderly there are two major types of dementia. The first is primary degenerative dementia with senile onset, commonly known as senile dementia, and the second is multiinfarct dementia. Senile dementia and multiinfarct dementia may look a good deal alike and thus have not been viewed as mutually exclusive from each other until recently.

Senile dementia refers to a usually chronic progressive decline in mental functioning associated with changes in the brain, primarily the dissolution of brain cells themselves. The disorder occurs much more frequently in women than in men, probably because women have a greater life expectancy than men. The average age of onset is 75 years, with a range of 60 to 90 years of age. However, sex linkage itself may be a factor in senile dementia.

Older people may move slowly from normal old age to senile dementia with no abrupt changes. However, the older person with multiinfarct dementia may pass abruptly from old age to severe stages of the disease. Also, significant memory impairment is more common in older women than in older men of the same age. Friends and relatives gradually notice small differences in physical, mental, and emotional functioning as well as previous personality traits becoming exaggerated. Finally, a host of emotional reactions are possible, with depression, anxiety, and irritability being the most frequent. In addition, hallucinations can be present, especially at night. Sleeplessness and restlessness are common, and there is frequently loss of bladder and sphincter control.

Senile dementia is eventually fatal, with a fairly steady and progressive course. Persons may live 10 or more years, but average survival is 5 years. Typically personality fades away or dies before physical death occurs.

Multiinfarct dementia, as previously mentioned, is also a chronic disorder that usually shows an uneven and stage-like downward progression, as compared to the more steady decline seen in senile dementia. The disorder is associated with damage to the cerebral blood vessels through arteriosclerosis (i.e., a narrowing and closing of the vessel itself). The blood flow to the brain is interfered with and, as a result, insufficient oxygen and nutrients reach the brain. Hypertension and/or diabetes are frequently present. Typically, age of onset is between 50 and 70 years, with an average age of 66. It is much less common than senile dementia and is found more often in men than women. The cause of the arteriosclerosis is still unclear, although many hypotheses have been offered such as smoking, lack of exercise, diet, environmental pollution, and so on.

Early symptoms of multiinfarct dementia are dizziness, headaches, and decreased physical and mental energy, and the onset can be gradual or sudden. However, approximately 50% of the cases occur acutely in the form of a sudden attack of confusion. Individuals who have a more gradual onset often look much more like those with senile dementia than multiinfarct dementia. There is usually a gradual loss of intellectual ability, and memory loss is incomplete rather than complete. That is, the individual is unable to remember one minute and regains total capacity the next. The course of the dementia is up and down rather than progressively downhill. In addition, there are often speech disturbances, abnormal gait with short steps, and hallucinations. Unfortunately, paranoid reactions are often misdiagnosed as multiinfarct dementia as a result of careless examinations and unclear diagnostic thinking.

In treatment there is also a great need for special medical care because of the critical physical involvement in multiinfarct dementia. If and when remission occurs, the person can often benefit from psychotherapy, physical therapy, and recreation. Physical abilities are often a greater problem than intellectual capacities, although intellectual damage can be profound after massive or repeated cardiac attacks or strokes.

Presenile dementia includes a group of cortical brain diseases that clinically look like the senile dementia seen in older people; however, they occur earlier, in the 40- and 50-year-old age groups. Intellectual deterioration and personality disintegration are two predominant features, just as they are in senile dementia. Alzheimer's disease has become the name applied to the most frequently seen type of presenile dementia, although comprehensive data on incidence are not available (Butler & Lewis, 1982). Behaviorially with Alzheimer's disease there is rapid mental deterioration, beginning with marked mental losses as well as tendencies toward agitation. It proceeds toward more severe symptoms such as incoherence, gait disturbances, and convulsive seizures. Later the individual becomes rigid and may be unable to stand or walk. Finally, utter helplessness prevails, with incontenence and progressive emaciation. The average age of onset is 58 years, and an individual seldom lives longer than 5 years after the illness begins. However, remissions do occasionally occur.

In conclusion, there is little yet known about the cause of Alzheimer's disease. However, it is suspected that three elements play a role: (a) the process of aging, (b) genetic factors, and (c) pathogenic factors in the environment (i.e. toxins and/or infection).

CONSEQUENCES FOR THE FAMILY SYSTEM

To begin with, empirical and clinical evidence has made it clear that most older people are not isolated from their families. Therefore, one must go further and assume that any problems, crises, and changes affecting an older person also affect his or her entire family system. Even the youngest family members will be reacting to the events in the lives of grandmother and grandfather. It is through these experiences that they learn firsthand about aging, and many of their attitudes toward older people and their own eventual aging will be modeled after the situations and attitudes in the family system.

Caregiving for chronically ill persons is often extremely taxing and exhausting. The caregiver, usually the spouse or adult daughter, often faces the prospect of social isolation, lack of time for self and friends, and unrelieved physical labor in caregiving (see, for example, Brody, 1981). The fact that families maintain primary responsibility for the care of chronically ill elderly members is well established (Monk, 1983). However, the consequences of their caregiving behavior for the entire family system are not well understood.

Some research has shown that some members find caregiving to be burdensome (see, for example, Brody, 1981), while others derive satisfaction from caregiving (see, for example, Seelback, 1978). All too often, however, the effects of the chronic health problems of older adults on the family system are overwhelming. Family members report increased personal stress and disruption in normal family life and routine (Brody, 1981). Health problems may increase as the accumulation of stress begins to wear on family members, who frequently express feelings of frustration and helplessness. They find themselves torn between compassion and love on the one hand and guilt, anger, and frustration on the other. It may be at the risk of their own well-being that family members assume the care of a chronically ill family member. Yet many are motivated by their genuine concern and love and their need to be useful and helpful in any way they can.

The caregiver's emotions may also include denial, shame, embarrassment, fear, frustration, anger, depression, and guilt. Other family members may experience similar emotions, but the timing of their emotions may be different from those of the central caregiver. Understanding anger as a reaction to frustration is important and may enable the caregiver to deal with the situation in a more adaptive way. While anger can be a constructive force, it may become destructive when a caregiver shows anger toward the parent or spouse with a chronic illness, and some caregivers wind up hating themselves for their behavior. Caregivers may also limit their capacity to help the older person when anger replaces the loving feelings of the past. In addition, caregivers are apt to feel guilt when they are out of control. However, they can often learn to manage and use their anger in the interest of their survival as effective caregivers. In order to accomplish this task, the family and caregiver must first decide to take care of their own needs, understand their own emotions, and feel comfortable with these behaviors and feelings.

If both the chronically ill older person and the family and caregiver become depressed, professional counseling can help them and the entire family system. Sharing feelings is very helpful, especially when expressions of empathy are offered.

Feelings of guilt may also trouble the caregiver and the family. This guilt may arise from disturbed family relationships of the past, traits ignored in their parent or spouse, or errors in treating the parent or spouse. It may also arise when the constant frustration of tending to the chronically ill person's needs causes them to neglect or abuse him or her. In addition, guilt over institutionalizing a relative may be the most difficult feeling to dissipate, and professional intervention may be necessary in order to work through these feelings. It is important that those who deal with chronic illnesses must recognize that both the older person with the illness and the caregiver and family are victims of the condition and that adequate treatment should involve the entire family system. Assistance should be offered in practical terms, enlisting as wide a support network as possible, including the mobilization of community resources.

In addition, although feelings of affection and obligation toward elderly parents and the perception of parental dependency by adult children may lead to increased helping behavior, one cannot exclude the existence of conflict between adult children and elderly parents as a possibly significant factor in reducing helping behavior. The historical quality of the relationship between adult children and elderly parents must be considered. If there has been a long history of rejection, alienation, or interpersonal conflict, there may be little willingness for adult children to provide services or for elderly parents to accept them. Even appeals for affection or duty may include little motivation.

Also, problems may well arise when adult children have been deeply enmeshed with their nonaging parents and have struggled earlier to obtain their own independence and autonomy. Caregiving responsibilities may threaten reenmeshment, which can have negative effects on the entire family system, including marital and parent-child relationships, for generations to come. However, a positive relationship with an elderly parent is not a necessary prerequisite for an adult child to provide care and help to that parent. Thus, it is unclear from the admittedly too-limited literature whether a relationship with a history of conflict between adult child and elderly parent would lead to increased or decreased helping behavior to the elderly parent. Such a history may even be unrelated.

Another aspect which must be considered is that conflict may lead not only to less helping behavior but to increased abusive behavior toward elderly parents, although it may seem paradoxical that the family can be a source of love and care as well as a source of conflict and even violence. However, the results of the few studies of adult children's help to parents tend to be different or inconsistent, and many times such differences are related to background variables or factors.

The socioeconomic status of the family appears to be an important factor in determining adult children's aid to elderly parents. Middle-class adult children tend to provide more financial aid, while working-class adult children provide more services, although this is partially influenced by the fact that working-class adult children tend to live closer to their elderly parents. However, even if middle-class children live closer, they are often too busy in demanding occupations to provide direct services rather than financial aid. Thus, they may hire someone to provide the direct services.

Middle-aged daughters tend to have closer relationships with their elderly parents than do sons (Troll, 1971). Also, Troll (1971) points out that daughters traditionally provide more help to elderly parents than do sons, particularly in areas of homemaking and personal care. Lopata (1973) also found in a study of the Chicago area that widows' sons were helpful in practical matters, such as financial dealings, while their daughters fostered closer emotional ties by giving services and visiting. As increased numbers of women work and men take on more domestic duties, sex differences in help provided to elderly parents may be reduced. However, there is no indication that this is currently the case.

There is likely to be a wide age range among individuals with elderly parents, extending from early adulthood to early old age. A few elderly persons with minor children can be found. However, very little is known about how adult children's feelings toward elderly parents may vary with age or how helping behaviors may vary as well. In general, however, the ages of adult children and their elderly parents are correlated, so that older adult children are more likely to have older parents with greater needs for care and services. Yet it is difficult to reach any conclusions about the age trend in children's feelings in middle age toward elderly parents, since different studies have dealt with different populations and have used different measures.

It also needs to be pointed out that many elderly parents who are well into old age take care of their own needs and do not need help from their children or other service providers. However, most elderly parents will need help from others at a point when the illnesses of aging become too great for them to handle alone. Often adult children anticipate what their response to such future parental need will be, and if their commitment to help is sincere and realistic, it is likely that it will be translated into actual helping behavior when the need arises.

Since most elderly people want to be self-sufficient and independent for as long as possible, adult children should adopt a more preventive approach to their elderly parents' needs by helping them find ways of learning and growing to meet their own needs both before and during the period of decline. By so doing, the adult children may in the long run be forestalling decline. Many adult children at present tend to place too much emphasis on "support" strategies of helping in which they try to provide whatever they think the elderly parents need. This may lead to learned helplessness and dependency, while training and motivational strategies may be more effective in prolonging independence and self-sufficiency.

Adult children can help their parents to help themselves as long as possible and as much as possible rather than allowing them to depend unnecessarily on family or society. Adult children can provide the resources and support to promote parents' self-care rather than emphasize direct services. Such an approach could pay unexpected returns for adult children in later years through the changed attitudes with which they confront their own aging. However, it is imperative that one remember that not all adult children are capable of providing resources and support, as they too may be dealing with the issues of aging such as retirement, ill health, and so on.

In conclusion, there is much to be done in exploring the critical questions of long-term care as related to families so that improvements based on accurate knowledge can be made. Whatever the nature of the strains on the family system, it is clear that knowledge about the lag between needs and family-oriented programs is great. Without an adequate knowledge base, effective intervention strategies cannot be designed or implemented.

Alzheimer's Disease and Ambiguous Loss

4

PAULINE BOSS, WAYNE CARON AND JOAN HORBAL

> *All the world's a stage*
> *And all the men and women merely players.*
> *They have their exits and their entrances. . . .*
> *(The) last scene of all,*
> *That ends this strange eventful history,*
> *Is second childishness and mere oblivion,*
> *Sans teeth, sans eyes, sans taste, sans everything.*

William Shakespeare, As You Like It

THE NATURE OF DEMENTIA

More than 3 million Americans have Alzheimer's disease, an irreversible form of dementia. Its symptoms include progressive memory loss, the loss of intellectual capabilities, and deterioration in the ability to perform even the simplest everyday activities, such as preparing meals, driving a car, grooming oneself, and, finally, even the ability to toilet and feed oneself. In addition, Alzheimer's disease can be associated with drastic personality changes. In its early stages, the caregiver is often the only one who sees these changes and is often not believed by other family members, since changes come and go. Only in the later stages of the disease are the signs of deterioration obvious to everyone. The patient requires constant supervision and care due to memory loss and then total helplessness. Throughout this process the caregiver perceives an increasing ambiguity in the boundary of his or her family: the patient is physically there but becomes psychologically absent. This phenomenon, called boundary ambiguity, occurs especially when there is an unclear loss in a family. Alzheimer's disease is such a situation—the caregiver and family do not know whether the patient is in or out of the system.

AUTHORS' NOTE: This chapter is based on case study material from the University of Minnesota and Veterans Administration Hospital Project Study on Alzheimer's Disease, 1P50-MH40317-01, funded by the National Institute on Aging. Dr. Pauline Boss is the Principal Investigator for the Family Project 5. Appreciation is expressed to Professor Vern Bengtson at the Andrus Gerontology Center, University of Southern California, where part of this paper was written.

THE THEORETICAL PREMISE

The thesis of this chapter is that this ambiguity in the boundary of the caregiver's family system is, in fact, the greatest stressor for the caregiver and the family. We propose that it is the ambiguity rather than the disease itself that wears down the caregiver. Many of us can deal with illness, even terminal illness, as long as we know the facts surrounding that situation and as long as the person we care for gives us some note of recognition and emotional response.

With Alzheimer's disease there is no clarity about the facts of the disease. The doctors cannot yet give us definitive information about the illness. They do not know what causes it, what prevents it, what eases it, what the pattern or rate of deterioration will be, or even whether an individual has it for sure. In addition, the degree of ambiguity increases as the patient becomes unable to interact emotionally with the caregiver and family. The patient becomes psychologically absent while physically present, and this incongruence between physical and psychological presence creates high boundary ambiguity in the family system and keeps the caregiver and family in a highly stressful state. The patient *is there, but not there,* in the sense that he or she no longer relates to the family in the old, familiar ways. The family, and especially the caregiver, is held in limbo. No resolution is possible when a family loss is ambiguous.

CAREGIVERS, BOUNDARY AMBIGUITY, AND CHRONIC ILLNESS

Although limited to idiosyncratic samples, previous research has established that the caregiving role for the Alzheimer patient is usually assumed by one family member: the spouse if alive, otherwise a middle-aged daughter (Brody, 1981; Soldo, 1980). Home care is often provided at great cost to families in terms of chronic fatigue, family conflict (Rabins et al., 1982), restriction in social life (Poulshock & Deimling, 1984), resentment toward other relatives who do not help, feelings of entrapment (Hartford & Parsons, 1982), and overall high levels of stress (Cantor, 1983; Lezak, 1978). Psychological, physical, and financial resources are strained, especially if the patient suffers from cognitive impairment (Johnson, 1983; Lezak, 1978; Lopata, 1973; Rabins et al., 1982).

Support from other family members appears, however, to mediate the relationship between caregiving and stress. Some families appear to become more cohesive and supportive in response to the illness, with a corresponding reduction in the caregiver's stress (Hayter, 1982; Zarit et al., 1980). For other families, however, caregiving is associated with increased levels of family conflict and thus with a negative impact on family relations (Poulshock & Deimling, 1984; Rabins et al., 1982). The relationship between caregiving and stress, therefore, appears to be conditional on some phenomenon within the family system that has yet to be identified.

Studies have shown the importance of family support, but more research is needed to empirically document the relationship between family health and the physical and mental health of the aged member. Fengler and Goodrich (1979) found that male patients with high life satisfaction were being cared for by wives who also had high life satisfaction. Hartford and Parsons (1982) reported that some members of a caregiver's support group noted improvement in the patient as their own mental health changed for the better. In some cases this improvement even included better cognitive functioning of the patient. There is, therefore, preliminary evidence that it would be fruitful to examine how the mental health of the caregiver affects the physical and psychological health of the demented aged member, and vice versa.

Families provide the bulk of care for dementia patients, sometimes at great personal cost. The literature suggests that it would be advantageous for both patient and caregivers if the levels of family stress and dysfunction could be lowered. We propose that a significant predictor of high stress and dysfunction is *ambiguity in the family boundary: confusion as to whether the patient is in or out of the family system.* As stated earlier, this ambiguity arises because a demented family member is psychologically absent from the family system while physically present. Indeed, high stress is routinely reported when family members are cognitively impaired (75%) while only 43% of family members report high stress when the patient is not cognitively impaired (Zarit, et al., 1980). It may be that the critical variable is boundary ambiguity.

History of Boundary Ambiguity Research

The variable of boundary ambiguity, used to explain and predict familv stress, was developed in clinical and research settings with families stressed by having physically or psychologically missing members (Boss, 1977, 1980a, 1980b, 1982, 1987; Boss & Greenberg, 1984, 1986). The original research focused on the families of men missing-in-action. Because there was no clear evidence of the father's death, for many of these MIA families he was psychologically present while physically absent.

Demented patients are another kind of missing family member. They are physically present but psychologically absent. They no longer perform the same roles that they previously performed, and they are less and less emotionally involved with the family. A reorganization is therefore required on the part of the family to maintain effective boundaries, but because the family member is not dead, family members are held in limbo. Because the facts remain unclear, it is only the family members' *perception* of the situation that can trigger a reorganization process (Boss, 1987). For this reason, we believe that identifying, validating, and clarifying as much as possible this ambiguous psychological boundary will be an effective way to intervene and support the caregiver and family of Alzheimer patients. Although the outcome of the disease cannot be changed, the caregiver's and family's perceptions of the demented patient's presence and role within the family can be altered.

CHRONIC STRESSOR SITUATIONS

Illness varies on the continuum of chronic to acute. As Boss states (1986), the presence of a family member with persistent kidney disease exemplifies a chronic event, whereas a child's breaking a leg represents an acute event. However, in Alzheimer's disease there are, according to caregiver reports, *both* chronic and acute stressor events. This overlay of chronicity and acuteness results in an even greater burden for these families than we had originally thought. Indeed, as a chronic situation Alzheimer's disease is a process that runs a long course, is difficult to amend, and has a debilitating effect on the family. There is uncertainty regarding the facts about the onset, development, and conclusion of the disease process. But there are also acute events that the caregiver can pinpoint. The following case illustrates this.

> Mrs. A was interviewed one year after the death of her husband, whom she had watched deteriorate over a 7-year period from the time of the initial diagnosis of dementia. She described this period as one long grind punctuated by periods of acute crisis as some new symptom or problem occurred. Sometimes it was a concrete problem such as George getting up at 3:00 A.M. and wandering outside or losing

control of his bladder and bowels. At other times the problems were more emotionally draining, such as when he no longer was able to recognize her and would demand she (his wife) take him to his wife! Looking back over the ordeal a year later, Mrs. A indicated she still felt tired and drained. She wondered if she would ever feel normal again.

When there is an ambiguous chronic stressor in the family, the possibility is especially high that the family will deny the illness (Boss, 1986). Given the long-term and ambiguous characteristics of Alzheimer's disease, the family may, in fact, reorganize itself without the affected member, thereby denying his or her presence in the family system. Or they may deny the illness, expecting the sick person to act as he or she always did. Although such denials may ease the tension in the family system for a short time, over the long run denial is harmful. When family members (a) deny that the illness exists or (b) view the affected person as already gone, the boundaries of their family system cannot be maintained; the system cannot function as it should in its daily activities or in critical problem-solving situations. Not having a clear picture about either the patient's presence or absence or about the disease itself, the family comes up with its own "reality" to make sense of the situation. They either deny that the demented member is physically present or they deny that the illness exists at all. Neither of these family perceptions of reality will hold up over time if the reality of the disease runs counter to their perception.

> The B family, when interviewed with Mr. B, who had been diagnosed with dementia 9 months earlier, seemed to choreograph their interactions around him. They addressed Mr. B only to tell him where to sit, ask him to put down a book he had picked up, and inquire whether he needed to go to the bathroom. In his presence family members talked quite freely about Mr. B and his condition but did not address him directly with questions or comments. When the interviewer directed questions to Mr. B, another family member would invariably answer for him. The family seemed to conspire to act as if Mr. B were not in the room. Comments such as "He doesn't understand what we are talking about anyway" and "We don't want to stress him by asking him to do things he can't do" demonstrated a shared perception by the family that Mr. B's mind was completely gone, even though psychometric testing indicated his dementia was at a relatively mild stage.
>
> Mr. C and his two daughters had some difficulty in agreeing on how

Mrs. C's dementia had manifested itself. Mr. C said he first noticed that his wife seemed to lose her place easily in conversations and would often ask the same questions repeatedly. The older daughter Catherine, however, asserted that her mother had always been a little scattered, and having trouble following conversations was nothing new for her. In response to Mr. C's description of an incident where Mrs. C became lost while driving the car home from a relative's house, the younger daughter Barbara recalled how she had always found that stretch of highway very confusing and noted that her mother didn't like driving anyway. Both daughters spoke of the diagnosis of Alzheimer's disease as "tentative" and, although two neurological exams had already been completed, the family had scheduled a third in an attempt to get another diagnosis.

What our early findings suggest, however, is that the family's perception of the situation may *change* over the course of the disease. According to Wikler (1981), who focused on the severe retardation of a child in the family, chronic stressors become "recycled" at each juncture across the life span when a developmental step would normally occur in that person. For example, when the retarded child reaches school age and cannot attend school, the family is reminded acutely of the retardation and will be reminded again at each successive developmental juncture where transitional behaviors should be forthcoming but are not possible.

We feel a similar recycling phenomenon happens to families of Alzheimer patients. In Figure 4.1 we illustrate what Alzheimer caregivers have told us is their perception of loss in similar stages. They report high stress at each juncture where a new loss occurs and say that the grieving stages occur over and over again at each step downward toward the ultimate loss, death.

In this paper we use family stress theory and case study material to inductively identify what appears to block coping and what appears to help in maintaining clear boundaries for caregivers and families of Alzheimer patients. We address these two questions: What are the differences between those families who overcome the hardships of ambiguous loss and those who are debilitated by it? And what are the variables most important to successful coping with an ambiguous loss? On the basis of family stress theory and our early findings, we present the following variables as offering answers to our questions. We present them with the hope that clinicians and researchers will test them in order to determine whether or not change in these variables matters to such troubled families. The

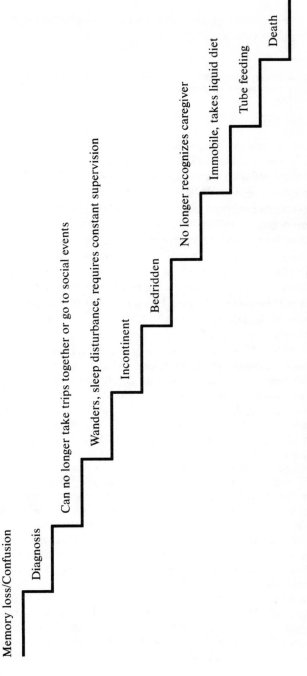

Figure 4.1. Stages of loss as perceived by caregivers of Alzheimer patients.

Memory loss/Confusion

Diagnosis

Can no longer take trips together or go to social events

Wanders, sleep disturbance, requires constant supervision

Incontinent

Bedridden

No longer recognizes caregiver

Immobile, takes liquid diet

Tube feeding

Death

variables are: (a) gender, (b) values and belief systems, (c) family rules and rituals, and (d) developmental tasks.

LIVING WITH AND SURVIVING CHRONIC AMBIGUOUS LOSS: WHICH VARIABLES MATTER

Gender Roles

On the basis of early clinical observations it appears that women caregivers operate differently than men caregivers do. As Carol Gilligan states, males and females may approach problem solving "in a different voice" (1982). Alzheimer caregivers are usually older, and therefore belong to a cohort with more traditional socialization regarding gender roles: men as instrumental, in charge, and active; women as expressive, supportive, and passive. Such socialization will, we propose, have a major effect on how the caregiver perceives and responds to the event of ambiguous loss. We therefore propose that *active* coping behaviors will be more functional for the caregiver than will be *passive* coping behaviors and that these behaviors will be, due to socialization, gender related.

Mary D expressed a good deal of pleasure in having us visit her at home. Although previously a very active and highly religious woman, she had discontinued almost all social activities, including church attendance, when her husband's dementia became more severe. She had devoted all her time and energy to caring for him, to the point of discontinuing her own blood pressure medication because she felt it made her drowsy and less able to care for him. Although he was now in a nursing home, she still had not resumed her former activities. She stated she didn't feel right going out by herself, and even going to church alone made her very uncomfortable. She tried to visit her husband daily, even though he no longer recognized her or seemed to notice her visits. She stated her greatest problem was filling up her time, and in response to a question about what was helpful to her, she said reading Zane Grey westerns was a major coping activity for her.

Mr. E, a retired professional man, maintained a relatively active life while providing in-home care for his bedridden wife. He considered it important, he said, to take a couple of hours every day for himself as a break from his caregiving duties. He used respite care from 1:00 P.M. to 3:00 P.M. so that he could visit friends, and golf. When queried about what was most helpful to him in coping, he brought us into his wife's bedroom to show us the Heyer lift, lamb's wool pressure pads, and other appliances which he used to provide home nursing care for his wife. He explained that these helped him cope because they eased his wife's pain while making his job easier.

In our early findings it appears that many female caregivers' coping mechanisms are, stereotypically, more passive, while male caregivers' coping mechanisms are more active and technology-oriented. We also note a gender-related difference in the types of social networks caregivers have. Male caregivers' social networks are often impoverished in terms of emotional support, while female caregivers' social networks are more often limited in the opportunities they present for respite and active recreation.

Given these early findings we propose that rigid, traditional gender role socialization is a barrier to coping not only with ambiguous loss but with all loss as life goes on. Given that loss is inevitable in marriage and family life, we propose that gender socialization needs to be less rigid and less dichotomous for *both* males and females. Females especially need to learn about active coping mechanisms and to learn that "taking charge" is neither unfeminine nor undesirable behavior. When one's spouse is chronically ill with a disease such as Alzheimer's, one cannot remain passive or there will be two victims, the caregiver as well as the patient.

Values and Belief Systems

In family stress theory values and belief systems play a major role in determining how a family responds to a chronic stressor situation (see Boss, 1986). If the caregiver values mastery over fatalism, action over passivity, or control over acceptance of "the way things are," those beliefs will make a difference in how the event of loss is perceived and responded to. We predict that those caregivers and families who have resources will be more mastery oriented and will rely more heavily on action and technology to resolve their problems; they will rely more heavily on self-help information than on groups where feelings are shared; they will tend to seek out information as their major strategy for problem solving and reducing stress. Research indicates that families in Western cultures are more mastery oriented than families in Eastern cultures. This may, however, be related to economics (see Boss, 1987). More specifically, we propose that the rich more than the poor and the male more than the female will be mastery oriented and active in their approach to lowering stress in families with ambiguous loss.

Mr. F, whose wife was assessed as mild to moderately demented, nevertheless took over all household tasks when the diagnosis was first made. He went into semi-retirement from the business he owned, spending 3 to 4 hours a day at the office. He explained the system he had for keeping up with all his tasks. In the morning he would throw a load of clothes in the laundry before he showered and shaved. By the time he had finished breakfast, the laundry was ready for the dryer. In similar ways, he integrated cooking and cleaning into a regular routine which allowed him to maintain the household in an efficient manner. He felt his wife benefited from not having to worry about these things, and he took great satisfaction in the way he had organized the household chores.

Passive coping strategies, on the other hand, are found in people with a more fatalistic orientation. Because of their value orientation, they have a lesser need to be in control and are more accepting of "the way things are." Such people are less likely to set limits on demands for their time and energy because they believe a higher power will take care of them. Although it may be that economic status is a primary predictor of value orientation, as previously stated, we do not know if a passive and fatalistic orientation *precedes* or *follows* being poor, having fewer resources, and therefore having less power. Having an incurable illness may be just such a situation of powerlessness. At any rate, determining the caregiver's belief system will, we believe, be paramount in determining, first, how he or she perceives the event of Alzheimer's disease in the family, and, second, how he or she will cope with it. The belief system will also determine what kind of support system or information system the caregivers will accept to ease their own stress.

Tom G maintained his job with the government in spite of continuing pressures at home that made it difficult for him to concentrate on his work. As his wife's dementia increased, she became more and more demanding and suspicious. She sought constant attention from him and followed him from room to room, unable to tolerate being alone. She frequently berated him for not loving her and trying to get rid of her. Although her confusion resulted in making many mistakes in recipes and sometimes forgetting things on the stove until they burned, she still did the majority of the cooking. In fact Tom seemed unable to set any limits with his wife. Tom's children were aware of these problems, but like their father they seemed unable to think of any solutions. No one knew how to tell Mrs. G she ought to no longer cook. He expressed an attitude of tired resignation and stated he would simply try to carry on with things as they were as long as he could. He was hoping for a miracle.

Family Rules

Family rules can be thought of as unexpressed, preconscious formulations of what is and is not acceptable behavior within the family system. Because these rules are unexpressed, it follows that they are not negotiated, discussed, or examined by the family.

Family rules appear to run along three directions: gender rules, generational rules, and communication rules. As we discussed previously, gender rules are those that prescribe what is acceptable and unacceptable behavior by men and women with the family. These rules tend to be more traditional for the social cohort which is affected by Alzheimer's disease and may include such rules as: "men drive the car while women ride," "men work and women stay at home," or "women can't go out alone socially." Over time there will be increasing pressure on the family to change due to the progression of the illness, and this, therefore, may force a change in the rule, e.g., the woman taking over the driving or the man being forced to retire. Gender rules can also be thought of as role-defining rules; that is, if the family rule is broken, then the role itself is challenged. For example, if the rule is that men drive and women ride, when the male Alzheimer patient can no longer drive and must turn over the keys to his wife, then the patient may lose part of his self-esteem and identity as the man of the family. But to his or her own detriment, the caregiver may go to great lengths to preserve traditional gender rules no longer functional in the family of an Alzheimer patient.

When asked to describe difficult events that had occurred related to her husband's Alzheimer's disease, Mrs. H talked about the trip back from their annual winter vacation in Florida last year. Mr. H was driving and, while going through Chicago, became quite confused and lost. Although clearly frightened by the experience, Mrs. H indicated that Mr. H would again be driving on their trip to Florida this year. She explained that she did not know how to tell him that he shouldn't drive and noted that she had never driven the car on long trips.

For Mrs. I one of the more difficult turning points came when she had to take over the family checkbook. Her husband, a retired accountant, began making serious mistakes in balancing the checkbook, sometimes paying creditors two and three times for the same bill. Mrs. I reported that this was very difficult for Mr. I to accept, and that on a recent doctor's visit when the issue came up, he explained that his wife was taking over the finances temporarily so she could learn how to do them. Mrs. I explained that she now writes checks for all the bills but has Mr. I sign them so he still feels he is in charge.

Generational rules are those that define the nature of the hierarchical structure of the family. For example, one common rule is that parents do not become dependent on their children. This results in the pattern of spouse caring for spouse when help from the adult children is obviously needed.

Mr. J was becoming increasingly difficult to manage, showing signs of paranoia and hallucinations and at times becoming threatening and violent with his wife, whom he no longer recognized. Although Mrs. J and her two sons agreed that she needed help, they seemed unable to organize any plan for this. One son, who lived next door, had volunteered vaguely that he would come over and sit with Dad sometimes when Mom needed a break, but in the last month he had not been asked and had not volunteered to do so. The older son stated that the greatest loss for him was that he could no longer turn to his Dad for the advice and guidance he had provided in the past. It appeared that no one in the family could bring him or herself to challenge the authority Mr. J had maintained over the course of the family's life.

And, finally, communication rules involve the shared understanding of family members about who talks to whom, what is permissible to be talked about, and the manner in which people talk with each other. Communication rules also include prescriptions about how the family talks or acts in public or with a stranger. For example, families have different rules about who may talk to the patient about the disease and what aspects of the disease may be discussed. In some families only the primary caregiver talks directly to the patient about the disease, serving as a conduit for other family members. In some families talk about the memory loss is allowed, but it is not permitted to talk about other aspects of the disease, for example personality changes or the inevitable ending of death. It is our belief that the more restrictive rules about communication are, the more difficulty the family has in coping with the stress of ambiguous loss.

It is important to point out that these three types of rules are both long-term rules as well as limiting rules. They are long-term because they develop gradually over time as the family develops, and limiting because they are related primarily to what persons do *not* do in the family.

Family Rituals

The most critical time to assess family boundaries (i.e., who is in and who is out of the family) is during family celebrations and rituals such as weddings, holidays, or birthday dinners. Family celebrations and rituals are times that family boundaries are symbolically demonstrated by who is included and who is excluded. In families where there is Alzheimer's disease, this demonstration of "who is in and who is out" is often painfully evident at ritualistic family gatherings.

> For the K family Christmas had always been a time when their large family gathered at the home of the parents. This year for the first time the adult children did not spend Christmas together, opting instead to spend it with their own families, and Mr. and Mrs. K went for the day to their eldest daughter's home. The family explained that the change resulted from their experience the Christmas before, which seemed too stressful and confusing for their father who has Alzheimer's disease. Normally he had held the central role in the gathering, deciding when presents were to be handed out and personally selecting each present from under the tree. Last year, however, he had been extremely irritable, had difficulty remembering why the family was gathered together, and spent the time when presents were distributed sitting in another room. The family had difficulty pinpointing how the decision to spend Christmas separately was made for this year, explaining that it simply seemed to be agreed on by everyone.
>
> Prior to her and her husband's wedding anniversary, Mrs. L contacted each member of the family to say she did not want to celebrate the anniversary this year. She explained that her husband would not remember the date and would feel confused and stressed if a fuss were made. But when the day arrived, her husband was confused about why the anniversary was not celebrated. He said, "I'm still here, you know." Although it was not discussed further at the time, each of the children separately identified the anniversary date as one of the highest stress points of the past year.

We propose that in families whose rules tend to be rigid and who emphasize togetherness at times of ritual or celebration, the likelihood of the caregiver and family prematurely closing out the ill member will be higher. We predict, therefore, that if family closeness is the rule, tolerance for ambiguous loss will be less. In such cases we propose that families and caregivers will work hard, sometimes at the subconscious level, to make their family "right again" by closing out the patient and clarifying their ambiguous loss. This is family boundary maintenance, but at the expense of the patient's premature expulsion from the system.

Clinicians and researchers alike must ask about these important ritualistic times in family life because they produce rich information about the family's perception of the patient and their own ways of coping. Families are systems that need to maintain their boundaries in order to continue functioning; at times of ritual and celebration, we can assess the health of those family boundaries where there is ambiguous loss.

Developmental Tasks

As family systems evolve through their life cycle, predictable transitions occur in terms of membership (entries and exits) and status. Previous work has established that these times of normal developmental transition provide a source of boundary ambiguity for the family (see Boss, 1980). Alzheimer's disease strikes a population which ranges in age from mid40s to the 80s and 90s. It can have an impact, therefore, on a wide range of developmental tasks in the family.

In cases where the illness strikes a young family, for example, the couple may be in the process of preparing to launch the last child and move into the empty nest stage of life. This is often a stage couples look forward to, when they can reestablish the close marital bond separately from the pressures of parenting. When dementia strikes during this "in-between" phase *before* the children are actually all launched, the anticipated transition is hindered, if not stopped, for the child as well as the couple.

> Mr. M and his wife had worked hard all their lives raising four children. Mr. M was self-employed and looked forward to the day when his youngest daughter would be out of the home. He planned an early retirement and thought he and his wife would travel. He was diagnosed as having Alzheimer's disease at the age of 55, when the youngest daughter was in her junior year in high school. Mr. M deteriorated rapidly and within the year had to be placed in a nursing home. The two older boys took over the family business, one of them quitting a job he had worked at for 8 years in order to do so. Mrs. M reports that the family has gotten much closer through the ordeal but notes that she sometimes gets sad when she thinks about the plans she and her husband had for spending time together before either of them was too old to enjoy it. She reports that the children seem to be coping but worries most about Julie, the youngest. At a recent support group

meeting that she and Julie attended, Julie spoke of feeling she had lost out on her senior year of high school because she needed to be with her mother and sick father. Julie had planned to go to a small private college out of state but has dropped those plans indefinitely to stay home. Mrs. M says she worries that Julie is drifting but doesn't know what to do. She acknowledges that she does not want any of her children to be away from her right now.

Other developmental tasks of the family, while less obvious than the launching of the last child, nevertheless represent important milestones for different family members. As the family remains caught in the limbo created by ambiguous loss, there are lost moments that cannot be regained.

Mr. N was diagnosed as having dementia 3 years ago, and his wife has recently been showing signs of memory loss and confusion. While a definitive diagnosis has not yet been made on Mrs. N, their middle-aged daughter Ann has resigned herself to having both parents becoming demented. She states that she does not mind the time and energy required to care for her parents but truly resents losing the ability to relate to them. She says she has looked forward to the day when her own children were all grown so that she and her mom could once again reconnect and spend time together. Now she feels that chance to reconnect with her mother is lost forever.

One particularly interesting pattern which appears to be emerging from our initial studies involves the apparent retreat of the caregiver from the role in a current life cycle stage to one from a previous stage which was more successfully managed. Caught in the grips of ambiguous loss due in part to an inability to define a new role for the demented family member, the caregiver falls back on the earlier role of parenting when the roles of spouse and peer no longer make sense.

Mrs. O was interviewed 9 months after her husband had died after being hit by a car while wandering away from home. This tragedy marked the end of what she described as 4 years of terrible pain. She reported first suspecting something was happening to her husband when he changed from a highly proper and somewhat reticent man to someone who was loud, brash, and given to uncontrollable rages. He received a diagnosis of Alzheimer's disease and was forced to accept early retirement. Very quickly he required full-time attention and care. He lost his ability to control his bladder and bowels, which forced

Mrs. O to keep him in diapers. While he lost his ability to perform sexually, Mrs. O reports that he became obsessed with sexuality and was constantly making sexual remarks or gestures to any woman who was around. Mrs. O stopped having friends over, and when her husband began wetting the bed at night, moved him into a separate bed. Mrs. O stated that she began to think of Mr. O more as "my big two-year-old baby" than her husband. She stopped wearing her wedding ring, and reported no longer really feeling married. She focused her energies on "mothering" Mr. O. When he was killed, she once again began wearing her wedding ring, and reported feeling that she could finally "really grieve for him."

Family systems consist of related persons each going through their own developmental transitions across the life cycle. The interrelationships of these transitions and how they can be disrupted by the ambiguity inherent in Alzheimer's disease will help determine the particular pattern of responses shown by the family. The resolution of the boundary ambiguity will be affected by both current developmental transitions of family members and previous transitions which were handled successfully. Both clinicians and researchers need to study these issues to fully understand family responses to Alzheimer's disease.

THEORY AND KNOWLEDGE TO TEST

On the basis of theory and knowledge thus far, we make the following propositions so that clinicians and researchers alike can test what works best to ease the stress for families of Alzheimer patients:

1. Those caregivers socialized to be instrumental, mastery-oriented, in control, and active in their problem-solving behaviors may need information for self-help more than peer support groups. Caregivers in this group may more likely be men and have higher incomes.
2. Those caregivers socialized to be more fatalistic in their beliefs, more expressive, more passive, and more accepting of things as they are may need support groups and may lean more on others to give them directions about how to problem solve. They will, in short, need more than information to ease their stress. Caregivers in this group may more likely be women and low-income people.
3. Those families whose rules about gender roles, generational roles, and communication are more flexible will be better able to mobilize their resources for effective coping.

4. Those families who have adapted their rituals and celebrations to meet the changing times and circumstances will show less stress than those families who maintained rigid rules about how celebrations are handled.

5. Alzheimer families experiencing family life cycle transitions will exhibit significantly more stress and will have greater difficulty coping than families at other points of the life cycle. The movement of the family to resolve boundary ambiguity through denial, premature closing out, or role redefinition will in part be determined by the history of that family in resolving key developmental issues and earlier transitions involving entries and exits of family members.

What becomes clear to us, however, as both researchers and clinicians, is that we must first do a microstudy of each family and caregiver before we even know what the critical variables are to test in larger sample studies. Clinicians have traditionally done a better job of this than have researchers. We can learn from each other. We need to ask each caregiver how he or she eases the stress and what helps the most. We need to explore each family's unique style of maintaining its boundary in spite of the ambiguous loss. We cannot begin to do this until we have sorted out the source and pattern of stressors in relation to the progression of the disease. Of specific importance is the pattern of timing for disease-related events. Based on one caregiver's description of how he saw the events of Alzheimer's disease as they occurred with his wife, we present Figure 4.1. Exploring the unique characteristics of such patterns for each family will better allow us to understand the particular response of each caregiving system. In the end we may find a similar pattern of perception exists in many caregivers' minds, but we begin inductively in order to bring to the surface new information that can then be tested. The ideas proposed in this paper are to stimulate new variables and new approaches which can be tested deductively.

SUMMARY

Families with ambiguous loss are more troubled than families with a clearcut loss. Alzheimer's disease is one such ambiguous loss. Alzheimer's is incurable, irreversible, and terminal. Nevertheless, there are steps that can be taken to minimize the stress associated with the disease. Research has given us indications that family variables may be as crucial or more crucial than variables associated with the degree of burden in understanding why some caregiving systems cope while others suffer. We propose that it is the ambiguous nature of the loss as it influences the family's sense of self-definition that is the strongest predictor of stress. This variable we call boundary ambiguity.

Accordingly, intervention should include measures designed to alleviate the boundary ambiguity of the family system. From this it follows that interventions should be made at the level of the entire family—children and siblings as well as spouse. Interventions ought to be tailored to the unique nature of each caregiver and family system.

Although we focused here on families where a member has Alzheimer's disease and is therefore psychologically absent while still physically present, the same theoretical premise is useful for understanding and helping any caregiver or family where it is not clear whether a member is in or out of the system. Not all illnesses exhibit this phenomenon, but when they do, the family is more likely to be in trouble. Boundary ambiguity is presented as a critical variable which encompasses a range of challenges presented to families struggling with dementia. Helping families deal with the ambiguous nature of their loss may be even more critical in reducing stress than focusing on the illness itself.

5

Psychotherapy with Families Caring for a Mentally Impaired Elderly Member

MARILYN J. BONJEAN

Perhaps the most feared illness of late life is dementia—losing one's cognitive and physical abilities as well as being lost intellectually and functionally to family members. The National Institute of Neurological and Communication Disorders and Stroke estimates that dementia, a global and progressive impairment of intellect, affects 15% of the United States population over 65. It is the fourth leading cause of death in the elderly, claiming 120,000 lives each year. Estimates place the incidence at about 3 million, indicating the involvement of approximately 12 million family members (Mace & Rabins, 1981). The prevalence of dementia rises with age to about 20% among those 80 and over (Gurland et al., 1980), which is also the most rapidly growing segment of our society. Over 5 million people or 1% of the population are now over 85, and by the year 2000 this number will increase to 5.4 million (Soldo, 1980). It is these older adults and their families who will turn to mental health professionals to provide services when a dementing illness is diagnosed.

The objectives of this chapter are to provide a profile of the challenges facing family caregivers of dementia patients and to outline a model for psychotherapy with these families. It is often assumed that little can be done for victims and families because dementia is a progressive condition, and existing brain damage cannot be reversed. However, the family as a whole may grow stronger from the experience of successful care provision, and many of the problems involved in caring for a demented person can be managed through consultation and support. The model provided in this chapter is offered to assist psychotherapists in increasing the family's ability to manage problems and choose practical alternatives which serve the best interest of all its members.

UNDERSTANDING DEMENTIA

The first task of the psychotherapist is a basic understanding of dementia. Since the prevailing societal myth is that mental confusion is a normal part of late life, it may be diagnosed in patients with no real dementia at all or in those with some other treatable condition.

There are two major subtypes of dementia. The most common is Alzheimer's disease, Senile Dementia of the Alzheimer's Type (SDAT), which accounts for 60% of the dementia cases of those over 65. It is characterized by abnormal brain structures of unknown causes: senile plaques, neurofibrillary tangles, and granuovascular structures (Gurland et al., 1980). It follows a progressive course of gradual decline and is terminal.

The other major dementing illness is multiinfarct dementia, which accounts for approximately 20% of cases. Multiinfarct dementia occurs after a series of strokes or infarcts due to occlusions of arteries in the brain. A stroke may be so small that it is not obvious when it occurs or large enough to cause paralysis. The location and size of affected arteries will determine the side effects of the stroke. Dementia does not always follow a stroke, and its causes are not known. Multiinfarct dementia follows a step-by-step progression and is not necessarily fatal.

Dementia is a very difficult disease to understand, and its diagnosis is often made after excluding all other possibilities. The recommended diagnostic procedures include a statement of current symptoms, history, mental status examination, face-hand test, and neuropsychological tests. A laboratory examination includes complete blood count, serology, liver function tests, organ-specific serum enzyme studies, and measurement of E.S.R., thyroxine, triiodothyronine, vitamin B_{12}, folic acid, and drug levels (Dahl, 1983). For further information Zarit et al. (1985) provide an explanation of psychological testing, and the dementia diagnosis and medical evaluation are thoroughly discussed by Katzman (1986).

THE CAREGIVING FAMILY

After reaching a basic understanding of dementia and its diagnosis, the therapist will need an understanding of the experience of families caring for a demented member. The four-generation family is becoming more normative, and it is to this family that older adults often turn for assistance. Between 1900 and 1976 the number of people under age 15 who experienced the death of a parent dropped from 25% to 5%, while the number of middle-aged couples with two or more living parents increased from 10% to 47%. Ten percent of all people 80 years or older have an adult child over the age of 65 (Uhlenberg, 1980).

It is difficult to estimate the number of persons engaged in caring for an older adult family member, although a rough estimate is provided by various research studies. For every person residing in a nursing home, two or more equally impaired elderly live with and are cared for by their families (Comptroller General of the United States, 1977).

Myllyluoma and Soldo (1983) report that over a million households contain an older person in need of assistance with activities of daily living or mobility—a skilled care level of assistance. Brody (1985) estimates that when those providing care but not residing with the relative are considered, 5 million people are involved in parent caring at any given time. Stone et al. (1986) report that in 1982 approximately 2.2 million caregivers aged 14 or older were providing assistance to 1.2 million noninstitutionalized elderly disabled persons. They also state that these figures underestimate the population of informal caregivers to impaired elderly.

As families move through their life cycle, each generation is concurrently attempting to accomplish its own developmental tasks. For the elderly generation, adjusting to the aging process is a crucial task for the evolution of the entire family life cycle. The older adult generation is engaged in maintaining individual, couple, parental, and other functioning in the face of physiological decline; exploring new familial and social roles; supporting a more central role for the middle generation; learning to convey wisdom and experience; grieving the loss of a spouse, other family members, and physical and/or mental functions; and preparing for death. Reviewing the past and integrating the successes and failures of a lifetime into a meaningful whole which gives hope and direction to the remainder of life is a primary challenge for this generation. The midlife generation, in contrast, is engaged in launching children, renegotiating marriage, incorporating in-laws and grandchildren, and accepting appropriate responsibility for older generations as well as the disabilities and death of parents. Young adults are beginning to shift some concern toward the older generation and stretch the family boundaries to accommodate their experiments with intimacy and distance (Carter & McGoldrick, 1980). Today accomplishing these tasks takes place within an emotional context of three or four generations. If they are accomplished, it will be a gift to future generations, serving as a model for behavior and engaging family members in their own tasks to become responsible yet individuated persons.

As the family progresses through its life cycle, there will be stress from normal transitions and changes. However, families with older adult members are increasingly being called upon to manage the disruption of chronic physical and/or mental impairment. Accomplishing these generational tasks is much more complex when one generation requires extraordinary care as in the case of elderly dementia victims. Family life is radically altered by this commitment, as a balance of energy and resources must be maintained while providing care for the demented member.

Profile of the Caregiver

The type of care provided by families is changing. Because medical science has increased longevity, families provide more difficult care over a much longer time period than in the past, including a majority of the medically related and personal care, household tasks, transportation, and shopping (Doty, 1986).

Although the whole family is affected by a member's chronic mental impairment, there is usually one primary caregiver who may receive some help from other family members. A primary caregiver is at least twice as likely to be a woman as a man, and a male care recipient is most likely to be cared for by his wife and a female care recipient by a daughter or daughter-in-law. This reflects both the greater longevity of women and their traditional role of personal care provision and nurturance. Women often have a career of lifelong care provision to the family, first for children, then for parents, husbands, and other relatives. These women are likely to be 65 years of age or older if caring for a spouse or mid to late 50s if caring for parents.

While the nurturant aspects of women's societal roles and self-expectations have remained essentially the same, increasing numbers of women have entered the labor force. From 1940 to 1979 the proportion of working married women between the ages of 45 and 54 increased fivefold. At present 42% of women aged 55 to 64 are in the work force (United States Bureau of Labor Statistics, 1984), and these daughters as well as elderly spouses are the traditional providers of elder care. Predictably employment and caregiving duties can create tremendous stress and decreased productivity at work as well as at home. In a study profiling caregivers for 6,400 impaired older adults, Stone et al. (1986) noted that approximately 9% reported they left the labor force to care for a disabled relative, one-fifth cut back on time, 29.4% rearranged their schedules, and 18.6% took time off from work without pay. Wives were more likely than husbands to rearrange their schedules, and daughters were more likely than sons to experience all three types of work conflict.

Spouse caregivers had the same probability of terminating employment to provide care, while daughters (12%) were more than twice as likely as sons (5%) to do so.

Although women provide the majority of caregiving, elderly husbands also represent a target group for intervention. In the Stone et al. (1986) study husbands constituted 13% of the caregivers. They were the oldest subgroup of caregivers and reported the most extra hours in caregiving activities. More than one-half provided care with no informal support or paid assistance. Since more women than men are diagnosed with Alzheimer's disease and more midlife women are entering the labor force, it is likely that more husbands may assume the caregiver role.

Caregiving changes the whole lifestyle of the responsible person. Leisure time, privacy, social contacts, physical well-being, and emotional stability are all affected (Tusink & Mahler, 1984; George & Gwyther, 1986; Zarit et al., 1986). Memory disturbance is the most problematic behavior for caregivers of elderly persons (Zarit et al., 1986). Grad and Sainsburg (1963) compared families caring for a cognitively imparied member with a control group not doing so. They found that study families had more neurotic symptoms, less social activity, more disrupted households, more disrupted work routines, and lower income. Many caregivers find themselves isolated from social contacts which would allow reality testing of their feelings, reactions, and decisions as well as supportive reassurance (George & Gwyther, 1986). Clearly those caring for a dementia victim are themselves at risk of mental and physical health problems, and, indeed, mental health concerns are those most commonly reported by family caregivers (Brody, 1981; George & Gwyther, 1986). The sugested treatment plan for these problems has been a combination of education, problem solving, and support.

TREATING THE CAREGIVING FAMILY

Medical Treatment

Medical science has yet to discover a successful treatment for dementia. Various approaches have been tried such as tranquilizing and stimulating medication, vasodilators, vitamins, and hyperbaric oxygen. Since an acetylcholine deficit has been discovered in SDAT, supplementing this chemical has been attempted but without success (Funkenstein et al., 1981; Thompson et al., 1976; Jarvik and Kumer,

1984a, 1984b). Multiinfarct dementia may be contained through measures to treat the causes of infarcts in the early stages of the illness, and medication and environmental adaptation can sometimes minimize or manage agitation, depression, and paranoia. If other illnesses contribute to impaired functioning, these can often be treated. Since no effective biological treatment of SDAT exists at present, however, efforts must be directed toward the psychological adjustment of the individual and the family.

Individual Treatment of the Dementia Patient and Primary Caregiver

Those with a dementing illness are not usually considered appropriate candidates for individual psychotherapy. While there has been little research regarding the benefits of psychotherapy with patients or of the usefulness of including them in family therapy, several authors have suggested this may be of benefit. Goldfarb (1967) believes that individual therapy with the impaired person in the early stages is useful. Verwoerdt (1981) also underscores the importance of individual psychotherapy relationships with impaired clients in which a positive, realistic, consistent approach is used. He stresses the creation of prosthetic environments and approaches which reduce the client's reliance on the capacities which are impaired. Brody et al. (1971) reported research indicating that individualized treatment plans have the potential to decrease the excess disabilities of mentally impaired older adults when their unique traits, personality, history, and potential strengths are utilized.

Various authors have emphasized the importance of psychotherapy for the primary caregiver. Groves et al. (1984) reports that spouses receiving psychotherapy showed symptomatic relief and that in some cases there was a successful resolution of a focal conflict with a demented relative. Zarit and Zarit (1982) recommend individual psychotherapy for caregivers before joining a support group. They found caregivers requesting help at times of such great stress that they seemed to benefit more from the immediate relief of individual sessions. Toseland et al. (1984) and Ware and Carper (1982) have also suggested benefits of individual therapy.

Intergenerational Family Therapy

The model proposed in this chapter is based on this author's clinical experience utilizing a theory of the family system which assumes that family process is not static and that families are evolving groups influenced by multigenerational dynamics and are interdependent upon their environment. It proposes that primary caregivers are members of a family interactional system spanning several generations which influences the development of problems, resources, and effective solutions. The stress of caring for a dementia victim will affect each family member's relationship to the patient and to each other. Changes in communication patterns, role relationships, and family structure may be necessary to successfully care for the patient. Previous conflicts may be reawakened under the stress of caretaking and need to be addressed so that a useful care plan can be developed.

Since caring for a dementia patient in the community or in the nursing home takes place within a family context, the problems arising from care provision can best be managed by involving the kin network from which the primary caregiver may gain emotional and material support. The first contact with the therapist is usually made by an adult child who is the primary caregiver or is concerned about a parent caring for an impaired spouse. The therapist must discover who is part of this family and therefore needs to be included in at least some of the therapy sessions.

Members of caregiving families who enter therapy generally do so at a time of high tension around the diagnosis or progression of their relative's dementia. The therapist will need to take a very active approach which accepts as normal the diverse feelings of members and their reactions to caregiving. This supportive stance may encourage a less self-critical attitude within the family. The first session requires careful management so that family members can unburden some of the concerns regarding caregiving and yet are guided to be specific about treatment goals.

Creating Rapport

Each family member will have a unique world view and a language which expresses that view. To form a working relationship with the family, the therapist will need to understand how each member thinks about the illness and his or her contribution to caring for the demented person. Each may see it differently: as a punishment for past misdeeds, a cruel joke beyond comprehension, an act of fate or of God, a way to find additional meaning in life, or an experience that when shared may be of help to other families

George and Gwyther (1986) describe the way spouses as primary caregivers think about their roles. Some emphasize role obligations:

"When we married I promised him for better or worse, and I keep my promises." Others use terms of social exchange: "She was always a good wife and would do the same for me if I were ill." Still others demonstrate family solidarity: "I was in love with Bill for 60 years, and I want to do what is necessary for him."

Adult children as primary caregivers often raise more questions about creating a balance between parent care and their own lives, spouse, and children or managing a long-term imbalance in resources. They report intense guilt, grief, and emotional exhaustion from conflicting demands. "I love my mother but I hate her illness. I can be patient when I help her, but I am also deeply angry with her for having Alzheimer's disease and changing. You shouldn't get angry with someone for having a disease, should you? I cry more now. My children and grandchildren won't know her the way I had hoped they would. No matter what I do, she gets worse. My husband and children are getting shortchanged. Not that they've complained, but I feel it. I'm so tired, I'd just like to go to sleep. That's selfish, isn't it?"

Secondary caregivers' experiences are quite different from those of primary caregivers because they assist the primary caregiver and do not usually live with the demented person. As contributors to care, they often question how large a part they should play in care decisions. "I know Mom has a difficult time caring for Dad, but when I try to help it is never good enough. I think she should bring in more outside help, but she says she should be able to rely on her own children." or: "My sister lives closest to Mom and Dad and does a lot for them, and I know she thinks I don't do enough. She wants to tell me what to do but never asks for my opinion." The conflicts for secondary caregivers often involve their relationships with family members other than the dementia patient and reveal the dynamics of the broader kin network under the stress of caregiving.

Daughters-in-law typically carry out the caregiving duties when the responsibility falls on a son. They also question the duration and amount of contribution to impaired parents and voice mixed feelings about the extent to which they should be involved in decision-making. "I do a lot for John's parents, but his family doesn't acknowledge my help or include me in any decisions." Others feel differently. "Bob will have to talk to his mother about home health care. I don't voice any opinion, because he may blame me if it doesn't work out."

Sons-in-law may question the imbalance in emotional and material resources committed to their wives' families. They may resent the interruption in plans for the future and the effect of caregiving on the marital relationship. "Jane is so exhausted from concern about her parents, she seems to ignore our relationship, and we certainly can't travel the way we wanted."

Each family member must have an opportunity to express viewpoints, beliefs, or cultural prescriptions about the care of the impaired person. If the unique views of each member are not considered, an apparently sensible plan may not be acceptable to individual family members and may have little chance of success. If the assessment of the family system is limited to only one member, the therapist will get a more limited understanding of the problem and resources for problem-solving. When the views of several members are included, the therapist can help the family integrate this broader understanding of the situation so that a more workable plan can be developed to manage the caregiving.

Giving Information

Often the dementia patient's loss of memory and judgment have occurred so gradually that family members are quite confused when they enter treatment. The therapist will want to examine whether medical and psychological assessments have been conducted to develop a careful diagnosis. This is very important, because many treatable conditions may include some degree of memory disturbance. Even if a thorough medical assessment has taken place and the physician has explained the diagnosis to the family, misunderstandings about causes and symptoms may still exist. Families are typically under such tremendous stress when a dementia diagnosis is explained to them that issues and questions often arise later. Each family member will have a personal timetable for absorbing information. Rather than a denial of reality which the therapist must overcome, this is a healthy response, used to regulate stress and maintain a functional status. Continuing to give accurate information throughout the course of therapy is important.

Questioning family members about how the illness is understood will give the therapist information about how each sees the world and his or her particular strengths, problems, and misunderstandings.

1. How have you tried to make sense of this illness?
2. What have others told you?
3. How do you explain your relative's condition to others?
4. How do you think about the future?
5. Who has been most helpful to you? Least helpful? How do you account for this?

Exploring the Problem Situation

When family members come for consultation, they are usually experiencing a crisis in adjusting to the dementia diagnosis or managing the behavior of the demented person. Both the disease which renders the patient in need of assistance and the coping mechanisms the patient uses to adapt to those impairments may mean difficult behaviors for caregivers to manage. Depression, hypochondriasis, paranoia, excessive dependency, or the unreasonable refusal of aid are common problems. Managing wandering, incontinence, constant repetition, self-endangerment, or assaultive behavior is both physically and mentally wearing. Difficult behaviors brought on by the demented person's inability to accurately perceive the environment or perform self-care activities may produce strong emotional responses in caregivers which can be perceived as problems. Love, anger, satisfaction, guilt, embarrassment, admiration, fatigue, tirelessness—caregiving can be an emotionally confusing process.

Relationships among family members can range along a spectrum from very positive to extremely pathological. Care decisions are made in the context of each individual's and family's history, qualitative relationships, and coping capacities. Even the most healthy of families will find care provision a tremendous challenge, and others will experience a reawakening of relationship problems. Caregiving can be undertaken because of a sybiotic relationship, gains from being the burdened one, an unfilled need for parental approval, competitiveness with siblings, a wish to control the patient, or guilt over past behavior. Spouses may have a painful marital history, or children may actively dislike their parents and find no pleasure in their company yet believe they ought to do things for them despite these feelings.

It will be very important for the therapist to define with family members what behaviors will be realistic and responsible for them. For example, a daughter who has had an abusive relationship with her mother and deeply resents her may nonetheless plan to care for the mother in the daughter's home despite the objections of her husband and children. The therapist will want to examine with family members the probable success of such a plan and offer alternatives such as community services in the mother's own home, a group home, or a nursing home. Monitoring such a care plan while not providing the direct care herself might allow the daughter responsible action with a greater probability of success and support from her husband and children.

When family members enter therapy they may feel overwhelmed, panicky, and out of control. The calm, empathic stance of the therapist can enable family members to express the problem together, ventilate strong emotions, and begin to perceive themselves as able to act on their situation. Beyond supporting family members, the therapist's active focus on emotions in the initial interviews may convert the overwhelming force of these emotions into energy for managing caregiving problems and improving family relationships (Schmidt et al., 1986; Gwyther, 1985).

As the therapist proceeds with initial sessions, a clear, behavioral statement of the problem will be elicited as well as a description of any "exceptions" to the problem. An "exception" is what is happening when the problem does not occur (de Shazer, 1985). For example, when Mrs. Adams and her only daughter and son-in-law entered therapy, Mrs. Adams was being urged to place her husband in a nursing home because of his increasing incontinence at night. When asked to describe a typical night she said that John would wet himself two or three times, she would scold him, and then she would have to change him and the linens. Mrs. Adams reported that on nights when she could stay calm, there were few episodes. She also reported that talking things over with her daughter and feeling supported helped her be calm, but she added that her daughter seemed angry with her lately and her son-in-law did not seem to care the way he used to. At this point the therapist has information about an exception which may be the beginning of better management of the problem. Mrs. Adams had handled the incontinence better at previous times when family members were more supportive. The therapist can now explore the factors which would enable the family to use this successful pattern again or would necessitate using a new pattern of behavior.

When the therapist can discover an exception to the problem, this difference can be amplified to promote a more fluid situation than the "stuckness" the family has been experiencing. The therapist is then increasing the speed of movement toward solution which the family has already begun. Reflecting change as already begun is a useful frame of reference for families that often feel frustrated and powerless (de Shazer, 1985).

At times family members will not be able to identify any exceptions. Then the therapist may be able to encourage imagining what exceptions would be like. If a focus on exceptions is not possible with a family, the therapist can trace the cycle of family interaction around the problem. The therapist will then plan an intervention somewhere in the cycle to begin change.

Family members will need help in setting realistic goals. Some aspects of the illness and its progression cannot be changed. However, the perceived stress in the caregiving situation can change. Goals need to be small and behaviorally defined so that both therapist and family will have a sense of progress. It will be important for the therapist to convey realistic hope appropriate to each family's situation.

The following questions are useful for finding exceptions to problems and planning goals:

1. Most families have gone through a crisis of one kind or another. How have you and your family coped with crises in the past?
2. How are you trying to cope with the problem which brought you here?
3. Is this any different from the way you have coped with problems in the past? How is it different/similar?
4. What prevents you from using the coping mechanisms that helped in the past?
5. Are there any times when you are more successful in dealing with the problem than others?
6. What is different about those times when you are handling things better?
7. What would have to happen for you to do more of these behaviors that help you manage the problem?
8. Who will have the most difficulty adjusting to that change? How?
9. How will you know when the problem has improved a little? When it is gone?

Homework Assignments

At the end of the initial session the therapist will have some information about each family member's world view and special language. Exceptions have been identified which can be amplified to continue change, or a cycle of family interaction has been identified which appears to underly the problem and might best be interrupted. A homework assignment is then developed which will make sense to each family member because its language and presentation are carefully tailored to fit. The homework begins with a "compliment" portion which focuses on what the family members are doing right. Then a request is added for each to do or not do, think about, or observe something. For example, when the Allen family entered therapy, the three adult children expressed concern about their mother's lack of respite from caring for their father. Mrs. Allen was unsure about whether more respite was really necessary.

The following is a homework assignment the therapist might suggest: (Compliment) I am very impressed with the way each of you children is able to talk frankly about how you think your father's care should be arranged. Although this may sometimes seem meddlesome, Mrs. Allen, you and your husband certainly did many things right to raise such concerned children. I think they see how physically exhausted you have become and are afraid you will become ill too. (Exception) You and your children have noticed that the care goes better on days when the visiting nurse comes and you can go out for a few hours. I think using her services has been a useful care plan, and now your fatigue and your children are telling you it is time to add more respite to your plan. (Task) You mentioned having discussed use of adult day care, and I think you need more information before you can judge its usefulness. Between now and the next time we meet, I think it would be useful to look over this list of day care centers and decide which family members should go for a tour. We can discuss more about evaluating centers in our next session.

Subsequent Sessions

The therapist focuses in each session on family members' problem-solving abilities and incremental progress toward therapeutic goals, and setbacks are predicted as part of the normal course of progress. Sessions begin with a careful inquiry into the homework assignment. If a positive change has occurred, the therapist will focus on this and further positive steps. If no change is reported, the therapist will explore what will need to happen for change to occur. When family members are stuck in nonproductive patterns, the therapist may suggest doing something different. "Whenever the problem occurs between now and the next time we meet, I would like you to try something different from what you have been doing." Each session will end with a homework assignment to reinforce positive changes or introduce new behaviors. The emphasis in all sessions is on identifying any change or improvement, building upon this, and reinforcing any progressive steps taken. Behaviors may be suggested, but the emphasis is on identifying the family members' own solutions and successes.

Referral to Community Resources

Although many families may organize around a primary caregiver who links them with the formal and informal care system, a well-defined plan of care will include shared responsibility with other family members and use of community resources. A discussion of respite care for the primary caregiver, a break from the constant attention to the patient, may give secondary caregivers an opportunity to make important contributions to the quality of life for patient and caregiver. Contributions can be made by materially and emotionally supporting the caregiver, staying with the patient, or paying for home or community services. Family members often need assistance in understanding the community service network and in accepting the use of formal services. When Stone et al. (1986) questioned over 6,000 caregivers, only 10% were using community resources. In a recent study of 289 caregivers (Chenoweth & Spencer, 1986), none reported being given information about home services when the diagnosis and care plan were discussed with the physician.

The therapist may need to make referrals to a variety of community services, and adult day care can be an especially useful respite resource for caregivers. In a profile of 346 centers, Mace and Rabins (1984) found that many clients who could make the adjustment showed improved behavior and peer friendships. While some patients are not able to utilize day care because of transportation problems, disruptive behavior, or the severity of their illness, these patients might be served by home health care, in-home respite, home-delivered meals, and special transportation services. Nursing homes are also necessary community resources which have a place in many care plans. Deciding ahead of time on the signs that will indicate that home care is no longer possible seems to allow for a little less guilt in making the decision to utilize a nursing home. In addition, referral to mutual support or self-help groups may be a useful complement to family therapy. These groups can relieve social isolation, provide information, assist in problem solving, and offer support from others with similar experiences. The therapist will also want to refer family members for financial and legal consultation. There are a number of alternatives which allow a designated person to handle the patient's affairs, planning the estate so that full use is made of entitlement programs, assets are preserved, and decisions can be made regarding medical care (Gilfix, 1984).

Planning for the Future

As family members progress through the course of therapy, "relapses" or "setbacks" are discussed as part of the normal adaptive process. Family members are asked to identify what might be a setback, how it can be recognized early, and what will be done to overcome it.

Because the condition of the demented person and resources of family members will continue to change over time, the therapist can help family members prepare for the future by including in any present plan the signs that will indicate that once again changes are necessary. This will help family members expect future changes and engage in contingency planning.

Family reorganization must also allow for rest and renewal of the primary caregiver. Utilization of purchased services such as day care or home nursing care may permit the caregiver to be responsible but not overburdened. Further, family members must be prepared by the therapist for more cycles of ambiguity—not understanding new changes in the demented relative, gathering information, and incorporating new situations into family functioning. Finally, family members should finish therapy with an appreciation of their strengths and ability to solve problems. Although they may always feel some guilt about not doing enough, may grieve over continued losses, or have ambivalent reactions, they can behave in a responsible manner.

SUMMARY

In designing psychotherapy for family members of dementia patients, consider these steps:

1. Establish rapport with family members by gaining an understanding of their world view and explanation of the illness and the influence of the family's spiritual, religious, ethnic, and cultural background for each person.
2. Normalize the emotional reactions family members will have to the demented relative. Guide the expression of these emotions in a constructive way which allows this energy to be directed toward problem-solving.
3. Confirm each family unit's unique way of organizing to respond to the needs of the demented person.
4. Obtain a clear, behavioral description of the problem situation and the cycle of family interaction around it.
5. Identify any exceptions to the problem situation which indicate that change has already begun and can be amplified by the therapist.
6. If no exceptions to the problem are noted, identify the cycle of each family member's interaction around the problem and prescribe behavioral changes to modify this cycle.
7. Clarify realistic goals for therapy and signs of progress that goals are being reached.
8. Create a flexible plan of care which will be responsive to the changing needs and resources of patient and family members as the illness progresses. Be ready to make referrals to community agencies and teach advocacy skills.

6

The Impact of Developmental Disabilities and Other Learning Deficits on Families

ROBERT F. SCHILLING, STEVEN PAUL SCHINKE, AND
MAURA A. KIRKHAM

BACKGROUND

Most of the responsibilities of parenthood are directly or indirectly concerned with the child's dependency. For parents, siblings, and other family members who must care for a developmentally or learning disabled child, dependency has particular import. This chapter examines how this dependency affects such family members in various domains and periods of life.

The authors being with the definition, scope, and causes of developmental handicaps and learning disabilities. The characteristics of families with disabled children are noted, followed by a discussion of recent and future trends in the demography of such families. Next, the authors describe the challenges facing parents and other family members who live with a special needs child. Finally, the chapter examines coping and adaptation in families with disabled members.

DEFINITIONS

An historical review of the methods and terminology used to describe and define intellectual and learning impairments reveals the limitations of any single classification system. Diagnostic schemes are based largely on etiological, sociobehavioral, and intelligence criteria. Typologies that depend on etiological indicators overlook the majority of developmentally disabled children whose condition has no known cause. Behavioral classifications require observation of behavior that is difficult to obtain and measure. Measured intelligence is more reliable but may correlate poorly with adaptive behavior (Huberty, Koller, & Ten Brink, 1980).

Seltzer (1983) presents three approaches to the classification of disabilities. The oldest approach relies on categories that define an individual as disabled according to the absence or presence of traits or characteristics such as an IQ score or genetic markers. Alternatively, the functional approach emphasizes behavior over cause or condition. Finally, the social systems approach considers the behavior of the person in the context of social roles. Diagnosticians have increasingly come to rely on behavioral and social indicators in determining whether a person should be considered disabled. Although IQ tests remain important components of most developmental assessments, all classification schema in use today include adaptive behavior criteria.

In the past educators and psychologists were more concerned with determining mental retardation and measured intelligence and gave relatively less attention to the broader implications of a disabling condition. Over the past 20 years the focus has shifted from mental retardation to developmental disability as a more encompassing and less arbitrary construct. Depending on the definition used, developmental disability may or may not denote intellectual impairment. But the trend in legislative definitions has been to include any disabling condition that constitutes a substantial limitation in several areas of life activity (Seltzer, 1983). Definitions that emphasize function would seem to be better than definitions that focus solely on measured intelligence or observable indicators of a given condition. But the imprecision of functional classification systems has unintended and potentially adverse consequences for developmentally disabled persons (Zigler, Balla, & Hodapp, 1984). Whatever its scientific merit, any proposed return to a more rigid definition of developmental disability would be met with strong opposition.

The authors of this chapter have chosen to delineate learning disabilities apart from developmental disabilities for two reasons. First, many persons, especially parents, believe strongly that learning disabilities should not be grouped with developmental disabilities, either in practice or in theory. Second, many learning disabilities are relatively mild, and the definition of a developmental disability becomes unacceptably broad if such persons are included. To be sure, any denotation of a learning or developmental disability will be imperfect, but it seems unwise to cast a definitional net that is too wide (e.g. Summers, 1981).

Developmental Disabilities

The most widely accepted definitions of developmental disabilities stem from federal legislation of the 1960s and 1970s. The American Association on Mental Deficiency defines a developmental disability as:

A disability associated with mental retardation, cerebral palsy, epilepsy, or other neurological condition of an individual that is closely related to mental retardation or requires similar treatment and that originates in early childhood, is likely to continue, and constitutes a substantial handicap to the individual (Grossman, 1983, p. 168)

This definition is more restrictive than some definitions that emphasize functional limitations without mention of specific neurological condition. It is necessarily general, as developmental disabilities include a wide range of diseases, conditions, and deficits. The mention of neurological criteria excludes some, but not all, chronic illnesses that are covered in other chapters. For example, neuromuscular diseases (Gilgoff & Dietrich, 1985) and spina bifida (Myers & Millsap, 1985) are chronic illnesses that also conform to the definition of developmental disabilities used here. The developmental limitation leaves out conditions that occur during adulthood, although the term "early childhood" is open to interpretation. Similarly, "substantial handicap" is vague but presumably excludes minor developmental limitations affecting perhaps one in five children during part of their formative years (Suran & Rizzo, 1979).

Learning Disabilities

If developmental disabilities are imprecisely defined, learning disabilities (LD) are even less well conceptualized. Federal regulations use the term "specific learning disability," defined as:

A disorder in one or more of the basic psychological processes involved in understanding or using language, spoken or written, which may manifest itself in an imperfect ability to listen, think, speak, read, write, spell, or do mathematical calculations. The term includes such conditions as perceptual handicaps, brain injury, minimal brain dysfunction, dyslexia, and developmental aphasia (U.S. Office of Special Education and Rehabilitative Services, 1982, p. 786).

One uncomplicated definition states that "a learning disability describes a condition or a series of specific conditions that interfere with the normal learning process in a child who is of average or above average intelligence" (Lamm, Fisch, & McDonagh, 1982, p. 1). The American Association on Mental Deficiency (Grossman, 1983) and others (Hammill, et al., 1981; Phipps, 1982) give at least limited support to the notion that learning disabilities exclude mental retardation, and this distinction is emphasized by parents and by learning disabled children themselves. Other observers find that learning disabilities are not distinct from mild mental retardation (Leinhardt, Pullay, & Bikel, 1981; Sinclair, 1983). The Canadian Association for Children With Learning Disabilities (McElgunn, 1984) states that LD may occur concurrently with but not as a primary result of mental retardation. A recent analysis of children in special education (Edgar & Hayden, 1984–85) found that mild retardation and learning disabilities were difficult if not impossible to define and that developmental classifications can be shifted for many reasons unrelated to diagnostic advances or changes in measured IQ.

SCOPE

The scope of developmental disabilities varies according to the definitional criteria applied (Polloway & Smith, 1983; Summers, 1981). One review of 10,000 children in special education found that only 1.6% of such students had quantifiable handicaps (Edgar & Hayden, 1984–85). Estimates are further complicated by the lack of any nationwide system for reporting developmentally disabling conditions (Edgar & Hayden, 1985–85; Martini & MacTurk, 1985). A report on the school-age handicapped found that such children are indeed difficult to count over time, in part because of changing definitions of handicapping conditions. One of the major shifts occurred in the number of students receiving services under the multi-handicapped category:

> It is apparent from inspection of trends in individual state counts . . . the changes over time are so abrupt that they may well be due primarily to changes in administrative procedures and in classification practices of state educational agencies, rather than to changes in the number of multihandicapped students in the population (National Center for Education Statistics, 1985, p. 6).

The proportion of public school children receiving special education in this country has been steadily increasing and now stands at 11%, or 4.3 million students. Of these children, nearly 22%, or 923,000, are categorized as mentally retarded, hearing impaired, visually handicapped, multihandicapped, or deaf/blind (National Center for Education Statistics, 1985). More than half of the remaining children in special education are categorized as learning disabled, and the balance are classified as speech impaired, emotionally disturbed, orthopedically handicapped, or health impaired.

Mentally Retarded Children

Simple calculations reveal that mentally retarded children are otherwise classified. In 1976–77 some 959,000 students were receiving special education for mentally retarded children; by 1982–83 this number had dropped 21% to 757,000 students (National Center for Education Statistics, 1985). Census data (U.S. Bureau of the Census, 1984) show that 39,691,000 children were enrolled in public elementary and secondary schools during the 1982–83 academic year. If IQ scores alone are used to determine mental retardation, about 3% of the population would be judged to be mentally retarded. Assuming that large numbers of mentally retarded children are not systematically placed outside the public school system, it then follows that about 1,188,930 of the children in public schools would be classified as mentally retarded. Yet only 757,000 children are categorized as mentally retarded (National Center for Education Statistics, 1985). To be sure, about 61,000 mentally retarded children are living in institutions (Hauber, et al., 1984), but many of these would be enrolled in public schools. Allowing for the fact that some severely mentally retarded children are placed in deaf/blind or multihandicapped classrooms, there remains a large gap between the estimated and the categorized numbers of mentally retarded children.

Learning Disabled Children

Official reports indicate that learning disabled children are growing in number. By 1982–83 the learning disability category had grown to nearly 41% of the 4.3 million handicapped students in U.S. public schools (National Center for Education Statistics, 1985). Certainly the heightened awareness of parents and educators accounts for part of this increase in students identified as learning disabled. But as noted above, the learning disability classification has become the catchall for students who, for a variety of reasons, are not placed in categories that more accurately reflect their disabling conditions. Still, it is safe to conclude that children who are placed in learning disability classes have significant learning problems affecting family adaptation.

Children Over Age 21

Although independence for most youths begins sometime in the late teens or early 20s, these milestones may have little developmental significance for many handicapped persons. Zetlin & Turner (1985) interviewed 25 mentally retarded young adults who were living independently and their parents. Ten were described as independent, nine depended on their parents in virtually every area of their lives, and six were enmeshed in conflict-ridden relationships with their parents. An accurate census of families with a developmentally disabled child would find a larger proportion of such families than expected, because many handicapped children require care or supervision well beyond childhood (Hirst, 1985a; Schalock & Lilley, 1986; Winik, Zetlin, & Kaufman, 1985).

Because learning disabled adults often have difficulty in obtaining and maintaining employment, their parents may also have extended careers as caregivers (Goodman, et al., 1984; Telzrow & Hartlage, 1984). Unfortunately, estimates of families caring for disabled children over the age of 21 are not available. Although the imprecise definitions of learning and developmental disabilities preclude accurate counts of families caring for disabled dependents, crude estimates can be made. If developmentally disabled or learning disabled children are found in about 10% of U.S. families with children, then more than 3 million families are so affected.

FAMILY CHARACTERISTICS AND TRENDS

Handicapped children are disproportionately represented among low-income (Roth, 1982), single-parent (Colletta, 1983; MacKinnon, Brody, & Stoneman. 1982), and ethnic and racial minority families (Grossman, 1983; Ramey et al., 1975; Zigler, 1984). The underlying causes of this association between developmental handicap and sociocultural variables are far from understood, and available evidence is subject to misinterpretation and misuse. Hurley's (1969) unequivocally stated position on poverty and mental retardation is buttressed by less polemical evidence of the adverse developmental effects of poverty (Farran, Haskin, & Gallagher, 1980; Grossman, 1983; Nihira, Mink, & Meyers, 1985). It should be emphasized that children with developmental and learning disabilities are distributed across all levels of society. Moreover, many children in so-called "disadvantaged" families do not have serious learning disorders or developmental handicaps. Many poor children, particularly minority students, continue to be unfairly labeled as handicapped (Edelman, 1980; Edgar & Hayden, 1984–85; Tucker, 1980).

Taken by themselves, gross demographic characteristics are weak predictors of childhood disability. But to ignore the association between developmental disability and socioeconomic indicators is to overlook variables that interact with family adaptation (Bee et al., 1986). It is unlikely that children are referred to special classes unless they are having difficulty learning in the regular classroom setting. Without question, a child may come to be labeled as learning disabled or mentally retarded primarily due to some undetermined combination of early deprivation and institutional racism. Nevertheless, this same child may be functionally indistinguishable from classmates who are disabled due to some congenital or genetic defect. Families with such children may suspect that prejudice and bias are major contributing elements to observed developmental or learning problems, but they experience the same frustrations and stressors that challenge other families with disabled children.

The paragraphs that follow describe the difficulties that families with handicapped children must confront. Many of these challenges are made more difficult by the forces of racism, sexism, and poverty (Eheart & Ciccone, 1982; Johnson, 1983; Schilling, Kirkham, Snow, & Schinke, 1986). So it is of no small consequence that developmentally disabled and learning disabled children are disproportionately represented among ethnic and racial minorities, single-parent families, and low-income populations.

STRESSES AND CHALLENGES

Family members of handicapped children, particularly parents, must endure extraordinary stress and shoulder inordinate responsibilities. In addition to the normal demands that all parents face, parents of developmentally disabled children experience periodic crises, daily hassles, and chronic worries that are unique to their special circumstances. Although families with learning disabled members experience somewhat different stressors, the delayed onset and subtlety of learning disorders are in themselves stressful.

Discovery

The first of these challenges is the realization that the child's development is abnormal. Advances is prenatal diagnosis mean that a few families learn of a handicapping condition months before the child is born, although such procedures are usually provided only to parents who are willing to terminate the pregnancy if abnormalities are found. Some parents may be told of a child's disability soon after the birth. Mothers and fathers of Down's syndrome infants, for example, typically learn of the child's condition within hours of the birth, even though definitive blood tests are not completed until several days later (Bernheimer, Young, & Winton, 1983). For other parents the fact of a developmental disability may be suspected for years but only confirmed after the child enters the school system (Robinson & Robinson, 1976). Most parents of mildly retarded and learning disabled children learn of their child's disability in bits and pieces, painfully observing that something is not right and finally confirming their fears in encounters with developmental and medical specialists (Quine & Pahl, 1986).

Caregiving Implications

Family members may experience different kinds of stress in the months and years following the initial shock and disappointment. As the child passes chronological milestones, fails to make hoped-for gains, or comes in contact with nonhandicapped peers, parents and other family members must repeatedly confront the meaning of the child's disability. The full ramifications of the child's limitations become more apparent as the family contemplates the years of extensive care that lie ahead. For parents of moderately or severely handicapped children, daily care routines may involve enormous effort. Burdens of lifting, feeding, bathing, and toileting may extend for years beyond the stage when most children master these skills. Families often have to put aside plans for vacations and careers, develop restricted schedules, and take on lifestyles that revolve around the handicapped child's needs.

Behavior Problems

Developmentally disabled children are prone to behavioral anomalies that further tax the coping resources of family members.

Blacher (1984) and Wasserman, Allen, and Solomon (1985a) have found that the limited response repertoire of developmentally disabled children may adversely affect the bonding process. Breslau's (1985) comparison of children with four congenital conditions indicated that physical and mental abnormalities were associated with psychiatric disturbance. Studies of mildly handicapped children have consistently shown a relationship between disability and behavioral problems (Epstein & Cullinan, 1984; Polloway, Epstein, & Cullinan, 1985; Wasserman, Allen, & Solomon, 1985b). Thus, family members who must care for handicapped children, more often than their counterparts in families with nondisabled children, have to deal with a range of behavioral and emotional problems (Breslau, Staruch, & Mortimer, 1982; Quine & Pahl, 1985). These problems may interact with other challenges that confront parents and other caregivers. For example, developmentally disabled children may have little patience for learning motor, self-help, or cognitive skills that parents desperately want to teach them (Schilling & Schinke, 1984b; Schinke, Blythe, Schilling, & Barth, 1981).

Obtaining Services

Second only to meeting the child's immediate needs is a strong parental desire to find an exact diagnosis and provide the best possible medical care and developmental programming (Bernheimer, Young, & Winton, 1983). Parents may harbor ill feelings for physicians if the explanation of the diagnosis is not handled with sensitivity or if a diagnosis or cause cannot be identified (Quine & Pahl, 1986). Mothers and fathers typically wonder whether their child is getting the right kind of services. Many parents continue to seek out promising new treatments or educational improvements, and the more desperate may grasp at interventions that have little foundation. In their own research the authors have found that parents often have intense negative feelings toward social service and educational professionals who are seen as withholding needed services. Parents sometimes engage in lengthy procedural battles with teachers or administrators who must parcel out scarce educational resources.

Marital Adjustment

An extensive literature, based primarily on clinical impressions and uncontrolled studies, indicates that parents of disabled children often have unhappy marriages that frequently end in divorce (Love,

1973; Reed & Reed, 1965). The more recent data, however, do not point to higher rates of divorce among families with disabled members (Bristol & Gallagher, 1986; Darling & Darling, 1982). Some families report that caring for a disabled child gives meaning to their lives, and this appraisal of a difficult situation could have a positive effect on marriage. In one study (Krause-Eheart, 1981) some parents reported that a handicapped child was a source of marital strength, while others believed that their handicapped children had adversely affected their marriage. Certainly marital bonding has been found to be a source of strength for the parents of handicapped children (Friedrich, 1979; McCubbin, Nevin, Cauble, Larsen, Comeau, & Patterson, 1982), but positive marital relationships are coping resources in all families.

A reasonable hypothesis is that the stress of rearing a handicapped child will have an adverse effect on marriages. However, increased marital tensions need not result in higher rates of divorce. In some cases parents may weather relationship crises because they recognize the difficulty of rearing a disabled child alone. Unfortunately, the literature on marital adjustment in families with handicapped children offers more conjecture than carefully controlled studies. The effects of a learning disability on marital disruption are unknown, and the effects of specific developmental disabilities on marriages have received inadequate attention.

Recent data do not suggest a relationship between degree of handicap and marital adjustment (Blacher, Nihira, & Meyers, 1987). Marital harmony is a difficult construct to define and measure, and factoring in the effects of a disabled child adds to the methodological challenge. Future studies should focus on how spouses facilitate or impede coping and how the stresses of rearing a disabled child jeopardize marital stability. Without question the impact on the parents' marriage of a child with a handicapping condition will have differential effects depending on many factors such as the nature of the condition, the psychological and social characteristics of each parent, available family system resources, and additional familial and marital stressors.

Siblings

The effect of a developmentally disabled child on the family may extend beyond the additional care required of the parents. Although carefully conducted studies of siblings of handicapped children are scarce, observers have suggested that such brothers and sisters have more difficulties than their peers in families without handicapped members. Siblings may receive less attention because of the care and stimulation given to the developmentally disabled child. Increased child care responsibilities are borne by siblings, especially by sisters. Observers have argued that psychological and behavioral disorders result from this deprivation, stress, and responsibility (Schild, 1971; Trevino, 1979). Some studies have found that the siblings of disabled children are at risk of such damage (Breslau, 1983b; Gath, 1973), while others have found that siblings of chronically ill children do not exhibit psychologic impairment (Breslau, Weitzman, & Messenger, 1981; Drotar, Doershuk, Boat, Stern, Matthews, & Boyers, 1981). A blanket assumption that siblings are adversely affected by the presence of a handicapped child is simplistic and likely incorrect (Glidden, 1986). Future research in this area should be theoretically grounded, rely less on parent reports, and use methods that capture sibling behavior and attitudes within situational and developmental contexts (Brody & Stoneman, 1986; Simeonsson & Bailey, 1986). Evidence that younger siblings are more apt to be affected by the presence of a handicapped child (Simeonsson & Bailey, 1986) points to the salience of life cycle issues in studying the effects of a handicapped child on the family. As with marital relationships, how siblings are affected by the presence of a developmentally disabled child depends upon many intervening variables.

Family Life Cycle

The aging U.S. population has stimulated research on the adult years of the life cycle. Once concerned only with childhood, developmental researchers have begun to turn their attention to the life cycles of adolescents, adults, and families (Cobb, 1982; Olson, McCubbin, Barnes, Larsen, Muxen, & Wilson, 1983; Schultz & Rau, 1985). Researchers have recognized that special needs children and their families are enmeshed in a temporal network composed of the life cycles of the family as a whole, the parents, and the individual members (Bristol & Schopler, 1984; Wikler, 1986). Families experience different stressors over the life cycle, and they appraise their situation differently at various points in time (Blacher, Nihira, & Meyers, 1987). Family life cycles can be visualized as a series of stages or as developmental transitions (Turnbull, Summers, & Brotherson, 1986). For example, parents might be better able to adapt to the challenges of rearing a handicapped child if they have already had other children and have achieved a certain maturity and economic security. Similarly, families may reach a homeostatic balance during the handicapped child's school years, only to lose their sense of control and purpose when confronted with the meaning of disability as the child approaches the age of majority (Wikler, 1986).

Increasingly studies are designed to disaggregate data drawn from developmentally heterogeneous populations. Cross-sectional studies allow for comparisons across age groups, but correlational inferences between life cycle stage and adaptation must be made with caution. For example, cohort effects cannot be separated from age effects in such research designs. Differences attributed to life cycle stage may in fact be due to cohort-specific experiences. Longitudinal studies that measure the same sample at different points in time offer advantages over cross-sectional designs in the study of the life cycle. To be sure, such research is expensive, time consuming, and fraught with many potential problems such as attrition and the influence of unplanned events beyond the investigator's control. But many questions about families with disabled members can only be answered with complex designs and multivariate analytic strategies that reflect the complexity of relationships between family members, age, and intervening events (Vietze & Coates, 1986).

Gender Issues

Many role-related stressors that interact with life span development also have gender implications (Goldberg et al., 1986; Rossi, 1985). In a recent review (Schilling, Schnike, & Kirkham, 1985), the present authors found that mothers and fathers of handicapped children, like their counterparts in families without handicapped children, differentially appraise their situation through a filter composed of their past experiences and social roles. For several reasons role differences tend to be exaggerated in families with disabled children. First, the increased childrearing demands in special needs families discourage role reversal and role sharing, because parenting activities tend to be more specialized and less flexible than in other households. In-home teaching, feeding, toileting, housework, and transportation to school and developmental specialists may depend on schedules, relationships, and commitments that are not easily passed back and forth between caregivers. Second, the mothers of disabled children tend to feel obligated to protect and care for a special child even more than is the case in families in general. One result is that the mothers of handicapped children usually have different career paths than the mothers of nondisabled children.

Career and Economic Implications

A frequent concomitant of rearing a disabled child is reduced career opportunity. Promotions, transfers, entrepreneurial risks, extra hours—all of these career-related options may be put aside because of the energy and attention required by the handicapped child (Schilling, Schinke, & Kirkham, 1985). Mothers, who may feel responsible for the child's condition, typically exercise their strong commitment to providing the best possible care for the child at the expense of their career aspirations (Hirst, 1985b; Ungerson, 1983). Thus, studies of families of handicapped children find that mothers spend large amounts of time on child care and household tasks (Breslau, 1983a) and tend to work in the labor force less than mothers of nonhandicapped children (Baldwin, 1985; Breslau, Salkever, & Staruch, 1982).

Families with reduced career opportunities obviously have lower incomes than other families (Chetwynd, 1985). Added to these financial difficulties are the expenses of caring for a handicapped child (Chetwynd, 1985; Buckle, 1984). A British study (Baldwin, 1985) compared the earnings and expenses of some 400 two-parent, special-needs families with the income and expenditures of about 600 control families. First considering only earned income and disability allotments, the study found that middle- and upper-income families were adversely affected by the presence of a handicapped child. In addition, parents of disabled children tended to lose financial ground over time in that their standard of living was flat, whereas parents of nondisabled children became more prosperous as their children matured. Acknowledging that the methods for determining costs were crude, the author found that the index families had many additional expenses associated with the child's special needs. Families with disabled children are also more likely to live in public housing and in overcrowded accommodations (Cooke & Lawton, 1985).

These findings suggest that families with disabled children, particularly those with severely handicapped children, will fare worse economically than other families. Although the studies above give clues to the economic burdens of American families in the same circumstances, they are no substitute for data based on a U.S. sample. Comprehensive, controlled studies are needed if U.S. policymakers are to understand the financial implications of caring for a disabled child.

Social Integration

One possible result of having fewer discretionary dollars is reduced opportunity to participate in social activities. Financial hardship may in part explain why families with handicapped children are less integrated into the social fabric than other families. The reasons for this separateness are complex, but a rich anecdotal literature provides some insights. Families of mentally retarded and other handicapped children often feel stigmatized by society (Berger & Foster, 1976; Carver & Carver, 1972; Schild, 1971). Insensitive queries, born of ignorance more than of ill will, come from strangers and acquaintances. Many parents believe that neighbors, friends, and relatives withdraw from them because of their special circumstances. Conversely, some families may reject offers of help or friendship because they believe either that such gestures are insincere or that they would not be able to reciprocate. Finally, the practical requirements of handicapped children, such as special transportation and child care needs, adversely affect family members' integration in the community (Chetwynd, 1985).

Secondary Outcomes

The adversity experienced by parents and other caregivers of developmentally disabled children may result in untoward outcomes that are permanent or longlasting and may affect the parents, the children, and society. The parents may become chronically depressed. Their self-esteem, damaged when they learn of the child's condition, may be further harmed by the rejection they feel as the child matures. Or parents may direct their anger at school officials, social workers, neighbors, friends, relatives, and other potential helpers. Such parents may turn away offers of assistance and lose the ability to positively interact with others (Schilling, 1987).

Both handicapped and nonhandicapped children in the family are affected when parents are without hope. Such parents are less than ideal role models and are likely to have reduced energy required for childrearing (Kirkham, Schinke, Schilling, Meltzer, & Norelius, 1986). Removed from sources of information, these parents will have few options in the way of developmental programming, medical care, and recreation. In some instances frustrated parents may resort to maltreating their children (Rose & Hardman, 1981; Schilling & Schinke, 1984a).

Society is deprived of invaluable human resources when parents and other family members are unable to cope with the challenges of rearing a child with special needs or when the burden of care falls disproportionately on individual family members. For example, parents are unlikely to participate in community activities when all of their energies are expended at home or when they feel that society offers little to families of handicapped children. More obvious is the waste of the career talents of those parents (most often mothers) who would prefer to work outside the home if adequate family support and child care were available (Baldwin & Glendinning, 1983; Quarm, 1984).

The preceding observations do not outweigh the reality that families with developmentally disabled children are in most ways not unlike other families. Too much emphasis could be placed on anecdotal reports of parental distress or on comparative studies that report significant differences based on small effect sizes (Rubin & Conway, 1985), when most such parents appear to cope quite successfully (Busch-Rossnagel, 1984; Kazak & Marvin, 1984). Nevertheless, families with handicapped members must face challenges that begin with their initial worry and disappointment and which may extend indefinitely. In a society that values independence, achievement, and family sovereignty, parents of developmentally disabled children are apt to be at a distinct disadvantage. Rearing a child who by definition will be less independent than other children, and who, by societal standards, may achieve relatively little, parents are expected to manage the family with little outside help. The task for social workers and other human service workers is to design interventions that address the needs of families with developmentally disabled members. The following chapter will consider these issues.

7

Helping Families with Developmentally Disabled Members

ROBERT F. SCHILLING

BACKGROUND

The preceding chapter described the challenges and difficulties of families with developmentally handicapped and learning disabled children. Always problem-focused, social workers and other human service workers have increasingly come to rely on theoretically and empirically grounded interventions. Yet practitioners know that social problems demand attention long before they are fully understood. Indeed, the roots of social work can be traced to pioneer helpers who were called to act before science was applied to human services.

Underlying this chapter is an assumption that practitioners will always have to operate on the basis of incomplete knowledge. This necessity for action in the face of many unknowns, however, is not license to intervene solely on hunches or good intentions. To the contrary, the limitations of the behavioral sciences demand that practitioners continually draw upon the best knowledge available. All forms of professional intervention depend on a mixture of empirically derived strategies, clinical judgment, and practice wisdom. Effective practice draws on the latest intervention research while retaining compatible elements of the intervention process that have yet to be empirically validated. Thus, social workers and other helping agents who work with handicapped children and their families should be aware of extant interventions, the emerging needs of special needs families, and promising new applications. This chapter first describes the range of interventions for families with handicapped and learning disabled members. Then the needs and adaptive resources of families are discussed. Addressing these needs, the author then examines promising new family-focused interventions and offers an interventional model based on original pilot work.

EXTANT INTERVENTIONS WITH SPECIAL NEEDS FAMILIES

Diagnostic Teams

Diagnostic teams have been evaluating developmentally disabled children for more than two decades. Such teams came into existence as medical, educational, and developmental specialists recognized the necessity for the interdisciplinary evaluation of handicapped children and their families (Koch & Dobson, 1976; Lynch, 1981). To be sure, social workers and other family-focused professionals had been working closely with physicians for many years. But multidisciplinary diagnostic teams were heralded as important advancements when the Developmental Disabilities Assistance and Bill of Rights Act was passed in 1967. An extension of the Mental Retardation Facilities Construction Act of 1963, this legislation—along with amendments to Title V of the Social Security Act—provided support for community services in mental retardation facilities (United States Department of Education, 1980).

During the years that followed, interdisciplinary clinics were formed in university-affiliated programs for persons with developmental disabilities across the nation. Today children with developmental anomalies and learning disabilities are evaluated by teams of professionals assembled by hospitals, universities, and health departments. The principal objectives of such teams are to accurately diagnose children's handicaps and to recommend optimal intervention for remediating or managing disabling conditions. Implicit in these aims is the goal of helping parents understand and manage the child's disability. Ideally, findings are explained in terms that are meaningful to family members. Parents and extended family members ask questions, learn about resources, and most often come away with a better understanding of the nature and treatment of their child's condition. Families typically feel assured that they have sought the best possible advice and have investigated all avenues of help.

Although beneficial to most parents, the diagnostic evaluation process has many limitations. Evaluation is essentially child focused in that social work is often the only discipline that routinely assesses the family. A relatively small amount of time is allotted to family issues, even though the family may be the most salient contributor to the child's well-being and development. Because assessment of family functioning relies on interviews, the data may not give an accurate picture of the family. Recommendations are sometimes vague, e.g., "family counseling" or "contact local mental health center." Follow-up is often minimal, as local school districts and agencies are expected to carry out suggested interventions.

Counseling

Under this broad rubric are various therapeutic interventions that involve a professional, e.g., social worker, rehabilitation counselor, or psychologist, and one or more family members. In earlier decades counselors assumed that parents and siblings of handicapped children were pathologically affected by the presence of a handicapped child in the family (Tymchuck, 1983). Professionals emphasized parental grief and believed that parents progressed through predictable stages of the grieving process. Even today debate on the validity of the stage model of grieving finds its way into the literature (Allen & Affleck, 1985; Blacher, 1984).

Descriptions of the process of counseling with parents of developmentally disabled children emphasize traditional insight therapies and general counseling principles (Gargiulo, 1985; Stewart, 1978). Problems are described in such terms as denial, guilt, ambivalence, and anger (Collins-Moore, 1984; Menalasceno, 1977). That these feelings merit attention is unarguable, and insight-oriented counselors have undoubtedly helped many parents deal with such challenges. Unfortunately, insight therapies too often rely on a weak empirical base (Baker, 1984; Tymchuck, 1983). Such interventions have also been criticized as expensive and ineffective with low-income populations (Luborsky & Spence, 1978; Parloff, Waskow, & Wolfe, 1978). While family therapy may prove to be a useful form of counseling for families with handicapped members (Berger & Foster, 1986; Tymchuck, 1983), it is rich in theory but still an art with unproven effectiveness.

Group Counseling

Developmental disability specialists have also employed groups as vehicles for helping parents. Although descriptions of groupwork with parents of developmentally disabled children tend to lack specificity, such groups are often formed to deal with assumed dysfunction or pathology. Undoubtedly groups can be potent interventions for parents of handicapped children who often feel isolated and powerless. Relying on group dynamics to effect change, counselors typically encourage self-disclosure and expressions of emotional support. Group leaders facilitate the sharing of feelings and anecdotes so that members learn that other parents also experience fear, pain, disappointment, and hope (Bywater, 1984; Whittaker, 1979). Ideally, group participants also share helpful strategies for coping with difficulties, passing on tips on programs for developmentally disabled children and suggestions for obtaining services.

Groupwork with parents of handicapped children has its limitations. Leaders who stress the importance of letting the group develop its own norms and topics may waste precious time. Groups that fail to move beyond sharing and emotional support may have no lasting effects. Unfocused groups may degenerate into gripe sessions and may lose members. In some instances groups may harm individuals who feel slighted or attacked by other members. Unfortunately, outcome data on the efficacy of such groups for parents of handicapped children are scarce. Indeed, specification of the independent variable, a crucial element of any applied research undertaking, is difficult if each group differs according to the norms and direction established by the members.

Parent Training Groups

The bulk of the parent groups described in the literature on developmental disabilities are designed to increase participants' skills in teaching and managing their handicapped children (Cunningham, 1985; Prieto-Bayard & Baker, 1986). One review found that all studies of group behavioral training with parents of mentally retarded children reported favorable outcomes (Hornby & Singh, 1983). Even though behavioral methods and parent training are more easily measured than other forms of intervention, the reviewers judged the evidence of behavior change in parents and children to be unconvincing. Parent training groups may include social support objectives, but strategies and outcomes that reach beyond the child's behavior or parents' management skills are typically given only brief mention (e.g. Feldman, Manella, & Varni, 1983; Firth, 1982).

Advocacy Groups

In recent years a number of advocacy organizations have been formed (Gartner & Reissman, 1984; Traunstein, 1984). Locally and nationally such groups have achieved considerable success in shaping laws and regulations. Handicapped children need advocates because they require special services that society is often reluctant to provide, so a major purpose of these groups is to teach advocacy skills to parents of developmentally disabled children. The advent of such groups can be attributed to several developments affecting handicapped persons and their families. The civil rights movement and landmark legislation providing access and education for handicapped persons have given parents legal and procedural tools to obtain services for their developmentally disabled children (Friedman, 1979; Hull, 1979). As deinstitutionalization has opened up many more opportunities for handicapped persons, it has also necessitated more action on the part of parents. Parents have learned that access to remedial classes and other special services may depend on the persistence and skill of a determined advocate. Effective advocacy can make the difference between an optimal and inadequate residential, work, or educational placement for the developmentally disabled person.

Advocacy groups differ in approach and content, but some common elements apply across all groups (e.g. Brightman, 1984; Des Jardins, 1980b). First, information is a critical aim of advocacy training. Participants learn about laws and regulations protecting the rights of developmentally disabled persons, which officials to contact, and how to initiate complaints, requests, and hearings. Parents learn how to gather information to document and support a position. Leaders typically cover strategies that parents can use on their own and also discuss ways of coalescing with other parents. Assertiveness is also an essential component of advocacy groups (Des Jardins, 1980a). Participants learn how to overcome feelings of inadequacy and how to differentiate aggressive and assertive responses. Finally, modeling and role playing are often used to help parents become proficient in using advocacy skills.

Proponents of advocacy training view such groups as empowerment vehicles. Underlying the advocacy model of parent assistance is an assumption that developmentally disabled children will benefit when parents are aware of their rights and have the skills to seek the best possible resources for their children. The benefits to parents are implied, but the family's overall well-being is not a primary objective of the advocacy model. The extent to which advocacy groups help parents is unknown, as advocacy has not been subjected to extensive outcome testing. In sum, advocacy groups have important but limited objectives that clearly benefit children through the actions of parents and other family members.

Parent-to-Parent Programs

Among the most noteworthy developments in developmental disabilities over the past two decades has been the spread of support
programs that are started and operated by parents of developmentally disabled children (Davidson & Dosser, 1982; Silverman &
Smith, 1984). Found in every state, parent-to-parent programs are
sponsored by Associations for Retarded Citizens, children's hospitals, school districts, and health departments. The objectives and
emphases of parent-to-parent organizations are varied and may reflect the aims of the sponsoring institution. For example, one school-
sponsored project (Parents Educating Parents, 1985) concentrates on
educational issues, especially parent-teacher relationships. In contrast, hospital-based programs tend to reach parents shortly after
they learn that their child is developmentally delayed. Some programs link an experienced parent of a developmentally disabled child
with an inexperienced parent. Other organizations rely on group
sessions to cement bonds between parents. Still other groups combine individual and group models. Most of these organizations boast
multiple purposes besides emotional support, such as advocacy,
lobbying, public education, and fundraising.

Notwithstanding these differences, most parent-to-parent organizations subscribe to certain core values and aims. Fundamental are
beliefs that parents of developmentally disabled children share a
common bond and that families with handicapped children can help
one another. Emotional support is an essential element of all parent-
to-parent program models. Such support may take the form of listening, praise, and encouragement. Informational support may include
suggestions for child care or pointers on how to obtain services for
developmentally disabled children. Other supports provided by parent-to-parent organizations are instrumental—sharing transportation, equipment, and child care. Finally, the supportive functions
served by social companionship should not be overlooked (Wills,
1983).

The objectives and methods of parent-to-parent organizations are
in many ways similar to the goals and strategies that characterize the
individual, family, and group services described earlier. In contrast
to agencies staffed by professionals, parent-to-parent organizations
operate with a sense of mission and a belief that certain universal
experiences are encountered by all parents of disabled children.
Without question, parent-to-parent groups have made the difference

between despair and hope for many parents of developmentally disabled children. They provide a form of understanding that can only come from a parent in the same circumstances, and they serve as a creative outlet for parents who seek meaning in their lives.

Yet parent-to-parent models of help also have their limitations. Some parents are simply not skilled in working with other persons in need. Although some programs have training sequences for would-be helpers, these brief courses are no substitute for formal training in social work, rehabilitation, or other helping disciplines. As Whittaker (1983) has observed, informal and formal helpers have complementary, not duplicate, roles.

Interventions With Siblings

Based on their own observations, some clinicians have developed intervention programs aimed at siblings of handicapped children. Most of these interventions have followed a traditional counseling format. In individual or group settings, social workers or counselors offer information on specific disabilities, suggestions for handling uncomfortable situations, and encouragement for expressing concerns about the disabled sibling (Chinitz, 1981; Murphy et al., 1976; O'Neill, 1965; Schreiber & Feeley, 1965).

The Sibling Information Network Newsletter is a quarterly publication with stories by siblings, lists of books for siblings, and descriptions of sibling workshops and intervention programs. The newsletter reaches 1,000 parents and professionals and periodically describes an intervention program (e.g., Fairfield, 1983; Feigon, 1981). "Sibshops" are meetings or workshops aimed at siblings of handicapped children (Meyer, Vadasy, & Fewell, 1985a). The goals of the sibshops are to provide such children an opportunity to meet other siblings, gain specific information on disabilities, and learn how others handle situations common to special needs families. Information is provided through the use of games, campouts, and panel discussions. Common concerns of siblings who attended these workshops have been assembled in story form aimed at other siblings of handicapped children (Meyer, Vadasy, & Fewell, 1985b). None of these intervention programs has been empirically evaluated.

Skrtic et al. (1984) call for interventions that: (a) focus on the relationships between the parents and the disabled child and nonhandicapped siblings, (b) evaluate how much responsibility the nonhandicapped sibling should take in the care of the handicapped child,

(c) develop relationships between nonhandicapped sibling and the disabled child, and (d) consider all stages of the life cycle. Powell and Ogle (1985) outline several intervention approaches aimed at siblings with handicapped children including information, group counseling, encouraging social interaction, and using siblings as teachers of the developmentally disabled child. Steps and goals for each area of intervention are outlined, but no evaluation component is offered.

Other Supportive Services

Not covered in the preceding discussion are several kinds of services that provide indirect or temporary assistance to families of developmentally disabled children. Respite care, specialized day care, sheltered workshops, and summer camps bring welcome relief to the tired and discouraged family members. Despite the obvious need for such supportive services, programs tailored for families with handicapped members are scarce (Castellani et al., 1986). Respite care is doled out in notoriously small allotments. Although preschool education for developmentally disabled children is mandated by federal and state laws, comprehensive day care is expensive and hard to find. Similarly, public schools provide for handicapped children during most of the day, but latchkey day care is difficult to arrange. Novel programs for families of handicapped children appear infrequently in the literature, and service offerings for families are sparse.

Summary

This overview suggests the rich variety of programs and services for families with developmentally disabled members. The review also points up the limitations of existing interventions designed for parents and other family members who care for handicapped dependents. Although all of the services reviewed have merit, no single approach is ideally suited to the needs of this population. Some services provide temporary help on an irregular basis; others target only specific needs. Still other programs offer family assistance that is incidental to child-related objectives. Given the observed limitations of extant services, it is useful to consider the needs of parents and other family members who provide care for disabled dependents.

NEEDS OF FAMILIES WITH DISABLED MEMBERS

Before turning to the needs of parents and other family members, the author will comment on the value of assisting the family of handicapped persons. With a few notable exceptions (e.g. Intagliata & Doyle, 1984), the literature implies that children should be the immediate or ultimate beneficiaries of interventions involving families with disabled members. Many articles and books discuss behavior management strategies that parents can use with their handicapped children. Educators develop programs that enlist parents' help in reinforcing classroom teaching. Even respite care services are viewed as escape strategies for parents rather than interventions that will effect lasting changes in families.

The present author advances the notion that parents and other family members of handicapped children have needs that should be considered apart from the child's developmental requirements. Professionals who subscribe to this position value programs for parents and other caregivers, even if such services have no immediate or long-term benefits for developmentally disabled children. By extension, this value stance deems it unnecessary to defend intervention strategies aimed at parents with such purported cost savings as prevention of out-of-home care for handicapped children. Of course, family-focused interventions may result in greater well-being and more independence for developmentally disabled members. Moreover, parents' sense of well-being has much to do with their ability to help the developmentally disabled child. But the efficacy of strategies to assist parents and other caregivers should not rest primarily on such outcomes.

Adaptive Resources of Family Members

The preceding chapter discussed the stressors and challenges faced by parents and other family members of children with learning disabilities and developmental handicaps. What resources do parents, siblings, and other caregivers need to meet these challenges and maintain a sense of well-being? First, they need skill and determination, a reservoir of personal coping ability. Second, they require positive human contact and assistance from others, a network of social support. Finally, they benefit from supports that are built into the larger environment—neighborhoods, communities, and society. Each of these needs is discussed below.

Personal coping

Lazarus and Folkman (1984) have defined coping as "constantly changing cognitive and behavioral efforts to manage specific external and/or internal demands that are appraised as taxing or exceeding the resources of the person" (p. 141). Personal coping refers to "efforts made by an individual acting as his or her own resource, rather than seeking support, assistance, or validation from the social environment" (Schilling, Gilchrist, & Schinke, 1984).

Personal coping strategies are used regularly by parents of children with handicaps. A study by McCubbin and his colleagues (McCubbin, Nevin, Cauble, Larson, Comeau, & Patterson, 1982) indicated that the parents of developmentally disabled children relied upon a wide range of personal coping strategies. Mothers valued routine medical care and carrying out prescribed medical treatments for their cerebral palsied children. Both mothers and fathers indicated that keeping the family stable was an important form of coping. Bristol (1984) found that of 45 coping strategies listed, all were used by at least some mothers. The most helpful coping strategies were believing in the program from which they were seeking help, learning how to help their children improve, and believing in God. Studies of family adaptation to children with cystic fibrosis suggest that endowing the illness with meaning (Venters, 1981), denial (Cowen et al., 1985), and praying, staying busy, crying, and hiding feelings (Hymovich & Baker, 1985) may be effective personal coping devices for parents. Still other studies of parents of developmentally disabled children point to realistic acceptance (Darling, 1979) and recognition of one's strengths (Bregman, 1980) as personal coping strategies. The range of these coping strategies suggests that adaptation varies considerably across families with different backgrounds, assets, and challenges.

Social support

An extensive literature lends credence to the notion that social support is a potent helping resource (e.g. Whittaker, 1983). According to one definition, "Social support describes the comfort, assistance, and/or information one receives through formal or informal contacts with individuals or groups" (Wallston, Alagna, DeVellis, & DeVellis, 1983, p. 36). As used by the present author, social support is distinct from personal coping in that the latter refers to internal helping strategies. However, it is recognized that in other schemes, social support is conceptualized as a particular form of coping in general (e.g. Ilfeld, 1982; McCubbin, Nevin, Cauble, Larsen, Comeau, & Patterson, 1982). Wills (1983) listed six functions of social support: esteem building, status, psychological benefits that derive from simply participating in a relationship informational, social companionship, and motivation. All of these forms of social support are sought and used by most parents of handicapped children.

A brief review of coping among families with handicapped members underscores the saliency of social support for this population. Venters' (1981) study found that cystic fibrosis families functioned better if they had familial and external supports. Another investigation of a similar population (Hymovich & Baker, 1985) asked parents what they had done in the past when they needed assistance regarding their child's development. Nearly all (92%) mentioned asking a physician, and 63% said they had questioned other parents of children with cystic fibrosis. Friends and relatives were approached by 55% of the mothers and 30% of the fathers.

Spousal support, not surprisingly, is frequently cited as the primary source of assistance for parents of developmentally disabled children (Gallagher, Beckman, & Cross, 1983). Friedrich's (1979) study of 98 mothers of handicapped children found that the mother's feeling secure in the marital relationship was a strong predictor of reduced stress. Families of autistic children reported that spouses were important coping resources (Bristol & Schopler, 1984). For women female friends are often the most frequently mentioned source of support (Chesler & Barbarin, 1984; Schilling, Schinke, & Kirkham, 1985). A study of families of children with cerebral palsy (McCubbin, Nevin, Cauble, Larsen, Comeau, & Patterson, 1982) revealed that mothers valued talking with friends about their feelings, whereas fathers turned to their spouses for discussion of feelings and concerns. Families with perceived social support may be less likely to place their developmentally disabled child in institutional care (German & Maisto, 1982). Although comprehensive empirically derived models of social support remain to be developed (Gottlieb, 1983; Levy, 1983), there can be little doubt as to the importance of social support for families with developmentally disabled members.

Environmental supports

Families with developmentally disabled members need more than personal and social resources. To function optimally, these families require a range of institutional and community supports (Whittaker,

1983). Families are better able to manage the burdens and stresses of a handicapped child when governments, communities, and neighborhoods demonstrate a sensitivity to their special circumstances. At the federal level the Supplemental Security Income (SSI) program recognizes the financial dependency of many disabled persons. State programs, often made possible through federal grants, include respite care, funding for special education in local school districts, and support of clinics for developmentally delayed children. Local services, both private and public, range from special camps to accommodative transportation.

At least as important as these tangible environmental resources are the many subtle supports that society may provide for families with disabled members. More easily described than defined, these supports are an expression of positive and caring community attitudes. For example, a family rearing a developmentally disabled child in Berkeley, California, has certain environmental advantages over similar families in other communities. Berkeley residents have grown used to seeing and interacting with disabled persons who have elected to live near the Center for Independent Living. Citizens and public officials in this community are thus likely to be responsive to the psychological, social, and economic needs of families with disabled members. When a community is aware of the special requirements of developmentally disabled persons, families with handicapped members will tend to be included, assisted, and accommodated—in friendships, in the commerce of daily living, and in the goals and operations of agencies, organizations, and governments.

Empirical backing for environmental supports is less available than evidence for personal coping and social support among families with handicapped children (Sherman & Cocozza, 1984). Surveys have established that parents desire more community services and parent groups (Eheart & Ciccone, 1982; Kornblatt & Heinrich, 1985) and that families benefit from outward-directed activities (Power, 1985), special subsidies (Zimmerman, 1984), and respite care (Halpern, 1985; Ptacek et al., 1982). Notwithstanding the promise of environmental interventions (Coulton, 1981; Grinnell, Kyte, & Bostwick, 1981; Jeger & Slotnick, 1982), few studies—theoretical, descriptive, or applied—have examined how families with developmentally disabled members interact with the larger environment. Notable exceptions are ethnographic studies conducted by Mink, Nihira, and Meyers (1983).

Integrating personal, social, and environmental resources

Families with developmentally disabled members require a range of resources to buffer the stresses of life. Although the scheme offered here comprises three domains, the boundaries between personal, social, and environmental spheres are blurred. For instance, social supports that take the form of transportation, information, or respite care might also be categorized as environmental supports. Similarly, neighborly assistance has the same result regardless of whether it is attributed to the kindness of an individual or to responsible behavior shaped by the values of a community.

Personal coping abilities, social supports, and environmental resources are interactive. Crnic, Friedrich, and Greenberg (1983) conceptualized familial adaptation to a mentally retarded child as a "response to stress moderated by the interaction of available coping resources and ecological contexts" (p. 133). The present author (Schilling, Gilchrist, & Schinke, 1984; Schilling & Schinke, 1984) has observed the interplay between social support and personal coping among families with developmentally disabled children. A review of gender-related coping among parents of developmentally disabled children suggests that role differences interact with appraisal of stress and with perceived avenues of coping (Schilling, Schinke, & Kirkham, 1985). For example, more than men, women are likely to realistically perceive that a developmentally disabled child is a potential threat to their careers, because gender roles tend to be traditional in such families. Women may also recognize that by remaining at home, they will be able to draw on social supports that are unavailable to mothers who work full time outside the home (Schilling, 1987).

Services for most human problems may be placed along a continuum. At one end of the continuum are services directed at changing the person to fit the social and economic environment. In the middle range are approaches that attempt to achieve a better fit between the individual and the immediate social environment. At the other extreme are strategies that seek to alter the environment to meet the needs of the individual (Mitchell et al., 1985). The next section describes programs that blend complementary personal, social, and environmental interventions. Income supports for families of handicapped children are omitted not because they are deemed unimportant. To the contrary, adequate income is often a prerequisite for even minimally successful adaptation. Income maintenance and employment, however, are major policy issues that cannot be addressed within the scope of the present discussion of practice with families with developmentally disabled members. (See Chapter 9 in this volume and Chapter 10 in Volume 1, which address policy issues of relevance to families with developmentally and learning disabled members.)

PROMISING MULTICOMPONENT INTERVENTIONS

In the opening pages of this chapter the author suggested that most services for parents would be more accurately called parent-mediated interventions aimed at children. Few programs designed for families with handicapped children address more than one of the three areas of need outlined above. A review of extant programs uncovered only a handful that attempt to systematically address the diverse needs of families with developmentally disabled members. These multiple-component programs, pilot projects, and services are of three kinds: therapeutic, instrumental, and skill-based.

Therapeutic interventions

Aside from parent training, parent-focused services for the most part remain group or individual counseling sessions that deal with grief or family pathology (Berger & Foster, 1986). These forms of intervention were mentioned earlier as single-purpose services. In fairness, it must be noted that some therapists combine insight and other intrapsychic interventions with efforts to expand families' social supports. Family therapy, in particular, affords possibilities for enhancing support systems. Unfortunately, strategies to alter social supports and the wider environment are poorly operationalized (Holland & Hattersley, 1980). Perhaps this lack of specificity is due in part to the low status that has been accorded to environmental interventions until recently (Grinnell, Kyte, & Bostwick, 1981). Psychotheraputic counseling could become more useful if professionals routinely combined person-focused strategies with interventions designed to enhance social supports or to make communities better places for families with developmentally disabled members.

Instrumental services

Other kinds of programs provide multipurpose services that help parents in some material or facilitative manner. One pilot project, the Foster Extended Family Model (Barsch, Moore, & Hamerlynck,

1983), provided resources to help foster families involve extended family and friends in the responsibility for caring for a handicapped child. This novel project recruited the assistance of friends, relatives, and neighbors of foster parents. Each extended family member agreed to perform a special role such as baby-sitting, overnight respite care, or transportation. Although the activities tended to be child-focused, most provided considerable help to the foster parents also. Case management, including contracting for supplemental payments, considered the needs of the entire family. A less comprehensive program in Minnesota (Zimmerman, 1984) provided a subsidy to families with developmentally disabled children. Covered services included camps, respite care, and counseling, all potentially of benefit to family members.

Skill-based models

A third kind of family-focused intervention is designed to effect personal, social, and environmental change through skill building (Schinke, Schilling, Barth, Gilchrist, & Maxwell, 1986). Parent training is not included in the present discussion of skill-based interventions for families, although parent training programs are among the most important developments in services for families with handicapped members. Such skill-building interventions may have secondary benefits for family members, but their primary focus is on the behavior and development of the handicapped child. It is clear, however, that parent training is entirely compatible with interventions designed to enhance familial and parental functioning directly.

The goal of the skill-building models described here is to provide parents and other care providers with a repertoire of skills to enable them to develop their own personal coping strategies, social support networks, and institutional and community supports. Before proceeding further, it is necessary to define these terms.

As defined earlier in these pages, personal coping denotes efforts of an individual acting as his or her own resource in attempting to overcome or adjust to the demands of a given situation.

A social support network is "a set of interconnected relationships among a group of people that provides enduring patterns of nurturance and provides contingent reinforcement for efforts to cope with life on a day-to-day basis" (Garbarino, 1983, p. 5).

Institutional and community supports include a range of specific services and accommodations such as day care, specialized public transportation, and barrier-free architecture. Less obvious but equally important aspects of a supportive "macro-environment" are community awareness of the needs of families with disabled children and positive attitudes toward disabled persons and their families.

Examples of skills-based models

A small but innovative pilot project (Intagliata & Doyle, 1984) provided parents with skills to enhance their social support networks. Drawing on the model developed by Platt, Spivack, and Swift (1973), the investigators taught interpersonal problem-solving skills to a group of five parents. The approach also used standard group counseling methods such as self-disclosure, sharing common experiences, and universalizing problems. Although the outcome data showed an improvement in problem-solving ability, the study did not measure whether improved problem solving led to enhanced social support networks.

Another skills-building approach (Kirkham, Schilling, Norelius, & Schinke, 1986) combined elements of personal coping, problem solving, communication training, and social support development. A planned pilot group of four mothers drew upon the groupwork traditions of mutual understanding and action (Toseland & Rivas, 1984) but incorporated added structure through time-limited, goal-oriented activities. In eight group sessions led by social workers, parents of developmentally disabled children acquired content through didactics and discussion, modeling, guided practice, and homework.

Participants first learned personal coping strategies and practiced them in the group, at home, and in the community. For example, one group member learned to remind herself of specific accomplishments of her child. At home, when she became saddened by the child's limitations, she substituted these positive "self-statements" for the negative thoughts. Problem-solving skills were described, modeled, practiced, and later tried out in real-life situations. Several mothers reported on specific incidents in which they used the SODAS problem-solving process to help them through challenging situations. Steps included *S*topping and identifying the problem, generating *O*ptions, *D*eciding on the best alternative, *A*cting on the decision, and reinforcing (*S*elf-praise) themselves for their actions.

Parents learned communication skills in like fashion, practicing their verbal and nonverbal skills with spouses, neighbors, and school administrators. Next, participants discussed social support and analyzed their own social support networks. Parents developed and carried out plans for enhancing their social support networks, using the newly learned coping, problem-solving, and communication skills. One mother joined an advocacy group, using problem solving to become informed about opportunities and drawing on her newly learned interpersonal skills as she approached the organization.

Three of four participants showed gains from pretest to posttest on measures of quality of life, perception of child behavior and disability, cognition, and life satisfaction. A fourth participant improved on only two of five measures. Although promising, results of any small pilot study should be interpreted cautiously.

PRESENT RESEARCH

A growing literature on coping, social support, and environmental intervention suggests that these areas hold promise for preventing and treating a range of problems. Building on the previously described pilot study with four mothers, the author conducted a larger test with two intervention groups. Not a controlled research design, the present investigation nevertheless represents a step in this direction. The intent was to examine the effectiveness of a skills-building group training model designed to enhance the personal coping, social support networks, and community involvement of parents of developmentally disabled children.

Subjects

Participants, 15 mothers of developmentally disabled children, were referred by school districts, developmental preschools, parent groups, hospitals, and social service agencies. Prospective participants were screened when they called to inquire about the project. All subjects had full-time custody of a 2- to 14-year-old handicapped child; 11 of the children were less than 9 years of age. The mothers indicated that six of the children were mildly handicapped, six were moderately handicapped, and three were severely disabled. All children had previously been assessed by physicians, educators, or psychologists. Primary diagnoses for most of the children were mental retardation, language delay, learning disabilities, or other neurological impairments. All but two of the children were initially diagnosed after their first birthday; six were diagnosed after they turned 3. None of the children was in a mainstreamed classroom, and seven were in completely self-contained educational settings with little contact with nonhandicapped peers.

All but three of the parents were married, 13 were white and 11 were not employed in the labor market. The mothers were between

22 and 43 years old, and all but one had between 12 and 17 years of education. Most participants owned their homes (60%). Reported family incomes ranged from less than $5,000 to more than $50,000 annually (median = $25,000–$30,000). The median score on the revised version of the Duncan Socioeconomic Index was 38.4 (SD = 25.7). Typical occupations in this range of the index are real estate appraisers, statistical clerks, and construction laborers. Thus, subjects were heterogeneous with respect to most demographic variables, especially income and occupational prestige.

Intervention

A social worker and an experienced parent of a developmentally disabled child led two groups of seven to eight mothers for nine, two-hour, weekly sessions. The purpose of the groups was to teach parents a repertoire of skills to enhance their personal coping, expand their social support networks, and increase their community involvement. Refreshments and on-site child care were provided. Methods included discussion, modeling, guided practice, and homework (Barth & Schinke, 1984). The curricula covered, in sequence, personal coping strategies for use at home and in the community, problem solving, communication skills, social support enhancement, and environmental change. Each set of skills was explained, discussed by participants, modeled by leaders, practiced by the mothers with coaching and feedback from leaders and participants, tried out at home by individual participants, and reported on in subsequent sessions. During the later sessions participants combined newly learned skills as they assessed their circumstances, planned strategies, and carried out individual and group tasks to enhance their lives.

Personal coping covered attitudinal, behavioral, or emotional strategies used by individuals to combat stressors. Parents learned to identify thoughts and feelings that increase anxiety and unhappiness, and lead to self-defeating responses to challenges from the environment. One participant, for example, was frequently upset by strangers' queries about her child's disabilities. Instead of continuing to fear social contact in public, this mother began guessing which strangers would speak to her and the kind of questions they would ask. By making a game out of an uncomfortable situation, she gained a sense of control and focused less on her own fears.

Problem-solving skills have been applied with many populations and problems. The SODAS model, detailed in the earlier description of pilot work with four mothers, gave participants an easily recalled series of steps to use in complex situations that call for various solutions to be evaluated, selected, and put into action.

Communication skills included a variety of interpersonal behaviors that enhanced participants' performance and sense of competence in situations requiring both initiatory and responsive communication. Parents learned effective body posture and eye contact and how to defuse criticism, assert themselves, and advocate for their children. Ways of negotiating, initiating requests, and compromising were also discussed, modeled, and practiced.

Participants used these skills to build their social support networks and enhance their environments. Using problem solving, parents learned to identify needs and evaluate possible solutions. Personal coping and communication skills helped parents overcome fears about acting on their plans and gave them interpersonal competence in dealing with network members, school personnel, and social service providers. Group members collaborated on environmental change projects. One group developed a summer resource bulletin for developmentally disabled children in a five-county area. Other participants prepared a community education pamphlet entitled, "Mother Taught Us Not to Stare at a Handicapped Person, but She Didn't Tell Us What to Do." Still other members planned strategies for improving public transportation for disabled persons in the community.

Measures

Dependent measures included six instruments with a total of eight summary or scale scores. These included open-ended assessments of self-talk and communication and four other instruments. The self-talk instrument measured the use of spoken or unspoken self-messages that either reinforce or guide an individual through difficult situations (e.g., "Now I will knock on the door" or "I really did a good job"). These responses can be useful for parents who sometimes feel overwhelmed and confused and who tend to criticize themselves. The communication scale measures such skills as paraphrasing and the use of "I" in interpersonal dialogue (Barth & Schinke, 1984; Schinke, Gilchrist, & Blythe, 1980). Responses such as these help parents clarify others' statements and avoid the often dysfunctional use of "you" in sensitive negotiations.

The Self-Reinforcement Attitudes Questionnaire (Heiby, 1982) is composed of 20 Likert-type items that assess the respondent's tendency to either self-praise or self-criticize. The Eyberg Child Behavior Inventory (Robinson, Eyberg, & Ross, 1980) asks respondents to assess their children's behavior and indicate whether given behaviors are a problem for them as parents. The Beck Depression Inventory (Beck et al., 1961) is a commonly used, 21-item checklist used to measure depressive symptoms. The Quality of Life measure (Olson, McCubbin, Barnes, Larsen, Muxen, & Wilson, 1982) asks respondents to rate their satisfaction with various aspects of family life.

The Feetham Family Functioning Survey (Feetham & Humenick, 1982; Schilling, Kirkham, Snow, & Schinke, 1986) asks respondents to assess their current and desired interactions and responsibilities within the family. A difference score is derived by subtracting the score on the desired scale from the score on the current scale and converting the result to an absolute value. This score is an indication of the degree of correspondence between a parent's ideal and perceived family life.

Results

Table 7.1 shows that the participants made observable, albeit modest, gains from pretest to posttest. Subjects scored higher on scales measuring self-talk, communication, and quality of life and lower on scales measuring negative attitudes about self and depression. Parents also showed decreased difference between their ideal and appraised family functioning. Changes in appraisal of the severity and number of the child's problems were, respectively, slightly worse and the same, following intervention.

The outcomes of this study are promising but also suggest the difficulty of changing attitudes in the face of challenging life circumstances. The mothers demonstrated understanding of self-talk, self-reinforcement, and communication skills and appeared to be more satisfied in several life domains. Attitudinal gains were generally small, and the apparently declining appraisal of the child's behavior is troubling. And, because testing effects were not measured, it is possible that the gains were attributable to practice or social desirability bias. The lack of behavioral indicators further limits any conclusions drawn from the study.

Prevention research may yield effects that are only about half as large as treatment research because participants in prevention programs are functioning well (Combs-Orme, Reis, & Ward, 1985; Giblin, Sprenkle, & Sheehan, 1985). Perhaps it should not be surprising that fundamental beliefs, attitudes, and feelings are not easily altered in the course of a few group sessions. Indeed, reviews of enrichment and treatment research have found that skills are influ-

Table 7.1
Pre- and Posttest Group Scores

Variable	Pretest		Posttest	
	M	SD	M	SD
Self-Talk	1.20	1.70	4.60	.91
*Self-Reinforcement Attitudes	2.23	.49	2.08	.38
Communication	1.80	1.50	3.73	1.40
*Eyberg	3.59	.89	3.74	.91
*Eyberg Problem Total	.41	.18	.40	.23
*Beck Depression Inventory	12.46	11.51	7.8	8.83
Quality of Life	2.86	.54	2.93	.51
*Feetham Difference Score	1.05	.59	.66	.44

*Reverse scored

enced far more easily than complex global characteristics (Giblin, Sprenkle, & Sheehan, 1985; Rubin, 1985). Even if attitudinal and affective changes were marked, it is not at all clear that such changes are associated with behavioral outcomes (Chilman, 1973). Still more elusive are indicators that specific disorders or undesired events in the family have been avoided as a result of the intervention described here. As Lorion (1983) has pronounced, "without evidence to that effect, prevention cannot be claimed!" (p. 265).

CONCLUSION

This overview of interventions with families of handicapped children suggests directions for future research. At the policy level studies are needed to better understand the scope of presently available services and the extent to which such services help special needs families. For better or worse, programs that support families with handicapped members reflect society's ambivalence toward national policies that support families (Kamerman & Kahn, 1983). Although scholars, community professionals, and parent groups have recognized the need for comprehensive, family-based services, all but a few policies and programs still focus on the handicapped child. With infrequent exceptions available services appear to ignore the needs and contributions of siblings, fathers, and extended family members.

Drawing on the advice of parents and other family members, researchers could develop and test model services that focus on families as open systems with their own internal dynamics that are affected by the larger environment. Findings and limitations of the author's study point toward new research possibilities. Random assignment to experimental and control conditions is a necessary and logical next step. Follow-up assessments should measure long-term outcomes, including variables not expected to change except over time and actual use of skills and knowledge. Community involvement and social support use and enhancement should be assessed, ideally using observational or unobtrusive indicators. Initial results, consumer satisfaction reports, and leader observations suggest the need for more sessions, perhaps scheduled as a booster series. Follow-up sessions could evaluate maintenance of earlier gains, help parents integrate earlier material with issues that arose since the earlier training, and provide needed booster practice to facilitate the use of skills in particularly difficult circumstances.

Although this study included a socioeconomically diverse sample, mothers from other than majority culture backgrounds represented only a small portion of the participants. Applied researchers who plan similar studies should consider ways of attracting parents of various racial and ethnic origins. Several men inquired about the present study, suggesting that fathers would be interested in participating in future studies. Couples groups merit consideration too, although the author's experience suggests that such ventures present difficult practical and clinical challenges associated with scheduling, child care, and group dynamics. Subsequent research should also attempt to address the special needs of single parents and parents who have neglected their handicapped children. The model might be adapted for use with parents of behaviorally disordered or other special needs children. Finally, cost-benefit analyses should be conducted if such intervention models are to withstand the scrutiny of policymakers.

The earlier sections of this chapter discussed that families with developmentally and learning disabled children face many kinds of challenges. They draw upon a variety of resources—themselves, their social networks, and community and institutional supports. Because children's handicaps, family coping patterns, and available resources vary considerably, it is likely that a range of practice approaches is needed. No one model or set of strategies will be useful for all families. Experienced practitioners recognize that not all familes with handicapped members need or want external assistance. Researchers and program developers could learn much from parents, siblings, and handicapped children who adapt to difficult life challenges on their own.

8

Implications of Chronic Illness for Family Treatment

WILLIAM J. DOHERTY

Chronic illness presents human service professionals with a special challenge. Accustomed to handling issues that are more narrowly considered mental health or social problems, we often feel out of control in a world where biological, psychological, social, and institutional forces interact in complex ways. Progress on one level is sometimes accompanied by decline on another. Medical professionals sometimes collaborate with, and sometimes vie with, family service professionals. This chapter discusses this unique context in which family professionals deal with families experiencing chronic illness.

The organization of the chapter follows these topics: first, the "therapeutic triangle" as a model to understand family treatment and chronic illness; second, the multiple contexts that family professionals find themselves in when dealing with chronic illness; third, the new systems created when the therapist joins the patient/family and the medical team in caring for the family; and fourth, special features of the therapist/family context in chronic illness. The chapter concludes with recommendations for conducting treatment that is sensitive to these complex contextual issues in working with families around chronic illness.

THE THERAPEUTIC TRIANGLE

The fundamental point of my work with Macaran Baird, a family physician/family therapist, has been that all health care goes on in triangles (Doherty & Baird, 1983, 1987). The idea of social triangles, of course, is fundamental in much family therapy theory, for example, in the work of Bowen (1976) and Haley (1976). In referring to physician/patient encounters, Baird and I have described the "illusion of the dyad"—the assumption that the real working group in health care is confined to the physician/patient relationship. We maintain that the minimum unit of health care is a triangle consisting of the physician, the patient, and the family, and that beyond this basic triangle are more complex multilateral configurations involving other health professionals, members of the family's environment, and institutions.

Extending the therpeutic triangle concept to family professionals and chronic illness, I propose that family professionals often make the same fundamental mistake that physicians make: viewing the professional/family relationship as bilateral instead of at least trilateral. The fundamental unit for treating families with chronic illness, then, is the triad consisting of the family professional, family, and the physician or health care team. Of course, the actual social complexity is much greater (for example, the patient and the family are not identical, and other forces such as insurance companies and governmental agencies are likely to be involved), but the therapeutic triangle outlined in Figure 8.1 seems a useful launching point into contextual thinking about these issues.

Just as physicians often find themselves undercut and ineffective when they ignore the family context, family professionals face the same consequences when they fail to systematically consider the medical treatment context. For successful treatment, the family professional's relationship with the medical team (the base of the triangle in Figure 8.1) in some cases is as important as the relationship with the family.

Although triangles function in virtually every treatment context, they are particularly important for the family professional in the area of chronic illness. By definition, a chronic illness implies an ongoing relationship between a patient and a physician. It might even be called a "chronic relationship." The family professional, then, is joining an already functioning relationship system. Furthermore, it is usually safe to assume that if all were well with this relationship, the family professional would not be called in. Referrals to family professionals are made when treatment problems are already present, or when past clinical experience has taught the medical team that family problems are likely to occur. An example of the former is the adolescent diabetic with repeated bouts of ketoacidosis and subsequent hospitalization. An example of the latter is the new diagnosis of severe disability in a baby. If the medical team and the family were feeling comfortable with treatment and prognosis, the entrance of family professionals into the therapeutic relationship would not be considered. One might wish that routine involvement by family professionals were more commonly requested, but such is not the normal current pattern of medical care for chronic illness.

From this core framework of the therapeutic triangle, the follow-

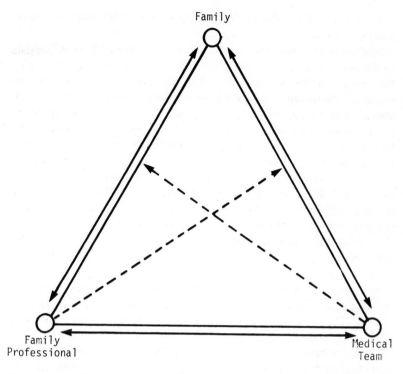

Figure 8.1 The family professional/family/medical triangle in chronic illness.

ing sections discuss the different relationships in the triangle, beginning with the relationship between the patient/family and the physician/medical team. For simplicity of language, I will use "family" to describe the patient and family and "physician" to describe the medical team. In reality, the patient and family may see things quite differently, and the medical team may consist of multiple physicians, nurses, and other professionals. However, the fundamental systems points ascribed to the physician/family relationship in this discussion can be applied, albeit with greater complexity, to these broader, multilateral relationships.

The Physician/Family Relationship

As mentioned previously, the family professional joins an ongoing relationship, the quality of which must be carefully assessed in the earliest phase of involvement. If this relationship is characterized by respect, trust, cooperation, and openness to examine both bio-medical and psychosocial issues, then the family professional is apt to be welcomed as a valued contributor of knowledge and skills that the primary physician does not have by training. In my experience, however, physicians who can manage clinical relationships of such quality and who sensitively involve human service professionals are both special and rare. But as will be discussed later in the chapter, physicians such as these become invaluable guides for family professionals into the Byzantine-appearing world of medical practice.

The "real world," as they say, is generally quite different. Based on my clinical observations and a modicum of literature, the following are common difficulties present in the physician/family relationship accompanying a referral to a family professional. Additional discussion and reference can be found in Doherty and Campbell's book *Families and Health.*

1. *The physician's bond with the family may be too tight.* Mara Selvini and her colleagues in Milan have described the roadblocks and land-mines experienced by their team in trying to build a therapeutic relationship with families who were enmeshed with the referring physician (Selvini-Palazolli et al., 1980). Over the years the physicians had become like a father or mother to the families, so an outside profes-sional was like an unwelcome stepparent. Selvini et al. believe that the family will comply with the physician's desire for a referral but only to please the physician. Having made contact with the therapist and engaged in only minimal effort to confront their family issues, the family feels free to return to the physician with the (good) news that the therapy referral did not work and that they are ready to reestablish the exclusive bond with the physician. The physician, too, may uncon-sciously contribute to and welcome the failed treatment, having satis-fied the professional duty of attempting a referral.

2. *The physician may be highly frustrated with the family.* In a case of his own, beautifully described by family physician Michael Glenn (1987a), the physician made the referral only after months of intense frustra-tion in his efforts to help the patient. The physician felt helpless to contribute what this dependent, multisymptom patient needed. In the macho culture of contemporary American medicine, helpless feelings quickly turn to angry feelings—anger at the perceived outside source of the helpless feelings. Families, readily sensing this frustration and resentment, may experience the referral as a rejection, a "dump." The family, too, feels frustrated and possibly resentful toward the physician for not being more effective. The referral thus becomes an admission

of failure to both sides. Not surprisingly, Dr. Glenn's patient failed to maintain a relationship with the referral therapist.

Such may be the state of the therapeutic system that the family professional joins when he or she blithely accepts a telephone referral from a physician!

3. *The family's belief system and the physician's belief system may coincide in creating a mind/body split and an individual/social split.* The most prominent cultural model in the Western world posits a dichotomy between the biological and the psychosocial dimensions of health and illness and between the individual and the social group (Capra, 1982; Bellah et al., 1985). Disease is either biological in origin and treatment (often called "real" or organic disease), or it is mental or psychological in origin and treatment (often viewed as "psychosomatic" or not "real" disease). Physicians are further socialized into this set of beliefs by rigorous biomedical training that systematically deemphasizes the psychosocial context of health and illness (Engel, 1977). Furthermore, both physical and mental health problems are thought to reside solely in individuals; families and other social groups are merely background considerations. Sharing the same culture with physicians and educated by physicians about health problems, families, too, may hold to these dichotomies. A consequence can be that a referral to a "psychosocial" professional may be perceived by the family as an accusation that the patient's problem is not *real*, that it lies in the "head" (the murky, immaterial world of psyche) instead of in the body where the family *knows* it really is. For instance, when the chronic pain patient is referred to a psychologist, both the patient and other family members may feel that the pain itself is being discounted. When family professionals are not attuned to these health beliefs of the physician and the family, they walk directly into the gulf between the biological and the psychosocial—and may fall into the chasm.

4. *The physician and the family may be ambivalent about the usefulness of psychosocial treatment.* This point flows from the other three. To exemplify the extreme form of this ambivalence, consider the physician who is too tightly involved emotionally with the family, who is feeling overly responsible for "fixing" the patient, and who senses that psychosocial problems are complicating treatment but feels inadequate to address them. Add to the picture the fact that this physician has never seen family treatment, does not know how it works, and doubts its efficacy. This ambivalence likely will lead to postponing the psychosocial referral until after all conceivable avenues of biomedical diagnosis and intervention have been tried. Having exhausted all options within the "hard" biomedical model, the physician turns to the "soft," uncertain world of psychosocial treatment. The family has probably been walking down the same ambivalent road with the physician. I have known patients and families who expressed relief at the

diagnosis of a terminal brain tumor as an alternative to the problem being in the head but not in the brain tissue. There can be an ironic sense of "safety" in even a severe biomedical diagnosis in comparison with the perceived dismissal of the patient's physicial pain and the feared unknowns of psychosocal diagnosis and treatment.

In addition to these general problems in the physician/family relationship at the point of referral, the family professional must also attend to contextual issues related to the specific disease process. Rolland's model (1984, and this volume) is quite helpful in specifying the psychosocial interface with disease. Rolland identifies illness types as progressive, constant, and relapsing. The physician/family relationship is apt to have different characteristics if the chronic illness is progressive (such as AIDS) rather than constant (such as spinal cord injury). In particular, the sense of urgency that the physician and family may experience with a progressive disease is apt to be greater than with a constant disease. Relapsing diseases such as systemic lupus erythematosus and multiple sclerosis may create a series of hopes and disappointments that threaten the long-term stability of the physician/family relationship. At every point of relapse the physician and family must decide whether to maintain the course of treatment or try another approach—or another doctor.

In summary, when engaging a family which has been in treatment for a chronic illness, the family professional is well advised to assess the dynamics of the family's relationship with the health care team. This discussion has focused on the physician, but the family's relationships with other health care professionals such as visiting nurses, clinic nurses who have regular contact with the patient, and physicians' assistants can also have important implications for the referral. For chronic medical problems that involve chronic psychosocial problems, it is not uncommon in my experience for the health professionals to have become incorporated into the problem-maintaining system with the family. The family professional who treats the family without attempting to deal with these relationships is cooking without all the ingredients.

THE FAMILY PROFESSIONAL'S CONTEXT

It is ironic that many human service professionals have spent considerable energy studying their clients' contexts while paying much less attention to their own. Many books, articles, and workshop presentations give advice on how to assess and treat families with certain kinds of problems but without systematic regard for the context in which the family professional works and in which the treatment occurs. Fortunately, this blind spot is receiving increasing attention in the literature. See, for example, books edited by Berger and Jurkovic (1984) and by Wynne, McDaniel, and Weber (1986) on the family therapist's role in different organizational contexts. In this section I will first summarize a model presented inititally in Doherty and Burge (1987) for delineating three contextual levels of family mental health care, each with its own implications for what the professional can do in working with families with chronic illness. I will then discuss some specific issues that I believe family professionals experience when they first begin to work with chronic illness.

Three Contextual Levels of Family Treatment

The basic idea here is that what the family professional does with the family depends not only on the needs and wants of the family and on the professional's training and skill but also on what part of the health care system the treatment occurs in. Sandra Burge and I have developed a model for family treatment that parallels the traditional levels of medical care: primary care, which provides general, office-based medical care for the population; secondary care, which provides community-based specialty and hospital-based care; and tertiary care, which provides highly specialized and technical treatment for serious and rare diseases. In the health care field, primary care generally is provided by family physicians, pediatricians, internists, and nurses who serve as patients' first contact with the health care system; provide inititial assessment and treatment for straightforward medical problems; refer more complex problems; and coordinate the care of patients who have multiple specialists treating them. Secondary level care is given by community-based specialists, often upon referral from a primary care physician. Examples are general surgeons, psychiatrists, and gastroenterologists. Tertiary level medical care generally is offered in medical centers whose primary purpose is training and research. Tertiary care is supervised by subspecialists whose work involves pushing the frontiers of medical knowledge in narrow fields of inquiry. Tertiary care is provided on a daily basis by teams of residents, medical students, and nurses. These tertiary care centers are generally connected with universities and are not typically found outside urban areas (Graham, 1983).

The analogous levels in family treatment are as follows: Primary family care is generally provided by professionals who do not consider themselves specialists in treating family mental health problems, most commonly by primary care physicians, clergy, and school counselors. These professionals are on the "front line"; they are the most accessible professionals to families, since little stigma is involved in seeing them. In addition to these three primary care professions, there is a growing number of mental health and social service professionals—trained in specialized family services—who are working in primary care settings. These family professionals inevitably deal with families in different ways than their colleagues do at the next two levels of family treatment.

The secondary level of family treatment is provided by social workers, psychologists, psychiatrists, family therapists, and other professionals who work in community mental health social service settings. These settings may be private practice arrangements, private clinics, or public agencies. These professionals work with families who define themselves, or have been defined by the referral source, as having serious psychosocial problems. However, at this level many professionals do not limit their practice to certain kinds of cases or to certain treatment modalities such as family therapy. County mental health center professionals, for example, are expected to treat whatever portion of a family comes for treatment, and to serve a broad range of individual and family problems.

The tertiary level of family treatment is provided by specialized family therapists at major training centers, some university-based and some at freestanding institutes. Prominent examples are the Ackerman Institute and Philadelphia Child Guidance Clinic. Here the staff professionals generally specialize in practicing and teaching particular models of family therapy. Clients tend to come from a wider geographical area than is true at the secondary and primary care levels. And, because they exist in universities or private institutes, tertiary care settings are less beholden to particular political constituencies than secondary care, community-financed settings are.

How do these distinctions apply to family professionals who treat families with chronic illness? To start with tertiary medical care settings, family professionals are apt to function as one specialty group called in by the physician in charge on certain cases. Or the family professionals may be regular members of a team in the psychiatric unit or units that treat patients, such as children with serious congenital problems who require ongoing social services. The "mental health team" in tertiary care medical settings is likely to be highly differentiated in role definition, thereby constricting the movement of the family-oriented professional. Typically on medical units psychiatrists handle serious mental health problems that are thought to require medication; psychologists handle testing, psychotherapy, and behavioral health consultations; social workers handle the family and referrals to outside agencies; and psychiatric nurses provide consultations to nurses on the unit. Furthermore, the mental health professional may not have a choice in accepting the referral from the attending physician, who may simply write an order for a "consult." In this tertiary care medical context the family professional must be continually alert to political issues among professionals while simultaneously trying to expand the acknowledgdment of families and the services to them. Dealing with these complex organizational issues requires as much creativity and effort as does working with the families.

Family professionals in secondary level medical settings typically work in community hospitals rather than in specialists' offices or clinics. While dealing with similar hierarchical and organizational constraints as the family professionals in tertiary settings, they have several advantages accruing to a smaller system. With perhaps only a few mental health and social service professionals serving a large population of inpatients and outpatients, providing direct service, and doing consultations for nurses and physicians, there often is room to explore different options in working with families with chronic illness. Furthermore, without the large contingent of transient residents and medical students to deal with, the family professional can develop collaborative relationships with some of the physicians who admit patients to the hospital. Such personal relationships allow for exploration of the context of the physician/family relationship that led to the referral. The setting also allows for follow-up contact with the physician after the family professional has seen the family. These secondary care settings thus allow more flexibility for the family professional. But if the setting is a hospital, the family professional's services to families may be limited to periods of exacerbations of the chronic illness rather than to more stable periods when other family issues may come to the fore.

Historically not many family professionals have worked in primary care medical settings. However, innovations in collaborative primary health care show promise of increasing these numbers

(Glenn et al., 1984; Glenn, 1987a). Family professionals working in family practice or pediatric offices have unique opportunities to work with families dealing with chronic illness. Because they are not hospital based, these professionals can encounter families at a variety of phases of dealing with the illness, from the point of diagnosis, through problems in initiating and keeping to the treatment regimen, to issues that arise when the chronic illness is stable, to problems associated with the decline and death of the patient.

The success of the family professional in gaining access to families depends crucially on the trust of the primary care physician to open up the doctor-patient relationship to the family professional. People with experience in these collaborative relationships attest that referrals to "in house" family professionals are far easier and more successful than referrals to family professionals operating at secondary level mental health centers—that is, to community mental health centers or to private practitioners. Because patients are accustomed to going to their primary care doctor at a general medical center, they do not experience the stigma attached to visiting a mental health or social service facility. Furthermore, their general trust for their doctor and the office health care team is likely to carry over to the mental health professional who has an office on site. Finally, it is sometimes possible for the physician to introduce the patient briefly to the family professional before the actual appointment is set up, thereby alleviating some of the patient's anxiety about the "stranger" to whom the referral has been made.

Along with easier accessibility and acceptance, however, come constraints not experienced as commonly by family professionals at the secondary and tertiary care levels of either medical care or family treatment. First, primary care patients and families are often ambivalent about whether they want or need more than one or two contacts with a family professional. Sometimes, indeed, they seem only to need brief work, but in other cases the family in primary care dips in and out of family treatment, only to wait for a later crisis to decide to get serious about working on its problems. Family professionals with experience in these settings learn to accept this wide range of motivation in families, confident that the family's ongoing relationship with the physician will provide another chance for contact if the need arises. Chronic illness in particular provides a special longitudinal link with a primary care setting. Family professionals working in secondary family treatment settings, on the other hand, frequently lose all contact with families who terminate treatment early. Primary care settings provide a unique perspective on the values of time and patience in providing family services.

The second major constraint concerns reimbursement. The solo family professional in a primary care clinic may not be eligible for third-party reimbursement, particularly for Medicaid and Medicare patients who may have the greatest need for services. Further, physicians in a constricting medical marketplace are often reluctant to subsidize a family professional's salary. These economic factors are a serious deterrent to more rapid development of this exciting prospect of multidisciplinary teams in primary care settings (Glenn, 1987b).

The other major category of settings for family treatment is the secondary level of family mental health care. Here community-based therapists provide treatment for families with chronic illness, sometimes but not always referred by a physician. In this context the family professional may have the advantage of full authority within the confines of the mental health context. Treatment is not as apt to be divided among a number of professionals unless the patient is being treated simultaneously with psychotropic medication. In other words, the family professional is not operating on "doctor's orders." However, it is much more difficult in these settings to assess the physician/family relationship that preceded the family's presentation to the family professional. Furthermore, the mind/body dichotomy is evident in the different buildings or parts of town for physical and mental treatment. The great risk to the family professional is to yield to the illusion that what the doctor is doing and how the family relates to the doctor is not important for family treatment. To be effective with families with chronic illness, the family professional must understand the dynamics of the physician/family relationship and must work to develop a collaborative relationship with the referring physician. The following case illustrates this point.

As a family therapist working in a primary care clinic, I sometimes received referrals from specialists at a nearby tertiary care hospital. With these referrals I generally did not have the opportunity to meet the patient first during a regular office visit to the physician, a practice I tried to do in the primary care clinic. This particular family had a 21-year-old daughter with Chron's disease, a chronic, often virulent bowel disorder, who also had a history of drug abuse. I saw her with her parents and her younger sister. The referral was made because her poor compliance with her diet and treatment regimens had led to repeated hospitalizations. The referring physician, a gastroenterology resident, was particularly concerned now about his patient's emotional stability. I won't give details of the approach I took except to say that I challenged the parents to stop indulging their daughter's dependency by supporting her without question every time she lost a job and even running interference for her with employers. Not surprisingly, this tack was not pleasing to the daughter, who proceeded to throw a temper tantrum in the session and tell her parents that they wouldn't get away with it. She sprayed me with a cola can she was holding, stormed out of the therapy room, but then came back and apologized for her outburst.

The parents for their part seemed encouraged to try to change their own response to their daughter's behavior. The morning after this evening session I called the daughter's physician to alert him to the likelihood that the women would call, complaining that the therapy was making her upset. I explained what happened and the rationale for my approach, assuring him that being upset was an inevitable by-product of her parents refusing to cooperate in her destructive life-style. The physician responded that indeed she had just called him (before 8 A.M.!) to report on how miserable the session made her feel and what a jerk the therapist was. The physician, who had previously thought that therapy should calm his patient down rather than stir her up, agreed with my approach, since he had experienced her manipulation in the past. He thanked me repeatedly for calling him, because now he could have a meaningful response to his patient's complaints. The therapy proceeded without disruption of the therapeutic triangle.

The family eventually began to get healthier as the parents joined together and the daughter started acting in a more adult fashion.

Challenges to the Family Professional's Training

Raised in a culture that splits mind/body and individual/group and trained in disciplines that traditionally have embraced the first di-chotomy if not the second one, family professionals bring several liabilities to work with families with chronic illness. These liabilities offer challenges for professional growth.

1. *Ignorance of physical aspects of illness.* Many psychosocial profes-sionals have limited understanding of the biological processes and natural histories of the illnesses of clients they are treating. This leads to a second problem:

2. *Attributional problems in explaining clients' behavior.* Does the cli-ent's chronic illness make him or her more susceptible to mood swings, as in multiple sclerosis? Is fatigue a natural part of the course of a disease or its treatment, as in certain forms of cancer and cancer treatment? How much of a family member's unwillingness to do

household chores stems from congestive heart failure and how much from interpersonal factors? There frequently are no easy answers to some of these questions, but a family professional who reads medical literature about chronic diseases and consults with physicians and other health professionals about clients with chronic illness can make more knowledgeable judgments about the sources of certain behavior patterns. For example, a multiple sclerosis client of mine occasionally came to a session during a crying spell that appeared unrelated to any particular incident in her life. I supported her own explanation that her disease was primarily responsible for her emotionality at these times. Clients and their families are one of the best sources of education for family professionals about living with chronic illness. It was this multiple sclerosis patient who first helped me see how disease processes can affect emotional expression.

3. *Fear of catastrophic consequences.* Ignorance of disease processes and medical treatments can lead family professionals to be buffaloed by families into believing that honest communication might bring on a deadly relapse. For example, few heart disease patients outside of intensive care units are such walking time bombs that honest confrontation of personal and family problems will precipitate a heart attack. To use another example, a therapist should understand that hyperventilation generally leads to a complication no greater than fainting. If physical illness remains a mystifying area to a family professional, then the fear of catastrophic consequences can prevent meaningful work with families with chronic illness. Parenthetically, knowing CPR is probably a good idea for a family professional, since knowing how to respond to the most grievous emergencies—blocked airway and cardiac arrest—makes the rest seem less frightening.

4. *Lack of mentors with experience in collaborative health care.* Despite early experiments (Ransom, 1981) there have not been many teachers of the issues discussed in this chapter. The field, therefore, is little tilled and quite ready for further research and clinical experimentation. But the absence of mentors means that family professionals are often left to learn by their mistakes and sometimes despair of progress, especially if they lack a trusting relationship with a physician who is also struggling with collaborative care. It is much easier to work with families with chronic illness within the confines of one's expertise than it is to venture into the collaborative, biopsychosocial frontier. Easier—but perhaps less challenging and effective?

SPECIAL ASPECTS OF THERAPIST/FAMILY CONTEXT IN CHRONIC ILLNESS

I want to highlight two additional aspects of a family professional's relationship with the family with chronic illness. Most aspects of the professional's actual work with the family are identical to working with any family. But two issues seem particularly important in chronic illness.

First is the problem of the lack of a clear contract, an issue discussed by Walker (1983). Families often want help with an illness, not with a relationship. They are referred to a family professional for reasons unclear to them but are willing to do whatever it takes to cure the illness or curtail the symptoms. The family professional may have an agenda of improving family relationships and the client's psychosocial functioning, whereas the family wants the client to feel better physically. The absence of a clear contract leads to misunderstanding about the direction of treatment (why are we talking about my marriage and not my headaches?) and to disappointment in the results. An approach to this problem will be discussed in the implications section of this chapter.

Second is the related issue of performance expectations by families toward the family professional. Weaned on the biomedical model where the problem is the physician's to solve, families may approach the family professional with the challenge to "fix" the problem. If the professional takes the "bait" (I'll succeed where others have failed), the family will return when the problem is not better, saying "Joe's headache is not better. What are you going to do now?" This performance expectation may be unwittingly communicated by an overenthusiastic referring physician who raves about previous "successes" of the family professional. Family therapists who accept this performance agenda will find their bag of tricks woefully shallow.

To recap the presentation thus far, the family professional dealing with chronic illness is involved in a complex of interlocking world views, professional turfs, family expectations, limitations of professional background, and the inscrutabilities of the biological, psychological, and social dimensions of disease. My main point has been that consideration of the multiple contexts of treatment is necessary for satisfactory approaches to intervention. The final section of the chapter describes specific, practical implications of the foregoing presentation.

IMPLICATIONS FOR TREATMENT

The following recommendations are based on the analysis in this chapter and on my experience as a family therapist in two primary care settings and two tertiary care medical settings. Naturally, readers will have to evaluate the suitability of these ideas for their own context.

1. *When taking a referral, find out whose agenda it represents—the physician's or the family's.* Too often physicians are trying to treat their own anxiety through a referral to a family professionial. With the "fix it" attitude of the biomedical model, even well-intentioned and compassionate physicians get caught in the trap of becoming more responsible for the problem than the family is (Doherty, 1986). One sign that the agenda is mainly the physician's is when the physician wants to set up the appointment for the family and resists the family professional's request that the family call directly for the appointment. Accepting a referral in this situation becomes covert treatment for the physician's anxiety. When I sense this dynamic, I try to deal overtly with the person who has the anxiety—the physician—by gently suggesting that the family has its own pace of change which the physician cannot control.

2. *Negotiate expectations with the physician and family.* For the therapeutic triangle to function effectively, all parts of it must have a common understanding of their respective roles and responsibilities. Given the likelihood of trouble within the physician/family relationship prior to the referral, the unwary therapist is likely to become caught in a struggle between the physician and family. Clear agreements about the goals of treatment not only facilitate treatment with the family but may help the rest of the therapeutic triangle to become healthier. For example, when a physician refers an obese diabetic woman because marital problems are presumably keeping her from controlling her weight and thereby her blood sugar levels, the therapist must establish clearly whether the goal of treatment is weight loss or relief from marital distress. I suggest that accepting the former agenda generally feeds into an existing power struggle between the physician and the patient and perhaps the family. The latter agenda, if owned by the patient, is the more appropriate focus of family treatment. It is essential to communicate what the family treatment can realistically hope to accomplish.

3. *When the family has a close relationship with the physician, consider a joint session with the physician at the outset of treatment.* This recommendation presents logistical problems but is well worth the effort in situations describe by Selvini-Palazolli et al. (1981) in which the family's close relationship with the referring physician might make them ambivalent about working with an "outsider." A joint session is also helpful when the family trusts the physician but is wary of therapists; the physician can "bless" the therapy by passing on the family in person. Further, having the family and the physician in the

same room can help the family professional assess the dynamics of their relationship directly. Not all physicians will cooperate with the request for a joint session, but many will consider it with families that are particularly troublesome to the physician and with whom much time has already been invested. Even if the physician does not stay for the whole session, the joint time together will usually be worth the effort.

4. *In acute medical situations do not proceed without ready access to and collaboration with a physician.* This recommendation is not only for the protection of the patient and family but also for the nonmedical therapist whose anxiety about florid signs of disease must be contained if treatment is to be helpful. Examples are patients with anorexia nervosa and unstable angina pectoris. The family professional is simply too vulnerable to charges of exacerbating a medical condition by pursuing psychosocial issues or to being manipulated by patients who sense the therapist's uncertainty and uneasiness.

For example, I once was referred a woman who could not swallow anything but water. While dealing with her and her husband about the psychosocial issues that had precipitated her problem (she had been checked out thoroughly by a throat specialist), I worked collaboratively with a family physician who weighed her, monitored her blood chemistry, and was prepared to hospitalize her if medically necessary. We both wanted to avoid hospitalization because this would reinforce her sense of helplessness. One day before hospitalization (and a feeling tube) was to be recommended, she began to eat; her new ability to swallow not surprisingly was associated with her experience of managing the household when her overprotective husband was forced to leave town to clear up a pressing family financial matter. The main point here is that I could not have handled this family without close collaboration with a physician.

5. *Keep in touch with the referring physician, especially when trouble occurs.* I previously touched on this recommendation. Physicians commonly feel left out by therapists to whom they refer patients. It can be hard for therapists to understand the ongoing sense of concern and responsibility primary care physicians feel for many of their patients and families. When they make a recommendation for family treatment, these physicians put themselves on the line with their patients, professionally, medically, and legally. They want to know how the treatment is going. Naturally, the family must give permission for the therapist to share this information with the physician.

6. *Express humility about "curing" medical problems.* Taking a one-down position is frequently very helpful here. Although successful psychosocial treatment not infrequently has payoffs for patients' disease processes and physical symptoms, generally these should not be a direct target of therapy. All the patient has to do to frustrate the

physician and the therapist is to not get better physically—not lower blood sugar or blood pressure, not reduce the intensity of headaches. And even if the patient and family are fully cooperating, the biological processes may not respond to psychosocial interventions. My practice is to identify the biomedical and psychosocial issues which the patient and family believe are hurting the quality of their lives and then to explore their openness to seeing a connection between the two domains. I then may suggest that improvement on the psychosocial front might improve the quality of their lives even if the biomedical problems do not change, and that, who knows, improvement in the psychosocial area may help with the biomedical. Medical progress thereby gets labeled as a possible fringe benefit of treatment rather than the essential goal. I communicate the same expectation to the physician. The point is to avoid psychosocial "hubris" about fixing complex biopsychosocial phenomena. In my opinion, a humble approach, as opposed to a macho one, creates the healthiest therapeutic relationships.

7. *Become better educated about medical conditions and the medical world*. Family professionals in medical settings or treating chronically ill people in mental health settings are involved in a world outside their normal training. It is important to become a sophisticated lay person in the area of common medical problems. Fortunately, there is a large lay literature on the most common chronic conditions. Furthermore, the family professional would be well advised to find an insider in the medical community who can serve as a guide or mentor into this alien world. Once having been guided in by a family physician, I found myself much less judgmental about physicians and more open to help them help their patients and themselves.

Collaboration, however, takes effort and accomodation on both sides. Physicians must give up some of their unilateral power, and psychosocial professionals must give up some of their righteous superiority in the interpersonal dimensions of patient care. I have written more extensively elsewhere about the problems and challenges of collaboration in biopsychosocial health care (Doherty, in press).

CONCLUSION

Working with families with chronic illness is one of the frontiers of family services in the last part of the 20th century. As family medicine and nursing edge toward a more comprehensive understanding of the family issues in health care, and as family professionals move toward more appreciation of the biological and medical aspects of family life, the frontier is open for new exploration. The roads are not well marked, and political and institutional forces offer continual resistance to new discoveries. But there is an emerging paradigm that proposes that we need different kinds of professionals and different kinds of families together in the wagon train if we are to make progress in understanding and improving the lot of people with serious chronic illness.

Public Policies and Families

9

CATHERINE S. CHILMAN

This chapter briefly discusses some of the salient aspects of public policies and families. It is a prelude to the next chapter, which is concerned with present and needed programs and policies to mitigate the health problems of families. It is very similar to a chapter with the same title in Volume 1 but is included here for the benefit of readers who do not have that volume.

DEFINITIONS OF FAMILY WELL-BEING

It can be argued that the chief goal of public policies concerning families is the promotion of family well-being. There are, however, conflicting definitions of this term, a term which often includes the words "strong families." To traditionalists strong families are apt to mean patriarchal ones in which members marry as young adults "until death do us part," have a number of children, refrain from the use of artificial contraceptives and abortion, follow traditional sex roles with husbands as the only (and adequate) wage earners and wives as full-time homemakers and mothers. Such families are often conceptualized as "stable and strong." They present a united front to the outside world, regardless of the divisions and conflicts that may occur within them.

A more modernist view is that strong families are ones that function in such a way as to promote the physical, social, psychological, and economic well-being of each person, both as members of the family and as autonomous individuals. This well-being is viewed in process terms, i.e. all family members, young *and* old, are capable (in fact, needful) of growth and development throughout the life span. The processes of this kind of family system support individual growth through respect for the autonomy of each family member and through the nurturance of each member as an integral part of a caring, interdependent, intimate family group. Following such a definition, family stability is not necessarily seen as desirable if stability means that marriages should be permanent regardless of their quality and parenthood should be perpetually selfless regardless of the problems that offspring may present in their adult years, as well as in their younger ones (Terkelson, 1980).

PUBLIC POLICY PROCESSES

As in the case of *family well-being,* the term *policy* has numerous definitions and interpretations. A full discussion of this topic alone could fill many volumes. For the present purposes, however, the term means public (i.e., government) policy and is conceptualized as a series of processes. Moreover, the primary emphasis is on *federal* public policies as constituting the most general approach. Public policy by itself might be thought of as a guiding principle of government, such as "every child in the United States shall receive a high quality of education," a familiar and enticing principle! However, the principle does not move beyond the enticement (and probably vote-getting) stage unless it is developed into legislative proposals, which then need to be passed by Congress and signed by the President.

The outcome of these processes is affected by highly political forces. Typically, numerous lobbying groups as well as individual citizens become involved. Action by Congress and the President is strongly influenced by these groups and individuals, especially by strong, well-financed, national lobbies.

The process is far from finished, however, even if legislation is approved and signed. Appropriations that provide *adequate funding* must be made by Congress, and this funding is strongly influenced by the nature of political support for and opposition to the legislation. Then, too, relevant federal departments must be provided with administrative personnel, processes that are also affected by political considerations. Following these steps, administrative guidelines must be developed.

The legislation then moves for its further financing and implementation to state levels. In turn, state governments must develop programs which are to be carried out by local units of government. These units, then, need to further develop and administer programs so that they actually reach the individuals and families for whom the legislation was intended. The degree to which this legislation is funded and implemented at state and local levels also depends on political considerations within the various units of government and, ultimately, on the views that individual local staff members may have about the matter. Even beyond that the ways in which these programs are used or not used by individuals and families is strongly affected by *their* particular attitudes, values, and behaviors in relation to the services offered. (Consider government-supported family planning programs, for instance.)

Furthermore, if it happens that some person or persons question the constitutionality of the law and this challenge reaches the Supreme Court, which in turn finds the legislation in violation of the Constitution, the entire process will be moved back to square one. In short, there is a long series of processes that must occur for a policy to have real effect: a study in the many trials and triumphs of a democracy in a national/state/local system![1]

Although ideally public policy development and implementation is a rational process based on the best scientific knowledge, rational process is only one piece of the much larger policy puzzle. For instance, findings from scientific research are often brought into the policy process to provide a patina of rational respectability to a piece of legislation that more fundamentally has pragmatic political purposes.

The complex, lengthy, political processes described above may well be discouraging to those who wish to affect public policies. To be effective, it is often useful for individuals to select a few policy issues that seem to them to be crucial, to affiliate with groups (often representative of one or more of the human services professions) which share their concerns, and to keep informed and politically active with that group or groups and follow the legislation through its many processes: congressional and presidential legislative actions, budget appropriations, development of administrative guidelines, state and local implementation, and court challenges. It also helps to know one's elected local, state, and federal representatives and to join and contribute to the political party of choice as well as campaign organizations for candidates supporting desired public policies.

In general, it is unproductive to complain, as many do, that public policies are "just a mess of politics." Within the American system of government "politics" is a process of democracy in action. As discussed above, the many processes involved are heavily affected by pressures from politically active individuals and groups. Thus, the way for human service professionals to affect policies is to become politically active themselves, especially through knowledgeable, well-organized groups. To simply criticize and stay outside of the processes is to pass the power to others who *are* actively involved and, furthermore, often involved with pushing agenda that are not in the best interests of families in trouble, especially poor and minority families who have relatively little power themselves.

A major point to the policy chapters in this series is to provide both the knowledge background and a stimulus to readers to involve themselves, to one extent or another, in political activities to affect public policies that play such a large part in the lives of troubled families. An ecological approach to services for families clearly implies that concerned human service professionals should involve themselves, to one degree or another, in policy- and planning-oriented political activities, as well as in the provision of direct services, which is the major focus of most practitioners serving families today.[2]

FAMILY-RELATED POLICIES

This leads to another definition: family policies or family-related policies. Again, the policies referred to here are public, i.e., government policies. And again, the term *family policy* has numerous meanings and involves numerous controversies. As of the mid 1980s the term was attracting increased attention, sparking heated debates covering the entire political spectrum from the extreme conservative political right to the extreme liberal left. Virtually everybody appeared to be "pro-family" and in favor of supports for family well-being, including supports for their economic and occupational well-being. But as we have seen, definitions of family and family well-being have many interpretations. To some the term *public family policy* may mean that certain kinds of families and family-related behaviors, as determined by government action, should be promoted and other kinds officially opposed.

On the other hand, many others hold that *family public policies* should be defined as including all government policies and programs which have an impact on families; they also tend to believe that government should not impose a particular standard of family roles and functions on its citizens. The concept that family policies consist of all policies affecting families has led in a number of directions, including that of *family impact analysis,* a term that became popular during the Carter-Mondale administration of the late 1970s (Zimmerman, 1982).

Family impact analysis takes a rational planning approach to family policy. It seeks to gather large bodies of data concerning numerous public programs that affect families and to assess their effects through complex statistical analyses of relevant data. Impact is measured by demonstrated or probable effects on birth, marriage, divorce, separation, illegitimacy, employment, and income. These statistics are primarily provided by the U.S. Bureau of the Census, the National Center of Vital Statistics, and the U.S. Department of Labor. Data from these government agencies are reported in some of the chapters in this book. Moreover, numerous studies of various aspects of family well-being and of program effectiveness of family life, broadly defined, have been carried out by numerous government agencies and universities as well as by human service public and private organizations. Findings from these investigations are also used to supplement the above data. Many of these studies are also discussed in the relevant chapters of this series.

Senator Patrick Moynihan, who has had a long-time interest in family policy, writes that in essence family policy focuses on the outcomes of other policies. He sees family welfare as being the business of numerous social and economic programs at national, state, and local levels and holds that their impact on families can be assessed, at least in part, by analyses of family data, as discussed above (Moynihan, 1986).

Kamerman and Kahn (1978), who have conducted extensive surveys of family policies and programs in this and other countries, define family policies in ways that are close to Moynihan's conceptions. They hold that family policy consists of activities funded and sponsored by government that affect families directly or indirectly, intentionally or unintentionally, whether or not these policies have specific family objectives. They write that family policy is both a perspective and a set of activities. As an activity it includes such family-specific programs as family planning services, food stamps, income maintenance, foster care, adoption, homemaker services, day care, child development programs, family counseling and therapy, and employment services.

All of the above views include, or can include, the concept of family impact analysis. This analysis has considerable merit primarily because it recognizes the huge network of government programs that impinge on families. This analysis also calls for the application of survey data as well as many kinds of research, both basic and applied, to the formation and analysis of public family-related programs and policies. However, family impact analysis by itself cannot be expected to change public policy. Those who apply its methods will have major problems if they fail to recognize and deal with the many political processes that are also necessary to actualize policies as shown above.

Also, family impact analysis is deficient if it merely takes the passive approach of simply analyzing what effects government pro-grams and policies will have or are having on families. An active approach is also needed, in which the needs of families are the primary consideration. Planning activities are then directed to for-mulating what programs and policies, both existing and not yet existing, are needed.

Another and far more conservative view of family policy was presented by President Reagan's Working Group on the Family in 1986 (Washington Cofo Memo, 1986). Their report called for less government infringement on the rights and responsibilities of fam-ilies. State-funded day care, income assistance through public family allowances for children, school feeding programs, and national health care systems were all seen as socialistic evils which under-mine American families and the larger society. The report called for local, volunteer assistance to families in lieu of federal/state govern-mental programs. On the other hand, government should take an active stand to affect cultural patterns perceived by the working group as being hostile to families; these patterns included drug use, pornography, and "bigoted" stands against religions.

The report also saw economic expansion as essentially a pro-family program. Such expansion could be brought about, the group stated, through such measures as low taxes, control of inflation, and the end of "social spending schemes." The report further stated that old principles need to be reaffirmed which prevent the erosion of family rights and responsibilities through court actions, dominance by public education, and control by social programs. Senator Moynihan called this report not so much an analysis of public policies and families as a "conservative tantrum." Indeed, it seems to reflect some of the main aspects of the extreme conservative position. Nonetheless, the report illustrates the principle that *all* aspects of the functioning of society can be viewed as relevant to family policies. It also shows that the field of family policy is highly sensitive and readily politicized.

Family issues deeply engage the heart as well as the mind. They touch upon the most intimate, significant aspects of our lives, the central identity each of us derives through our total development from infancy onward. Family issues include our most private and personal attachments, values, and beliefs. For many, probably the majority of Americans, family issues are closely intertwined with religious ones. And a basic principle of the American credo is a separation of church and state. Probably all religions see the guidance and succor of families as being central to their function and sharply different from those of government.

Furthermore, individual and hence family freedom from government interference is also basic to the American tradition. Millions of immigrants from the early 1600s to the present have come to this country in search of this freedom. Thus, the very words "family policy" can serve as a red flag to many of our citizens of all political persuasions.

Schorr writes that it is preferable to plan for a wide range of public policies and programs that families need rather than advocate for family policies per se, since the former term is less sensitive and controversial than the latter (Schorr, 1986). Moreover, many such programs can be offered as services that may be chosen or not, depending on the values and beliefs of individual families and their members, thus safeguarding principles of freedom.

FAMILIES VERSUS SOCIETAL RESPONSIBILITY

The concept of "family responsibility" is another controversial and complicated one that usually arises in debates about families and policies. It lies at the heart of many issues, including those concerned with poverty and public assistance. Although our traditional cultural patterns hold that it is desirable for families to be self-reliant and self-supporting, responsible toward each of their members, and independent of any public aid, virtually *no* family in today's highly urbanized, technological society is totally independent of the services provided by large networks of external systems, both private and governmental. Government aided and/or regulated systems within the country which are crucial to the well-being of virtually all families include transportation in its many aspects, water supplies, waste disposal, fire and police protection, dependable money supplies and insured savings bank deposits, public education systems, public health services, social security provisions, the court systems, and so on. And international programs aimed at implementation of foreign policy and national defense, as well as improved international trade, theoretically at least, provide important assistance for every individual and family in the country.

Although many of these forms of assistance are more or less taken for granted, sharp arguments quickly arise over such issues as special income, health, employment, housing, child care, and education assistance targeted to the poor and near poor. Such programs are highly visible, are incorrectly seen as inordinately expensive, and are often viewed as replacing family responsibilities—with many of these responsibilities fundamentally being the traditional functions of women, including child care, nursing care of the ill and disabled, and stretching the food, housing, and clothing dollar through home production. Some traditionalists claim that keeping these kinds of responsibilities within the family actually enhances the well-being of families. However, if we return to our earlier definition of family well-being, we can see that this well-being is eroded, rather than supported, if the basic survival and developmental needs of families and all their members, including wives and mothers, are not met. An overload of economic adversities or severe illnesses or handicaps may make it impossible for some families to handle problems such as these without the supplementary assistance of public programs. Although conservatives often argue that private voluntary efforts should provide the assistance needed, our society has become too urbanized, costly, and complex for these activities by themselves to make much of a dent on the host of problems that many families encounter today. As shown in more detail later, these voluntary efforts can be helpful as a supplement to, but not a substitute for, necessary family assistance programs.

As shown in the foregoing chapters, families in our complex, technologically advanced society have only limited control over their own physical health and over mobilizing the frequently costly resources for treatment of the physical illnesses and disabilities that may afflict family members.

A careful analysis of the points listed above can lead to the recognition that many of the health problems faced by families today are not solely a result of irresponsible actions on their part; rather, to a large extent they are a result of a combination of factors external to families. These include medical advances that have prolonged life so that more people are encountering the chronic health problems of old age; the steep rise in the cost of medical, hospital, and nursing home care; and the numerous stressors and hazards in the environment. Thus, a number of public policies and programs are needed to promote and support the health of families and their members, as will be discussed in more detail in the next chapter.

NOTES

1. Other legal challenges regarding legislation and its administration may be raised through the courts at various local, state, and regional levels, but a discussion of details concerning this and other issues affecting public policies transcends the space constraints of this chapter.

2. Although the foregoing paragraphs may seem like a high school lesson in civics, it is my experience that the majority of citizens, including graduate students, many academicians, and human service professionals, fail to understand many of the principles sketched here. These principles grow out of my experience and study as a university professor, as a former staff member of the (then) U.S. Department of Health, Education and Welfare during the 1960s, and as a former staff member of various state governments and private social agencies.

It was my common government experience during the 1960s that both academicians and human service professionals outside the federal government sought to impress me with their views of what policies and programs were needed because they assumed I was an "influential policymaker." In actuality, the executive branch of government (i.e., the President, his Cabinet, and the staff of the various federal departments) cannot create public domestic policies (with "domestic" referring to policies *internal* to this country) without supportive legislation and appropriations as provided by Congressional action. Also, any staff actions must be within guidelines provided by the relevant legislation. Furthermore, federal staff members need to be sensitive to the reactions of citizens, as groups and as individuals, at local levels since these citizens may protest to their elected officials in Congress if they object to any part of federal programs and the way they are administered.

Thus, it seems to me that the term "federal domestic policymakers" tends to be a fallacy if it refers to federal staff personnel, since their options are limited by many factors. In fact, given the constraints, it is something of a miracle that federal "bureaucrats" can act at all. Similar comments apply to local and state governments, but our focus here is on the federal government.

10

Social Policies:

UNDERSTANDING THEIR IMPACT ON FAMILIES WITH IMPAIRED MEMBERS

MARGARET WALKOVER

THE PROBLEM

Many families include members who are impaired. The Franklins' grandmother suffers from Alzheimer's disease. Lou Ferraro, a divorcé, is learning to care for his teenage son who was severely disabled in a car crash. David McCarthy, recently diagnosed with Acquired Immune Deficiency Syndrome (AIDS), has lost his job and now relies on his network of friends to provide care between periods of hospitalization. The Sanchez's 6-year-old daughter suffers from a congenital defect that leaves her unable to speak, move, go to the bathroom, or walk.

Each of these families must reorganize its economic, social, and emotional priorities around the needs of its impaired member. Each family suffers strain. It may use the services of physicians, nurses, caseworkers, counselors, and other professionals to help with medical needs, finances, children's school-related problems, marital difficulties, and the complicated demands of its sick family member (Jones, 1985; Doty, 1986). These families are not responsible for the event which severely disabled their grandmother, teenager, infant, or friend, and they deserve access to a health care and social service system that does not impose barriers to restoring the potential of their impaired family member.

These barriers exist, nevertheless, because: (a) the health care delivery system is primarily organized to meet the demands of acute illness, rather than the needs of the chronically ill patient (Somers, 1986; Rice & Estes, 1984), (b) government-sponsored insurance and private insurance rarely pay for the full range of treatment, which includes screening, diagnosis, and follow-up services (Ireys, Hauck, & Perrin, 1985; ICF, Inc., 1985), and (c) community resources are

AUTHOR'S NOTE: The author would like to acknowledge the assistance and support of Lorraine Klerman, Dr.P.H., and Wayne Praskins, M.A., during the preparation of the manuscript.

often limited. These resources include respite or therapeutic care, grants from nonprofit organizations to help pay for equipment, and even neighborly compassion (Kramer, 1981; Cantor, 1985).

These barriers prevail due to social policy decisions that determine which citizens will have access to specific levels of health care. In addition, these social policy decisions may also determine the degree of access vulnerable citizens have to the economic, political, and social resources they need to thrive in an increasingly competitive society.

Our nation's health care finance and delivery system provides many examples of the consequences that social policies have for some impaired citizens and their caretakers. The day-to-day challenges that vulnerable citizens face are often complicated by a fragmented system of health care financing. Financial assistance available to vulnerable persons is often inadequate because of its origin in a multitude of private and government programs, each with separate eligibility requirements.

For instance, individuals who worked prior to a disabling accident may receive a monthly sum from the Social Security Disability Fund which covers only a fraction of their medical costs. Retirees may be able to pay for a portion of their medical expenses with Social Security and pension payments. Low-income citizens are usually eligible for Medicaid, a public assistance program. Dependent children may only be partially covered under their parent's health insurance plan. These forms of revenue rarely meet the total needs of family members with chronic and debilitating illnesses.

In addition to the inequitable financing system, the impaired and their families must deal with an inaccessible system of health and social services. It is often difficult to find suitable health or social service providers. Families may find it impossible to coordinate the services of the myriad of agencies that do or should assist them. In some cases a funding source may not be accepted by the family's preferred health service provider. For example, Medicaid, the primary funding source for low-income citizens, is often not accepted by providers of long-term care services.

This chapter will attempt to provide a frame of reference for understanding the constraints that social policy decisions place on families made vulnerable by a complex and often inadequate social welfare system. This knowledge should improve the ability of practitioners to provide for their clients' needs. In the long run an improved understanding of social policy may enable human service professionals to modify those system elements that are dysfunctional, resulting in changes that will benefit future clients.

THE RELEVANCE OF SOCIAL POLICY TO THE HUMAN SERVICE PROFESSIONAL

Why should direct service workers be interested in a policy process that appears to be far removed from their work with clients? Caseworkers are not directly responsible for the design of social welfare policies, nor do corporations pay family counselors to propose improved employee benefit policies. Instead, human service practitioners deal with their clients' important day-to-day therapeutic and functional problems.

Human service professionals need to understand the impact of social policy on their work for four reasons. The first is that social policy affects the success of clinical interventions by altering the client's access to the resources of daily living. For example, public transportation policies that limit bus routes may make it difficult for patients to keep appointments. Restricted food stamp availability may increase the probability that a client will suffer from malnutrition, curtailing the effect of physical therapy. Economic policies may influence a patient's ability to obtain housing, education, or employment.

The second reason why an understanding of social policy is important involves the practitioner's role as advocate. An understanding of the policy process will help the professional decide how to negotiate the system. For example, a social worker may have a client whose depression is caused by the escalating emotional demands of a disabled child who cannot sleep at night due to physical discomfort. If the social worker understands the politics of insurance benefit regulations, he or she may be better prepared to pressure the insurer into funding a special bed for the uncomfortable child.

The third reason is related to the practitioners' role as a community resource. The public assumes that practitioners are experts on the problems experienced by the clients they treat. For example, community groups or business coalitions may ask a practitioner to help them decide which programs should receive their financial or volunteer support. Or a planning council may ask a social worker to evaluate whether a state-funded respite care program has benefited the elderly population in her caseload. Practitioners will be better prepared to interpret these requests if they have knowledge of program evaluation, which is a component of policy analysis.

Finally, social policies may affect clients' access to the services provided by human service professionals. Access can be restricted by limiting the kinds of practitioners for which the government program or private insurance plan will pay. These social policies reflect the extent to which the services of certain practitioners are valued by the organizations that lobby for the policies and by the decision makers that design and approve them.

Gilbert and Specht (1974) provide an excellent illustration of the effect that government policy decisions have on access to human service providers. Between 1962 and 1967 the federal government changed its policy toward the reimbursement of social workers. The 1962 amendments to the Social Security Act were well-funded and emphasized the importance of casework services for welfare clients. By 1967, however, government ideology had changed, and the 1967 Social Security Amendments deemphasized individual therapeutic interventions and withdrew the resources to support them.

As these examples show, changes in the financing of human services affect both client and practitioner. A knowledge of social policy can assist the practitioner in understanding how to pressure the policy process to act on behalf of both the human service professional and the client. The first step to becoming a skillful participant in the development and implementation of social policy is to acquire an understanding of its nature. The remainder of this chapter will prepare the human service professional to fulfill this objective.

SOCIAL POLICY DEFINED

Who Creates Social Policy?

Policy is a term that is used in many contexts. For the purpose of this discussion policies are created through institutional decisions originating in the private, for-profit; public; and private, nonprofit sectors of the economy. Social policy describes the net effect of these decisions on the welfare of citizens. This section will examine the contribution of each policy-making sector to the social policy process.

Private, For-Profit Sector

Business decisions made by for-profit corporations create private sector policies. Corporations generally prefer to make their business decisions in "free markets" without direct government regulation.

Our nation looks favorably on markets that are not only free but also competitive. Competitive markets are expected to have many advantages for society, including the production of low-priced goods and services and the efficient allocation of resources. Characteristics of competitive markets include the existence of many small, independent producers, buyers, and sellers who exchange money for goods or services voluntarily and on the basis of mutual advantage. Another important prerequisite to a competitive market are consumers who have the time, money, and information to make efficient purchases (Fuchs, 1986).

Advocates of decentralized "free market" arrangements believe that private policies reduce the need to use coercive government intervention as a tool to improve the public welfare (Savas, 1982). In the 1980s many academics, health care administrators, and politicians have vigorously argued that competition in health care is better suited than government regulation to encourage the development of cost-effective finance and delivery systems (Enthoven, 1980; Califano, 1986; Swoap, 1984).

Competition in the health care industry improves the health care finance and delivery system in at least four ways. The first is the cost savings for those who pay for health care services such as government, insurance companies, corporations, and patients (Langewell & Moore, 1982). Second, the need to compete for patient dollars has resulted in a reorganization of the health care delivery system to include a broad range of nonacute and outpatient services (Shortell et al., 1986). The third outcome of incentives to compete are innovative solutions to some social problems. For example, one interesting product is the "life care community," which sells apartments to elderly consumers who have the money to buy into these new housing/social service plans (Leutz, 1986).

Finally, from the perspective of the consumer, private, for-profit sector policies may result in the rapid distribution of new goods and services. The retail pharmaceutical industry offers several examples. In an effort to attract new customers, retail drug companies are creating subsidiaries that produce and widely distribute self-diagnostic products such as self-testing kits for pregnancy, diabetes, and colon cancer (Jones & Walkover, 1984), provide flexible financing for the rental or purchase of durable medical equipment, and sell specialized home health care services (Lindeman & Wood, 1985).

The expansion of social welfare activity sponsored by the private, for-profit sector is part of a general trend favoring the private provision of services that have traditionally been financed or administered by public or private, nonprofit sectors of the economy (Savas, 1982). For instance, some large corporations supplement their employee benefit packages with social services such as alcohol, drug, and psychological counseling; medical care; legal assistance; and loans with low interest rates. These employee benefits are believed to reduce absenteeism, contain health care costs, and attract the best employees (Chollet, 1984).

It should be noted that private, for-profit sector policies do not affect all citizens equally. Many of the previously mentioned innovative employee benefits are offered by a relatively small number of employers whose philosophy and financing capabilities support such programs (Health Insurance Association of America, 1984). For example, if a firm manufacturing artificial limbs cannot risk mass-producing an unprofitable mechanical hand, some disabled persons will remain impaired. Or an employer's decision to reduce manufacturing costs by using a toxic substance might result in an employee giving birth to a severely retarded child. In the face of this inequality, families with impaired members often turn to the public sector for assistance.

Public Sector

Public policy is an instrument used by government to implement social goals (National Conference on Social Welfare, 1985). Government policies can mandate the delivery of needed services that are not provided by other sectors of the economy (Marcus, 1980; Desonia & King, 1985). Public policies can also provide incentives for governmental agencies to form partnerships with private, for-profit and nonprofit sector agencies to deliver new services. Government leadership, expressed in the form of legislative policy, may also further social goals by creating programs which, for example, may increase family capacity and willingness to care for impaired members (Callahan et al., 1980). Citizens' rights to public education, a safe workplace, nontoxic air and water supplies, and health care are all protected to varying degrees by the public policy process.

Government-sponsored policies exist in the areas of education, economic development, and transportation, to name a few. These policies are formed through laws enacted by legislatures; through programs developed by government agencies on the local, state, and federal levels; and through judicial decisions.

It is difficult to design a public policy that will produce the desired outcome with precision. For example, the intent of the 1965 Medicare legislation was to increase access to hospital care for the elderly.

The politics of the policy process resulted in a payment system based on hospital charges, a system that helped to produce an unintended secondary outcome—an uncontrolled rate of medical care inflation (Medicine and Health Perspectives, 1985).

Problems in policy design have provided the impetus for research in the field of public policy studies (Bardach, 1977; Bauer & Gergen, 1968). Doubt regarding both the efficiency of government agencies and the regulatory process provides fuel for arguments concerning the appropriate role of government. One debate concerns whether government should promote a residual or an institutional model of social welfare. The residual model suggests that government programs act as a "safety net" to be used only when private for-profit and nonprofit policies have failed. The institutional model promotes government as a first line of defense, protecting citizens from the economic insecurity of modern industrial society via expanded social security programs and government regulations (Wilensky & Lebeaux, 1965; Titmuss, 1974).

The United States endorses a residual model of social welfare, and the size of the "safety net" of social programs is dependent on many factors. One major factor is the strength of the economy. In times of economic growth government support of services tends to increase. However, during periods of slow economic growth the safety net shrinks as the budget for health and welfare programs is cut (Berki, 1983; Morris, 1985).

Our health care finance and delivery system is currently faced with growing numbers of citizens who cannot afford to purchase services (Feder, Hadley, & Mullner, 1984). Their tragedy is increased by the shrinking safety net of government programs. A presidential commission reporting on the ethical implications of variation in the accessibility of services studied this dilemma and concluded that society, not exclusively government, has an ethical obligation to ensure that all citizens be able to secure an adequate level of care without excessive burden (President's Commission, 1983). This weak statement makes no promise of a strong government commitment to vulnerable citizens. It is clear that in the United States the government-sponsored system of social welfare will not always meet the needs of citizens who cannot afford health care.

Private, Nonprofit Sector

Private, nonprofit organizations are membership groups or societies which have a social purpose and seek to benefit their constituencies. They include mutual aid and self-help groups, service and fraternal organizations, religious and charitable societies, lobbying and educational groups, political parties, and unions. It has been observed that these groups provide citizens with a political voice that may serve as a mediating and empowering force between the individual, the state, and, most recently, large private corporations (de Tocqueville, 1848).

In the policy arena private, nonprofit groups may function as advocates for vulnerable populations, protectors of minority group interests, innovators of new programs, and providers of human services that government chooses not to support (Kramer, 1981). These groups have also traditionally played an important role for impaired individuals because of the free or low-cost volunteer services they offer (Kane & Kane, 1981).

Good examples of the activity of private, nonprofits include the programs of YMCAs and YWCAs. These community-based organizations often provide programs such as day care, youth activities, health care services, and family counseling on a sliding fee scale.

Private nonprofits are often used by the government to sponsor "demonstration projects," innovative social programs that are funded for limited periods of time in order to test new ways to administer social programs. The private, for-profit sector will sometimes market these services if their worth and potential to satisfy consumer demand has been established.

The home health care industry provides an appropriate example of this trend. In the 1960s home health care agencies were operated primarily by private, nonprofit agencies. However, after the Omnibus Reconciliation Act of 1980 made it possible for private, for-profit providers to receive Medicare reimbursement, the home health care market became dominated by for-profit providers who seized the opportunity to sell services to the growing elderly population (Lindeman & Wood, 1985). In this example, the private, nonprofit sector provided a "test market" for the for-profit health care providers.

The number and variety of services currently provided by private nonprofit providers are decreasing due to shrinking sources of revenue from foundations, government grants, and individual contributions. Private, nonprofit organizations have responded by carefully prioritizing the needs of the target populations or the locations they serve and redirecting their funds accordingly. As a result of an overall decrease in financial support for the activities of private nonprofit providers, the potential of the private nonprofit sector to assist families with impaired members has diminished (Kimmich, 1985).

Conclusion: The Development of Social Policy

Social policies may originate in different sectors of the economy, but they often develop interdependently (Lee & Estes, 1983). For example, access to perinatal services for a community's low-income women may be a product of the joint evolution of nonprofit, for-profit, and public sector policies. The nonprofit perinatal clinic's decision to have a sliding fee scale depends on the local business coalition's priorities for donations. In turn, the business coalition's incentive to donate to charity depends on the federal tax code's provisions for charitable contributions.

Each of the policy-making sectors is accountable to a different constituency. Corporations are accountable to stockholders; hence business policies are rarely implemented unless they will assist the firm in making a profit. Nonprofit groups are accountable to the benefactors who donate funds to support the mission of the organization. Governments developing public policies generally operate with some definition of "the public interest" in mind, but they must also respond to special interest groups.

Government has the broadest scope of accountability of the three sectors of the economy. In fact, public policy is often designed to provide the private, for-profit and nonprofit sectors with incentives to accomplish social goals that go beyond their usual scope of accountability (Schultze, 1977). Examples include special tax breaks for corporations who train and hire moderately impaired individuals or a county's technical assistance grant program that helps a community radio station provide closed captioned programming for the hearing impaired.

Some argue that social policies should be used to safeguard the social role of citizens made vulnerable by physical, emotional, or cognitive impairment (Goodin, 1985). One example of a safeguard is government tax policies encouraging private corporations to hire the physically disabled. Another is federal grants to the states which fund special lifts on buses enabling wheelchair-bound citizens to use public transportation. These examples are categorical in nature, funding specific needs of predetermined target populations. Safeguards providing increased security to a broader range of vulnerable citizens would include a system of national health insurance or a national public assistance program requiring the states to provide an adequate income for low-income citizens.

The latter examples are controversial. They are opposed by those who argue that the role of social policy is not to expand eligibility for social programs but to establish criteria determining which citizens have an appropriate level of need to qualify for programs that allocate scarce social, economic, and political resources.

In the face of perceived scarcity our society tends to use social policy in health care to decide whom to exclude as a beneficiary of public and private health care programs. These decisions are often tragic because of the inevitability that entire classes of citizens will be excluded in the process of deciding who will benefit from social programs (Calabresi & Bobbitt, 1978).

For example, United States society endorses a social policy on access to health care that uses employment status as a criterion for coverage. Individuals employed in organizations offering health insurance as a fringe benefit have relatively easy access to medical care. At the other extreme, however, chronically impaired citizens who are unemployed may not be able to buy health care services because they have limited or no income; jobs they can master are unavailable to impaired persons; or the government program or private insurance plan for which they qualify provides insufficient funds to pay for services they need.

Practitioners need to be aware of their active role in the social policy process, and this knowledge will help them find solutions to problems that are beyond the scope of the clinical setting. The next section of this chapter will present a conceptual framework explaining why social policies discriminate against some clients and favor others. This discussion should increase the practitioner's understanding of the limitations of some social policies.

SOCIAL POLICY ANALYSIS: WHO BENEFITS, WHO LOSES, AND WHY?

Private, for-profit; public; and private, nonprofit policies generate different systems of social welfare. The term *social welfare* is used here in its broadest sense and includes not only the provision of health and social services but also the availability of resources such as jobs, housing, and transportation. This section of the chapter will introduce some basic concepts which can be used to understand how and why social policies differ in their impact on families with impaired members.

Some Basic Concepts

Table 10.1 illustrates three *social welfare systems* generated by policies originating in the public; private, for-profit; and private,

Table 10.1
A Comparison of Three Systems of Social Welfare

Origin of Policy	Social Welfare System Generated by the Policy	Primary Allocation Principle(s)	Criteria for Access	Example
Public Sector	Universal	Equality	Normative	• Canada's health care system • Public education in the United States
Public Sector Private, Nonprofit Sector	Selective	Equity Adequacy	Needs Assessment • means-test • diagnostic differentiation • compensation	• Medicaid • Social services offered at a community YWCA
Private, For-profit Sector Private, Nonprofit Sector	Competitive	Efficiency	Capacity to Demand (i.e., pay for) Services	—Home care subsidiary of Johnson and Johnson Pharmaceuticals, Inc. —Home care subsidiary of Catholic Hospitals of America, Inc.

Policies originating in the public; private, nonprofit; and private, for-profit sectors generate different systems of social welfare (what will be delivered?). Each social welfare system has rules determining the total amount of goods and services to be delivered (how much will be delivered?). Eligibility for benefits is determined by access criteria (who will receive benefits?).

nonprofit sectors. These systems of social welfare need to be identified in order to understand the effect of social policy on citizens. Social welfare policies originating in the public sector are derived from either the universal or selective social welfare systems (Kamerman & Kahn, 1976). The private, for-profit and, most recently, the private, nonprofit sectors generate competitive systems of social welfare (Marmor, Schlesinger, & Smithey, 1986).

Each system of social welfare incorporates social values determining the *rules for allocating goods and services to specific categories of recipients*. For instance, the principle of equity implies that citizens should be allocated benefits proportional to the sum of resources they have already contributed to society, Therefore, if the salary of a professional is higher than the salary of a clerk because society places a higher value on the social contribution of professionals, unemployment benefit levels for lawyers will most likely exceed those of bookkeepers.

Access criteria determine which citizens are eligible to receive goods and services. These criteria are often used to ration scarce resources by identifying the "neediest" cases. Sometimes access criteria are used to offer benefits to populations who have previously been denied them. Access criteria differ according to the system of social values underwriting a social welfare program.

Each system of social welfare will now be examined in more detail, and the allocation rules and access criteria of each social welfare system will be explained. This discussion should clarify the implications of social policies made in the public; private, nonprofit; and private, for-profit sectors of the economy.

Universal Social Welfare Systems

Universal social welfare systems generate policies that make benefits available as a social right to the entire population or subsets of the population. For example, Canada's system of national health care is organized on principles of universality; health care is viewed as a right, and no one is denied access to the medical care system (Evans, 1984).

The primary allocation principle in a universal social welfare system is equality. Under this principle the same treatment is received by each member of a category of beneficiaries. A good example is the United States' system of public education, where every child aged 5 through 18 is guaranteed access to a public school. Special services may be provided to ensure that all members of the category "school-aged children" receive the benefit (e.g., free school bus service, free textbooks). The right of equal opportunity in education is extended to children with special needs through P.L. 94-142, the Education for Handicapped Children Act, which mandates that every local education authority provide the necessary educational resources to teach the handicapped.

In these examples access is based on a criterion of need that is normative; the level of benefits made available to a category of recipients is based on a notion of what they *should* receive, irrespective of existing political or economic barriers. For example, public education is based on the idea that everyone *should* have an opportunity to benefit from a formal education. If the criteria of need were not normative (e.g., economic status of families with school-aged children, intelligence of children as determined by an I.Q. score), citizens with low incomes or below-average intelligence would be prevented from receiving this public service.

Normative criteria of need apply to categories of potential recipients that vary in size and scope. For example, public education affects the entire United States. In contrast, a community fair may offer free blood pressure screening in only one town.

Selective Social Welfare Systems

Selective social welfare systems generate policies that make benefits available to subpopulations using predetermined criteria of individual need. Selective systems of social welfare are characterized by services that are financed and delivered in a fragmented manner. In addition, each social program has its own criteria for access.

The primary allocation principles used by a selective system of social welfare are equity and adequacy. Equity is sometimes confused with the principle of equality, which guarantees equal allocation of benefits to everyone, irrespective of differences in their levels of past contributions. Instead, the principle of equity generally means that benefits are allocated *in proportion* to past contributions.

The definition of equity can also be modified to mean an increase in allocated benefits to citizens who are not responsible for their inability to contribute. For instance, in 1972 the United States Congress voted to amend the Social Security Act and extend Medicare coverage to victims of chronic kidney failure. In 1976 the program cost $448 million for 21,500 beneficiaries. In this example a relatively small number of citizens received much more in benefits from the

Social Security system than the sum of their monthly payroll contributions to the Social Security Disability Fund.

Adequacy refers to the provision of a minimal level of goods and services. Variations in the definition of "minimal" produce unequal allocations of benefits. For example, states differ in their definition of an adequate level of economic need, resulting in public assistance programs whose benefits vary from state to state. In some states "adequate" means a public assistance income below subsistence level; in other states adequacy translated into enough funds to pay for food, clothing, and shelter.

Access criteria in a selective framework are used to decide who will be denied benefits. Consider the case of Jon Colman, who became a stroke victim at age 48. Jon was employed before his stroke, making him eligible for disability payments from the Social Security Disability Fund. However, these monthly payments will not cover his medical expenses. He needs physical and occupational therapy and is being denied eligibility for several rehabilitation programs. Jon was excluded from a state government rehabilitation program because his income was too high—he failed a means test of his economic need. His physician did not think his impairment was serious enough to justify entrance into a county occupational therapy program—he failed a test of diagnostic differentiation. The Veteran's Administration hospital would not give him free treatment—he failed to qualify for veteran's compensation because he did not have a service-related disability.

Access criteria are often arbitrary and applied in an imprecise manner. This causes some people who need services to slip "between the cracks" of the system and not receive care. Jon Colman certainly would have argued that he deserved access to these programs. But if he cannot find help, he will remain unemployed and lose his financial independence as well as his health.

Competitive Social Welfare Systems

Competitive social welfare systems generate policies that make benefits available to subsets of the population based on their ability to pay for services. A competitive system uses the allocative principle of efficiency, and efficient allocation of resources is accomplished as a byproduct of the transactions between producers and consumers in the marketplace.

Competitive systems of social welfare share many of the negative characteristics of the selective framework. For example, they are often fragmented and impose inequitable standards of financing and delivery. The major and most outstanding difference between the two systems is the nature of their access criteria; selective frameworks determine eligibility based on various categories of need, but competitive frameworks determine eligibility solely on the consumers' ability to demand (i.e., pay for) services.

When a system of social welfare becomes competitive, coexisting selective systems tend to erode. A good example is the evolution of the hospital industry in the United States (Starr, 1982). Prior to the 1980s the hospital industry was dominated by nonprofit providers. The growth of for-profit multihospital systems was, in part, spurred by a policy decision made by the Reagan administration, a decision that favored the production of goods and services through private markets rather than under the auspice of government (Havighurst, 1986; Ginsburg, 1983). The Department of Health and Human Services implemented this new philosophy by promoting health care policies that encouraged providers to compete for patients on the basis of price (Goldsmith, 1981; Davis et al., 1986).

Before this change in public policy private, nonprofit hospitals were the main providers of charity care in their communities.

However, heated competition between the for-profit and private, nonprofit multihospital systems has changed the access criteria used by private nonprofit hospitals because for-profits target the most profitable segment of a market, leaving the highest risk and the most expensive caseloads for their competitors (Townsend, 1986). Competition on the basis of price has made charity care a bad business decision (Wilensky, 1985). As a result, private, nonprofit hospitals have had to adopt the competive framework in order to survive (Yoder, 1986). The framework generating social policies has changed from selective to competitive, increasing the number of citizens without access to the range of services delivered in the hospital setting (Feder, Hadley, & Mullner, 1984).

Conclusion

In the United States families with impaired members are at the mercy of a fragmented finance and delivery system produced by disparate social policies resulting in conflicting systems of social welfare. Vulnerable families need practitioners who know how to realistically negotiate this system in their favor.

The tense relationship between the family and the state is one factor deterring systemic change in the social policy process. The next section will explore this and other factors that inhibit the development of effective policies.

THE FAMILY WITH AN IMPAIRED MEMBER AS A SOCIAL POLICY PROBLEM

How can we increase families' capacities to care for impaired members? Solutions to this problem are difficult to identify for at least three reasons: reluctance to reduce familial responsibility, conflicting definitions of family, and distrust of centralized control. The first two reasons address the relationship between the family and society. The third comments on our nation's reluctance to use social policy to mitigate the economic and political problems faced by individual citizens.

Reluctance to Reduce Familial Responsibility

The institution of the family occupies a sacred position in the political and economic culture of the United States. The idealized family is expected to instill in its members the qualities needed to fuel an economic system that relies on self-directed and independent citizens. Family members are socialized to become productive members of society through participation in the emotional bonds of family life: planning, saving, and sacrifice for the future.

This family ethic is so strong that when the family's ability to provide for its own breaks down, American social institutions are reluctant to provide assistance quickly and in a rational and humane manner. The relationship between the family unit and the public and private sectors becomes, at best, an "uncomfortable union" (Gilbert, 1983).

This uncomfortable union can stall the development of public policies that assist the family. The transformation of social policy proposals into funded programs is hindered when the autonomy of the family is threatened by the potential authority of government. For example, Pizzo (1983) provides an example of this pattern as she explains the slow development of comprehensive federal policies for children and their families. The author observes that whenever a Congressional policy proposal can be interpreted as an attempt to undermine parental authority, the proposal is made extremely vulnerable to legislative defeat.

The uncertain relationship between the family and the state is embodied in government programs presenting radically different conceptions of the role of government in family life. As a result, vulnerable families must deal with government-funded programs that assume inconsistent levels of responsibility for providing financing or services. Concurrent philosophies of the optimal degree of government intervention into family life include (Morris 1982):

1. Government should take minimal or no responsibility for the family. Instead, families should take complete responsibility for their impaired members through income generated by employment and through the sacrifice of their leisure time as they assume the role of caretaker.
2. Government should take primary responsibility for the needs of the vulnerable family member. An example is the creation of public institutions for the severely mentally retarded.
3. A third party, outside the jurisdiction of the family or government, should take primary responsibility for the needs of the vulnerable family member. The responsibility of government should be limited to funding and administering the program, and responsibility of determining eligibility (granting access) to a public program should be deferred to professional clinicians such as doctors, social workers, therapists, or probation officers.
4. The family and state should share responsibility for the ill family member. However, the state's role should supplement or complement the family unit, and substitution of state resources for family support should be avoided. The family unit is expected to meet its needs through multiple sources of aid outside of government programs. Examples of such role-sharing are found in studies documenting multiple sources of care used by the disabled elderly (Liu, Manton, & Liu, 1985; Leutz, 1986).

This list portrays real differences in accepted levels of government intervention. This disparity in part manifests our society's inability to make a commitment to a consistent family policy. Families must contend with a set of inadequate social policies that do not support the family as a caregiving unit, but instead randomly target the needs of individual family members.

Conflicting Definitions of Family

The development of social policies to assist families with impaired members is also frustrated by a lack of consensus on the definition of family. The following list presents examples of the proliferation of human relationships qualifying as families: (a) a nuclear group consisting of more than one generation; (b) divorced parents who remarried and are bringing up children in separate households; (c) aged or disabled parents who have adult children living in separate households; (d) a household that consists of unrelated and unmarried people; and (e) a network of close friends who are neighbors.

When the definition of family is fluid, it becomes difficult to establish policies that provide a similar level of access to different types of families. This dilemma is apparent in the long list of policy recommendations produced by the 1980 White House Conference on Families (White House Conference on Families, 1980). Some recommendations call for personnel policies (e.g., flex-time, parental leave) that would enable a family wage earner to work in addition to fulfilling her responsibilities to the impaired family member. Few recommendations encourage family members who wish to become full-time caretakers of the chronically ill.

This lack of definition may result in policies that support the social networks of some impaired persons but not of others. For example, new state regulations affecting employee benefit policies may allow a part-time worker to retain full health insurance benefits. This state regulation may aid a single working mother with a ventilator-dependent child but may also ignore the needs of an unemployed husband who is the sole caretaker of his wife with Alzheimer's disease. The variety of family constellations makes it difficult to develop comprehensive policies that will provide adequate levels of aid to families with impaired members.

Distrust of Centralized Control

United States society traditionally supports a decentralized social policy process that protects citizens from potential abuses of centralized authority. Our choice to split the development of social policy between the private, for-profit; public; and private, nonprofit sectors results in a trade-off between concentration of political and economic power and fragmentation of financing and services.

The fragmented nature of social service provision decreases citizens' awareness of the complex public policy process responsible for providing them with access to goods and services. Ignorance of the essential role of public policy facilitates the American ethic that stresses the virtue of self-reliance and distrust of government. These beliefs, combined with a fear of uncontrollable costs, prevent both lay persons and professionals from acknowledging that for most people personal security depends on a multitude of local, state, and federally funded government programs. All of these factors support the development of a social welfare system that places primary responsibility on individuals to care for themselves and their families in the event of disability or old age (Moroney, 1976).

This ethic of self-reliance in the face of adversity is a part of our national culture. It explains the complaint that it is unfair for middle-income workers in San Francisco to pay taxes that subsidize AFDC payments to poor mothers in Harlem. Yet if the middle-income worker develops multiple sclerosis, loses his job, and cannot support his family on disability payments, he expresses a latent desire to protect his "right" of access to a coordinated and rational system of social welfare.

In the 1980s access decisions are increasingly made on the basis of cost, discriminating against individuals without means of payment (Starr, 1986). The next section will define cost containment as well as discuss its implications for social policies that affect families with impaired members.

CURRENT POLICY PROPOSALS THAT AFFECT FAMILIES WITH IMPAIRED MEMBERS

Current policy proposals that aid vulnerable families are seriously considered only if they can demonstrate a capacity to contain costs (Steiner & Needleman, 1981). In addition, many of these social policies are actually designed to assist citizens whose need is less severe than the complex needs of the family with an impaired member. This section will introduce the concept of cost containment and then proceed to consider its implications for two policy proposals that are expected to assist one category of potentially vulnerable families, the elderly and their caretakers.

What Is Cost Containment?

Cost-containment mechanisms are currently included in almost all policies existing within the selective or competitive frameworks of social welfare. These mechanisms were developed in an effort to control the rampant health care inflation of the 1960s that resulted from private and public health insurance systems with limited cost controls (Schlenker & Shanks, 1983).

Cost-containment mechanisms are desirable because they force suppliers of health care to increase their efficiency. Three basic strategies are used by providers and payors of health care. The first is to deliver the same amount of services with fewer inputs (e.g., close down underutilized hospital beds). The second is to reduce the price paid for inputs (e.g., health care provider agrees to sell services to the payor at a discounted rate). The third is to deliver fewer services (e.g., shorten length of stay, give fewer diagnostic tests) (Fuchs, 1986b). The social policies discussed in this section use some or all of these methods.

Health care providers and payors are currently endorsing many new kinds of services and modes of financing because of their cost-saving potential. In some cases the cost-saving priority works to the benefit of the patient. For example, because an objective of cost-containment is to limit inappropriate utilization of health care, service delivery settings alternative to the hospital are gaining acceptance (Goldsmith, 1984). These alternative settings are now in demand by many health consumers and include innovations such as hospice care, adult day care, and outpatient surgery.

Program effectiveness is still judged primarily on the basis of cost rather than by the impact on patients and their families. Moreover, it is not clear that vulnerable families will have access to payors who reimburse for these services. Table 10.2 presents cost-containment mechanisms used by business and government.

These cost-containment mechanisms have five objectives: monitor and reduce utilization, deliver care in settings that are appropriate to the patient's severity of illness, increase the consumer's share of health care costs, allow employers to buy their employees' health care at discounted rates from providers who are believed to be cost-effective, and, finally, place a ceiling on the number of dollars spent for health care services. Hospitals, private employers, insurance companies, and the government are all experimenting with these forms of cost control. Payors and providers of services hope that these cost-containment strategies will not only eliminate unnecessary utilization of basic services but also control the use of expensive procedures and medical care.

Many of the services used by impaired persons with complex medical and social needs are not only expensive but are delivered in settings that are difficult to monitor by cost-conscious payors. In addition, many of the impaired person's medical needs present unlimited demand for home-based curative or supportive services. What criteria will be used to select populations who will receive less

Table 10.2
Some Health Care Cost-Containment Mechanisms
Used by Business and Government

Objective	Cost-Containment Mechanism
Monitor and reduce utilization of health care services	Preadmission testing
	Preadmission screening
	Discharge planning
	Hospital utilization review
	Hospital audit programs
	Peer Review Organizations (PROs)
	Second surgical opinions
Deliver services in settings appropriate to the consumer's severity and intensity of illness	Skilled nursing care
	Home health care
	Adult day care
	Hospice care
	Outpatient services (i.e., outpatient surgery)
Increase the consumer's share of health care costs	Deductibles
	Coinsurance
	Copayments
	Increased cost of health benefits if consumer does not practice health promotion (i.e. smokes, is overweight)
Allow employers to buy employee health care at discounted or fixed rates	Health Maintenance Organizations (HMOs)
	Preferred Provider Organizations (PPOs)
	Competitive medical plans
Place a ceiling on dollars spent for health care services	Diagnosis-related groups
	All-payor systems

care? What will happen to individuals who are chronically ill and need an array of medical care and social services?

These questions reveal a social problem of considerable magnitude when the current and future prevalence of chronic illness in the United States population is considered (Newacheck, Halfon, & Budetti, 1986; Waldo & Lazenby, 1984). It is inevitable that cost-containment strategies will restrict the range of services previously made available to certain categories of vulnerable citizens. As both the public and private health care delivery and finance systems become more selective, the impaired citizen's access to services will undoubtably decrease (United States Congressional Budget Office, 1985).

Cost Containment and Social Policy in Long-Term Care: Implications of Access to Care for Families with Impaired Members

The United States population is aging. This demographic change will increase the number of individuals who are disabled or functionally dependent as well as stimulate new markets for long-term care services (Rice & Estes, 1984). Long-term care describes the broad spectrum of services needed by persons who have lost all or some of their capacity to function due to a chronic illness or condition. In addition, chronically ill or impaired individuals often need services for an extended period of time. Government policymakers as well as private and public sector providers are under significant pressure to develop alternative means of delivering cost-effective care for this growing population. Two examples of policies that are currently being tested are private, long-term care insurance and Social Health Maintenance Organizations (Social HMOs).

Private, Long-Term Care Insurance

A number of commercial insurers and Blue Cross/Blue Shield plans are test marketing long-term care insurance for the elderly. These insurance plans provide coverage primarily for skilled nursing facilities but also include home health care and other support services (National Association of Insurance Commissioners, 1986). Trade organizations representing payors and providers of long-term care have undertaken an aggressive program to promote the development of such insurance benefits among their member organizations (Kirsch & Robertson, 1985). As a result of their efforts several insurance companies are test-marketing long-term care insurance products (Meiners, 1984). For example, 10 companies in four states are testing insurance for the chronically ill elderly that covers homemaker as well as home-health services (*New York Times*, 3/1/87).

Long-term care insurance may not be available to the majority of families with impaired members for three reasons. First, access to the insurance is limited to citizens employed by companies willing to provide such benefits. Because the cost of insurance bought outside of group plans is very high, few individuals will be able to afford its purchase (Knickman & McCall, 1986). Such barriers imposed by cost reinforce the notion that access to appropriate levels of health care should be made available to a privileged few. Access criteria based on employment status maintain a fragmented financing system.

Second, long-term care insurance for the elderly excludes over one-third of the population who are potentially in need of long-term care but are under age 65 (Weissert, 1983). Even if private, long-term care insurance for the elderly can be successfully developed, it is not clear that the nonelderly impaired will be sold policies to provide services during the youth, adolescent, or adult portions of their lives. The reason given by the insurance companies is cost. The elderly pay for their care by contributing premiums for many years. The insurers cannot afford to pay claims made by nonelderly persons with relatively short premium histories.

Finally, the future of private-sector-sponsored, long-term care insurance for the elderly is uncertain because insurance companies do not know how to price the product in order to guarantee a reasonable profit. For example, many goods and services needed by the chronically ill may not be covered because of an inability to price the beneficiary's unlimited demand (e.g., durable medical equipment, homemaker services (ICF, Inc., 1985). In addition, the inability to estimate the cost of long-term care insurance will restrict its availability to include only those elderly who are relatively healthy at the time the insurance is purchased. This is accomplished by not selling insurance policies to persons with potentially expensive preexisting conditions.

Long-term care insurance developed by private, for-profit sector organizations provides an example of a social policy originating in a competitive system of social welfare. A competitive social welfare system was defined earlier in this chapter as a system that makes benefits available to subsets of the population based on their ability to pay for services. It is clear that the underlying policy assumptions in private long-term care insurance will restrict its availability among many impaired persons who need services but do not have financial resources.

Social Health Maintenance Organizations

Health maintenance organizations (HMOs) are prepaid health plans that administer medical and preventive health services directly to consumers through specified providers. Consumers appreciate HMOs because they provide almost all basic medical care services for the price of the monthly premium. Health maintenance organizations were originally promoted by the federal government in the

1970s as a means of providing a cost-effective continuum of care with an emphasis on prevention and quality (Ellwood et al., 1973). In addition, they were expected to bring efficiency to the health care marketplace by providing a competitive alternative to traditional fee-for-service medicine (Brown, 1983).

Social health maintenance organizations (Social HMOs) were developed in the late 1970s by researchers at the Florence Heller School of Social Welfare at Brandeis University. The Social HMO augments the standard HMO model by providing a broader range of nonacute services. In 1980 the Health Care Financing Administration (HCFA) awarded the researchers from Brandeis a 3-year grant to develop the Social HMO concept into a model of service delivery for the impaired elderly. The Social HMO model was to become the cornerstone of a strategy to reform the United States' long-term care system.

The federal government supports the research and development of Social HMOs for two reasons. First, benefits offered to enrollees of Social HMOs include a full range of chronic care services, with an emphasis on community-based care. This service mix makes it possible for the Social HMO to provide appropriate levels of care for the impaired (Greenberg, Leutz, & Wallack, 1984).

Moreover, because Social HMOs assume complete risk for the health of the impaired enrollee, they have an incentive to deliver a range of services that will cover the enrollee's complex array of health care needs. This is to the enrollee's advantage because it is normally difficult to receive a broad range of case-managed services from separate providers under traditional health care financing systems (Greenberg & Leutz, 1985). In addition, Social HMOs make available at no or low cost items that patients require to proceed with the activities of daily living such as eyeglasses, walkers, and daily medications (National Association of Insurance Commissioners, 1986).

The second advantage of the Social HMO which motivated interest by the federal government was its promise as a tool to contain the cost of long-term care. Social HMOs are expected to control health care costs because payment for care delivered in a Social HMO setting is accomplished via capitation. Capitation is a form of financing where all services delivered by the HMO are purchased via a single prepaid fee. The financing principle of prepayment produces strong disincentives toward overutilization of health care services (Davis & Rowland, 1986).

In addition, Social HMOs control health care costs because the health plan's social services are used to substitute for more expensive (and inappropriate) medical services. The case management services of a Social HMO are also expected to control unnecessary utilization.

Social HMOs are currently a demonstration project funded by the federal government, and it is difficult to imagine their future in the health care marketplace after the government funding period is over. Because they are an alternative delivery system, Social HMOs must react to the competitive forces of the marketplace that force producers to be efficient. Competition comes from two major sources: standard HMOs and an additional form of alternative delivery system, the preferred provider organization (PPO), which lets the payor contract for health care services at a discounted rate.

The alternative delivery system industry is characterized by intense competition. Large insurance companies and multihospital chains have entered the HMO and PPO market, producing an oversupply of these delivery systems. The substantial financial and administrative resources of the large insurance companies and multihospital systems make it difficult for single marginal HMOs and PPOs to compete (Patricelli, 1986). For example, price wars waged by these alternative delivery systems make it difficult to compete for large employer contracts, which can guarantee enrollment of health care consumers (Gabel, et al., 1986; Billet & Cantor, 1985; Cost Management Report, 1986).

In addition, the alleged business strategy of competing alternative delivery systems is to enroll the healthiest strata of the population (Ginsburg & Hackbarth, 1986). Business sense dictates that individuals who are healthy enough to remain well after normal episodes of illness need fewer services. Healthy customers result in lower administrative costs, making it possible to offer potential enrollees a lower premium. Because the chronically ill population needs a wide variety of services, competing alternative delivery systems will not offer a full spectrum of services for the impaired.

Social HMOs will be left with the most expensive cases and will not survive in the marketplace. It will be difficult for Social HMOs to compete, because they are preferred setting for the chronically ill; the enhanced services of Social HMOs will inevitably attract patients who anticipate a need for medical care, increasing utilization costs. In order to make the services of Social HMOs available to the public, the government will have to subsidize the health care services delivered at rates that sustain the competitive edge of the Social HMO.

Respite Care: A Program in Search of a Policy

Respite care is offered as a benefit in some private, long-term care insurance proposals and in all of the Social HMO demonstration projects. This is fortuitous for two reasons. First, respite care is a service that appears to meet our social goal for vulnerable families—it directly promotes the family's autonomy by providing short-term substitute care that allows caretakers to resume their normal activities of daily living (Doty, 1986). Second, caretakers of the chronically ill prefer assistance in the form of services, such as respite care, rather than financial support (Horowitz & Shindelman, 1983).

The need for respite care is further substantiated by the high levels of strain experienced by caretakers (Brody, 1981; Cantor, 1983). Even though some families willingly provide for their impaired members (Liu, Manton, & Liu 1985), this strain can eventually destroy healthy patterns of family functioning, preventing the provision of care to impaired family members (Cantor, 1980). Respite care addresses this need by providing a psychological rest period from the stress of caring for vulnerable family members.

A strong cost-containment argument can be made in support of respite care services. For example, institutionalization of the chronically ill may be deterred or postponed by programs that increase the capacity of families to take care of their impaired members (Steiner & Needleman, 1981).

However, it is not clear that public and private policies will condone provision of this service. The reason given is cost; respite care presents unlimited demand for services in a setting that is difficult to monitor. In addition, a survey of substitute care in the adult day care setting demonstrated that government support of new familial support can lead to demand for expensive new public programs that compete for scarce public dollars (Harder, Gornick, & Burt, 1986). Some fear that the development of respite care services will likewise result in a new market for a service without sufficient private funding or cost controls.

There may be another reason why respite care is not fully supported in government and private plans; respite care can be perceived as a threat to the idealized role of the autonomous family in United States society. Those conservatives who oppose the public and private financing of respite care are concerned that the "substitute" quality of the service will encourage abandonment of family members and undermine the familial institution instead of providing an incentive to maintain the family's emotional health and equilibrium (Stone, 1985; Moroney, 1983).

Respite care is currently offered on a small scale by a handful of public and private providers around the country. However, until respite care programs are formally evaluated and shown to be cost effective, they will not be widely available to those in need.

CONCLUSION: PROMOTING FAMILY CAPACITY TO ASSIST THEIR IMPAIRED MEMBERS

Families with impaired members function in a political and economic environment that is biased against their interests. In an era of cost containment, the first priority of many social programs is to narrow the pool of potential beneficiaries by establishing restrictive eligibility criteria. As social programs become increasingly selective, vulnerable families may be excluded because they divert too many resources toward their catastrophic needs. The consequence will be a decrease in the capacity of these families to assist their impaired members.

Long-term care insurance and Social HMOs provide examples of innovations in long-term care that will inevitably exclude the most vulnerable citizens as long as these innovative systems exist in a competitive system of social welfare. Because services funded or delivered by these health care systems will be evaluated primarily on the basis of cost, many of the services needed by vulnerable families will not be provided. An example of this phenomenon is demonstrated by trends in the provision of respite care services.

Many services that might assist vulnerable families are not adequately funded because they are regarded as substitutes for familial responsibility. The perceived inability to prevent families from "abusing services" weakens an already inadequate social commitment to vulnerable families (Moroney, 1983). As a result, proposed social policies affecting families with impaired members are narrow in scope and tentative in commitment. This is expressed through inadequate budgets, narrow eligiblity categories, and short funding periods.

In this nation social policies affecting families are underwritten by a desire to return to the communal, voluntary model of service provision (Stone, 1985). This puts a damper on the hope that in the near future the public or private sectors will show a strong commitment to promoting a rational system of finance and delivery for families with impaired members. At its best, the role of social policy will be to increase the availability of selected support services to limited categories of potential recipients.

Until this nation supports a more universal system of social welfare, practitioners' obligations to their clients will extend beyond the clinical setting. Vulnerable families need practitioners who can successfully negotiate this nation's fragmented systems of social welfare for the benefit of the people whom they seek to help.

References

Adams, J. E., & Lindemann, E. (1974). Coping with long-term disability. In G. V. Coelho, D. A. Hamburg, & J. E. Adams (Eds.), *Coping and adaptation.* New York: Basic Books.

Allen, A. D., Affleck, G., Tennen, H., McGrade, B., & Ratzan, S. (1984). Concerns of children with a chronic illness: A cognitive-developmental study of juvenile diabetes. *Child: Care, Health and Development, 10,* 211–218.

Allen, D. A., & Affleck, G. (1985). Brief report: Are we stereotyping parents? A postscript to Blacher. *Mental Retardation, 23,* 200–202.

Anderson, B., & Palmore, Z. (1974). Longitudinal evolution of ocular function. In Z. Palmore (Ed.), *Normal aging.* Durham, NC: Duke University.

Anderson, B. J., & Auslander, W. F. (1980). Research on diabetes management and the family: A critique. *Diabetes Care, 3,* 696–702.

Anderson, B. J., Miller, J. P., Auslander, W. F., & Santiago, J. V. (1981). Family characteristics of diabetic adolescents: Relationship to metabolic control. *Diabetes Care, 4,* 586–594.

Antonovsky, A. (1979). *Health, stress and coping.* San Francisco: Jossey-Bass.

Atcherberg, J., Lawlis, G. F., Simonton, O. C., & Mathews-Simonton, S. (1977). Psychological factors and blood chemistries as disease outcome predictors for cancer patients. *Multivariate Experimental Clinical Research, 3,* 107–122.

Baker, B. (1984). Intervention with families with young, severely handicapped children. In J. Blacher (Ed.), *Severely handicapped young children and their families.* Orlando, FL: Academic Press, 319–375.

Baker, L., Minuchin, S., Milman, L. et al. (1975). Psychosomatic aspects of juvenile diabetes mellitus: A progress report. *Modern Problems in Pediatrics, 12.*

Baldwin, S. (1985). *The costs of caring: Families with disabled children.* Boston: Routledge & Kegan Paul.

Baldwin, S., & Glendinning, C. (1983). Employment, women, and their disabled children. In J. Finch, & D. Groves (Eds.), *A labour of love: women, work and caring.* Boston: Routledge & Kegan Paul.

Bardach, E. (1977). *The implementation game: What happens after a bill becomes a law.* Cambridge, MA: MIT Press.

Barsch, E. T., Moore, J. A., & Hamerlynck, L. A. (1983). The foster extended family: A support network for handicapped foster children. *Child Welfare, 62,* 349–359.

Barth, R. P., & Schinke, S. P. (1984). Enhancing the social supports of teenage mothers. *Social Casework, 65,* 523–531.

Bateson, G. (1972). *Steps to an ecology of the mind.* New York: Ballentine.

Bateson, G. (1979). *Mind and society.* New York: Dutton.

Bauer, R. A., & Gergen, K. J. (Eds.). (1968). *The study of policy formation.* New York: Free Press.

Beavers, W. R. (1982). Healthy, midrange, and severely dysfunctional families. In F. Walsh (Ed.), *Normal family processes.* New York: Guilford Press.

Beavers, W. R., & Voeller, M. M. (1983). Family models: Comparing and contrasting the Olson Circumplex Model with the Beavers Systems Model. *Family Process, 22,* 85–98.

Beck, A. T., Ward, C. H., Mendelson, M., Mock, J. E., & Erbaugh, J. K. (1961). An inventory for measuring depression. *Archives of General Psychiatry, 4,* 561–571.

Becker, E. (1973). *The denial of death.* New York: Free Press.

Bee, H. L., Hammond, M. A., Eyres, S. J., Barnard, K. E., & Snyder, C. (1986). The impact of parental life change on the early development of children. *Research in Nursing and Health, 9,* 65–74.

Bellah, R., Madsen, R., Swidler, A., Sullivan, W., & Tipton, S. M. (1985). *Habits of the heart: Individualism and commitment in American Life.* Berkeley, CA: University of California Press.

Berger, M., & Foster, M. (1976). Family level interventions of retarded children: A multivariate approach to issues and strategies. *Multivariate Experimental Clinical Research, 2,* 1–21.

Berger, M., & Foster, M. (1986). Applications of family therapy theory to research and interventions with families with mentally retarded children. In J. L. Gallagher & P. M. Vietze (Eds.), *Families of handicapped persons: Research, programs, and policy issues* (pp. 251–260). Baltimore: Brookes.

Berger, M., Jurkovic, G. J., & Associates. (1984). *Practicing family therapy in diverse settings.* San Francisco: Jossey-Bass.

Berki, S. E. (1983). Health care policy: Lessons from the past and issues of the future. *Annals of the American Academy of Political and Social Science, 468,* 231–246.

Bernheimer, L. P., Young, M. S., & Winton, P. J. (1983). Stress over time: Parents with young handicapped children. *Developmental and Behavioral Pediatrics, 4,* 177–181.

Bertalanffy, L. (1968). *General systems theory: Foundation, development, application.* New York: Brazillier.

Billet, T. C., & Cantor, J. A. (1985). Employers' experience with preferred provider organizations. *Compensation and Benefits Management,* (Autumn), 21–26.

Bishop, D. C., & Epstein, N. B. (1986). Family problems and disability. In D. S. Bishop (Ed.), *Behavior problems and the disabled: Assessment and management.* Baltimore, MD: Williams & Wilkins.

Blacher, J. (1984). Sequential stages of parental adjustment to the birth of a child with handicaps: Fact or artifact? *Mental Retardation, 22*(2), 55–68.

Blacher, J., Nihira, K., & Meyers, C. E. (1987). Characteristics of home environment of families with mentally retarded children: Comparison across levels of retardation. *American Journal of Mental Deficiency, 91,* 313–320.

Blackburn, J. A., & Chilman, C. S. (1986). *The probable impact of proposed legislative and budgetary changes on the lives of the elderly and their families.* Forthcoming.

Blumberg, E. M., West, P. H., & Ellis, F. W. (1954). A possible relationship between psychological factors and human cancer. *Psychosomatic Medicine, 16,* 277–286.

Blumenthal, M. D. (1969). Experiences of parents of retardates and children with cystic fibrosis. *Archives of General Psychiatry, 21,* 160–171.

Borrow, E. S., Avruskin, T. W., & Siller, J. (1985). Mother-daughter interaction and adherence to diabetes regimens. *Diabetes Care 8*(2), 146–151.

Boss, P. (1975a). *Psychological father absence and presence: A theoretical formulation for an investigation into family systems interaction.* Unpublished doctoral dissertation, University of Wisconsin-Madison.

Boss, P. (1975b). Psychological father presence in the missing-in-action (MIA) family: Its effects on family functioning. *Proceedings of the Third Annual Joint Medical*

Meeting Concerning POW/MIA Matters. San Diego, CA: Center for Prisoner Studies, Naval Health Research Center.

Boss, P. (1977). A clarification of the concept of psychological father presence in families experiencing ambiguity of boundary. *Journal of Marriage and the Family, 39*, 141–151.

Boss, P. (1980a). The relationship of wife's sex role perceptions, psychological father presence, and functioning in the ambiguous father-absent MIA family. *Journal of Marriage and the Family, 42*, 541–549.

Boss, P. (1980b). Normative family stress: Family boundary changes across the lifespan. *Family Relations, 29*, 445–450.

Boss, P. (1982). Family separation and boundary ambiguity. In I. Hultaker & J. Trost (Eds.), *The International Journal of Mass Emergencies and Disasters*. Sweden: International University Press.

Boss, P. (1983a). Family separation and boundary ambiguity. In O. Hultaker & J. Trost (Eds.), *Family and disaster: Vol. 1. The International Journal of Mass Emergencies and Disasters*. Sweden: International Library.

Boss, P. (1983b). The marital relationship: Boundaries and ambiguities. In C. Figley & H. McCubbin (Eds.), *Stress and the family*. New York: Plenum Press.

Boss, P. (1984, Fall). *Denial*. Agricultural Extension Service Publication (#HE-FS-2470).

Boss, P. (1984, Winter). *Ambiguity: A factor in family stress management*. Agricultural Extension Service Publication (#HE-FS-2469).

Boss, P. (1987). Family stress: Perception and context. In M. B. Sussman & S. Steinmetz (Eds.), *Handbook on marriage and the family*. New York: Plenum Press.

Boss, P. (1988). *Family stress management*. Newbury Park, CA: Sage.

Boss, P., & Greenberg, J. (1984). Family boundary ambiguity: A new variable in family stress theory. *Family Process*, 535–546.

Boss, P., Pearce-McCall, D., & Greenberg, J. (1986). *The normative stress of adolescents leaving home in mid-life families* (U.S.D.A. NC-#164 Regional Basebook Report). St. Paul, MN: University of Minnesota Agricultural Experiment Station.

Boss, P. G. (1979). Theoretical influences on family policy. *Journal of Home Economics*, Fall, 17–21.

Boszormenyi-Nagy, I., and Spark, G. (1973). *Invisible loyalties: Reciprocity in intergenerational family therapy*. New York: Harper & Row.

Bowen, M. (1976). *Family therapy in clinical practice*. New York: Jason Aronson.

Bowen, M. (1978). Theory in the practice of psychotherapy. In *Family therapy in clinical practice*. New York: Jason Aronson.

Boyle, I. R., diSant'Agnese, P. A., Sack, S., Millican, F., & Kulczycki, L. L. (1976). Emotional adjustment of adolescents and young adults with cystic fibrosis. *Pediatrics, 88*(2), 318–326.

Bracklehurst, J. C., & Hanley, T. (1981). *Geriatric medicine for students*. Edinburgh: Churchill Livingstone.

Bradley, C. (1979). Life events and the control of diabetes mellitus. *Journal of Psychosomatic Research, 23*, 159–162.

Bregman, A. M. (1980). Living with progressive childhood illness: Parental management of neuromuscular disease. *Social Work in Health Care, 5*, 387–408.

Breslau, N. (1983). Family care: Effects on siblings and mothers. In G. H. Thompson, I. L. Rubin, & R. M. Bilenker (Eds.), *Comprehensive management of cerebral palsy* (pp. 299–309). New York: Grune & Stratton.

Breslau, N. (1983a). Care of disabled children and women's time use. *Medical Care, 21,* 620–629.

Breslau, N. (1983b). Family care: Effects on siblings and mothers. In G. H. Thompson, I. L. Rubin, & R. M. Bilenker (Eds.), *Comprehensive management of cerebral palsy* (pp. 299–309). New York: Grune & Stratton.

Breslau, N. (1985). Psychiatric disorder in children with physical disabilities. *Journal of American Academy of Child Psychiatry, 24,* 87–94.

Breslau, N., Salkever, D., & Staruch, I. S. (1982). Women's labor force activity and responsibilities for disabled dependents: A study of families with disabled children. *Journal of Health and Social Behavior, 23,* 169–183.

Breslau, N., Staruch, K. S., & Mortimer, E. A., Jr. (1982). Psychological distress in mothers of disabled children. *American Journal of Disabled Children, 136,* 682–686.

Breslau, N., Weitzman, M., & Messenger, K. (1981). Psychologic functioning of siblings of disabled children. *Pediatrics, 67,* 344–353.

Brightman, R. P. (1984). Training parents as advocates for their developmentally disabled children. In J. M. Berg (Ed.), *Perspectives and progress in mental retardation* (Vol. 1, pp. 451–458). Baltimore: University Park Press.

Bristol, M. M. (1984). Family resources and successful adaptation to autistic children. In E. Schopler & G. Mesibov (Eds.), *The effects of autism on the family.* New York: Plenum Press.

Bristol, M. M., & Gallagher, J. J. (1986). Research on fathers of young handicapped children: Evolution, review, and some future directions. In J. J. Gallagher & P. M. Vietzer (Eds.), *Families of handicapped persons: Research, programs, and policy issues* (pp. 67–77). Baltimore: Brookes.

Bristol, M. M., & Schopler, E. (1984). A developmental perspective on stress and coping in families of autistic children. In J. Blacher (Ed.), *Severely handicapped young children and their families: Research in review.* New York: Academic Press.

Brody, E. M. (1981). Women in the middle and family help to older people. *The Gerontologist, 21,* 471–480.

Brody, E. M. (1985). Parent care as a normative family stress. *The Gerontologist, 25,* 19–29.

Brody, E. M., Kleban, M. H., Lawton, M. P., & Silverman, H. (1971). Excess disabilities of mentally impaired aged: Impact of individualized treatment, *The Gerontologist, 11,* 124–133.

Brody, G. H., & Stoneman, Z. (1986). Contextual issues in the study of sibling sociaization. In J. J. Gallagher & P. M. Vietze (Eds.), *Families of handicapped persons: Research, programs, and policy issues* (pp. 67–77). Baltimore: Brookes.

Brown, L. (1983). *Politics and health care organization: HMOs as federal policy.* Washington, DC: Brookings Institution.

Bruhn, J. G. (1977). Effects of chronic illness on the family. *Journal of Family Practice, 4*(6), 1057–1060.

Bruhn, J. G., Hampton, J. W., & Chandler, B. C. (1971). Clinical marginality and psychological adjustment in hemophilia. *Journal of Psychosomatic Research, 15,* 207–213.

Buckle, J. (1984). *Mental handicap costs more.* London: Disablement Income Group Charitable Trust.

Burish, G. G., & Bradley, L. A. (1983). Coping with chronic disease: Definitions and issues. In G. G. Burish & L. A. Bradley (Eds.), *Coping with chronic disease* (pp. 3–12). New York: Academic Press.

Burr, C. (1985). Impact on the family of a chronically ill child. In N. Hobbs & J. Perrin (Eds.), *Issues in the care of children with chronic illness* (pp. 24–40). New York: Academic Press.

Burr, W. R. (1973). *Theory construction and the sociology of the family*. New York: John Wiley.

Burton, L. (1973). Caring for children with cystic fibrosis. *Practitioner, 210*, 247–254.

Busch-Rossnagel, N. A., Peters, D. L., & Daly, M. J. (1984). Mothers of vulnerable and normal infants: More alike than different. *Family Relations, 33*, 149–154.

Busse, E. W., & Pfeiffer, E. (1973). Mental illness in later life. Washington, DC: American Psychiatric Association.

Butler, L. H., & Newacheck, P. W. (1981). Health and social factors relevant to long-term care. In J. Meltzer, F. Farrow, & H. Richman (Eds.), *Policy options in long-term care*. Chicago, IL: University of Chicago Press.

Butler, R. N., & Lewis, M. I. (1982). *Aging and mental health*. St. Louis, MO: C. V. Mosby.

Bywater, E. M. (1984). Coping with a life-threatening illness: An experiment in parents' groups. *British Journal of Social Work, 14*, 117–127.

Calabresi, G., & Bobbitt, P. (1978). *Tragic choices: Conflicts society confronts in the allocation of scarce resources*. New York: W. W. Norton.

Califano, J. A. (1986). *America's health care revolution: Who lives? Who dies? Who pays?* New York: Random House.

Callahan, J. J., Diamond, L. D., Giele, J. Z., & Morris, R. (1980). Responsibilities of families for their severely disabled elders. *Health Care Financing Review*, (Winter), 29–48.

Cantor, M. H. (1980, November). *Caring for the frail elderly: Impact on family, friends and neighbors*. Paper presented at the annual meeting of the Gerontological Society of America, San Diego, CA.

Cantor, M. H. (1983). Strain among caregivers: A study of experience in the United States. *Gerontologist, 23*, 597–602.

Cantor, M. H. (1985). Families: A basic source of long term care for the elderly. *Aging, 349*, 8–13.

Capra, F. (1982). *The turning point: Science, society, and the rising culture*. New York: Simon & Schuster.

Carter, E. A., & McGoldrick, M. (Eds.). (1980). *The family life cycle: A framework for family therapy*. New York: Gardner Press.

Carver, J., & Carver, N. (1972). *The family of the retarded child*. Syracuse, NY: Syracuse University Press.

Castellani, P. J., Downey, N., Tausig, M. B., & Bird, W. A. (1986). Availability and accessibility of family support services. *Mental Retardation, 24*, 71–79.

Cederblad, M., Helgesson, M., Larsson, Y., & Ludvigsson, J. (1982). Family structure and diabetes in children. *Pediatrics Adolescent Endocrinology, 10*, 247–254.

Cerreto, M. C., & Travis, L. B. (1984). Implications of psychological and family factors in the treatment of diabetes. *Pediatric Clinics of North America, 31*(3), 689–710.

Chenoweth, B., & Spencer B. (1986). Dementia: The experience of family caregivers. *The Gerontologist, 26*, 267–272.

Chesler, M. A., & Barbarin, O. A. (1984). Difficulties of providing help in a crisis: Relationships between parents of children with cancer and their friends. *Journal of Social Issues, 40*, 113–134.

Chetwynd, J. (1985). Incomes forgone in the home care of intellectually handicapped children. *Community Health Studies, IX,* 48–53.

Chilman, C. S. (1973). Programs for disadvantaged parents and their children. In B. Caldwell & H. Riciuti (Eds.), *Review of child development research.* Chicago: University of Chicago Press.

Chinitz, S. P. (1981). A sibling group for brothers and sisters of handicapped children. *Children Today, 10,* 21–23.

Chodoff, P., Friedman, S. B., & Hamburg, D. A. (1964). Stress, defenses and coping behavior: Observations in parents of children with malignant disease. *American Journal of Psychiatry, 120,* 743–749.

Chollet, D. (1984). *Employer-provided health benefits: Coverage, provisions and policy issues.* Washington, DC: Employee Benefit Research Institute.

Christensen, B., & DeBlassie, R. R. (1980). Counseling with parents of handicapped adolescents. *Adolescents, 15*(58), 397–407.

Cleveland, M. (1980). Family adaptation to traumatic spinal cord injury, response to crisis. *Family Relations, 29,* 558–565.

Cobb, S. (1982). Social support and health though the life course. In H. I. McCubbin, A. E. Cauble, & J. M. Patterson (Eds.), *Family, stress, coping and social support* (pp. 189–199). Springfield, IL: Charles C. Thomas.

Colletta, N. D. (1983). Stressful lives: The situation of divorced mothers and their children. *Journal of Divorce, 6,* 19–31.

Collins-Moore, M. S. (1984). Birth and diagnosis: A family crisis. In M. G. Eisenberg, L. C. Sutkin, & M. A. Jansen (Eds.), *Chronic illness and disability through the life span: Effects on self and family* (pp. 39–66). New York: Springer.

Combrinck-Graham, L. (1985). A developmental model for family systems. *Family Process, 24*(2), 139–150.

Combs-Orme, T., Reis, J., & Ward, L. D. (1985). Effectiveness of home visits by public health nurses in maternal and child health: An empirical review. *Public Health Reports, 100,* 490–498.

Comptroller General of the United States. (1977). *The well-being of older people in Cleveland, Ohio* (#R.D.-77-20). Washington, DC: U.S. General Accounting Office.

Congress takes on catastrophic illness. (1987, March 1). *The New York Times,* p. 5.

Cooke, K., & Lawton, D. (1985). Housing circumstances and standards of families with disabled children. *Child: Care, Health, and Development, 11,* 71–79.

Cost Management Report. (1986). Insurer-provider networks: A marketplace response. *Business and Health,* (January/February), 20–22.

Coulton, C. J. (1981). Person-environment fit as the focus in health care. *Social Work, 26,* 26–35.

Coupey, S. M., & Cohen, M. I. (1984). Special considerations for the health care of adolescents with chronic illness. *Pediatrics Clinics of North America, 31*(1), 211–219.

Cowen, L., Corey, M., Keenan, N., Simmons, R., Arndt, E., & Levison, H. (1985). Family adaptation and psychosocial adjustment to cystic fibrosis in the preschool child. *Social Science in Medicine, 20*(6), 553–560.

Crain, A. J., Sussman, M. B., Weil, W. B. J. (1966). Effect of a diabetic child on marital integration and related measures of family functioning. *Journal of Health and Human Behavior, 7,* 122–127.

Crnic, K. A., Friedrich, W. N., & Greenberg, M. T. (1983). Adaptation of families with mentally retarded children: A model of stress, coping, and family ecology. *American Journal of Mental Deficiency, 88,* 125–138.

Croog, S. H., Shapiro, D. S., & Levine, S. (1971). Denial among male heart patients: An empirical study. *Psychosomatic Medicine, 33,* 385–397.

Cunningham, C. (1985). Training and education approaches for parents of children with special needs. *British Journal of Medical Psychology, 58,* 285–305.

Dahl, D. (1983). Diagnosis of Alzheimer's disease. *Post Graduate Medicine, 73,* 212–216.

Darling, R. B. (1979). *Families against society.* Beverly Hills: Sage.

Darling, R. B., & Darling, J. (1982). *Children who are different: Meeting the challenge of birth defects in society.* St. Louis: C. V. Mosby.

Davidson, B., & Dosser, D. A., Jr. (1982). A support system for families with developmental disabled infants. *Family Relations, 31,* 259–299.

Davies, R. K., Quinlan, D. M., McKegney, P., & Kimball, C. P. (1973). Organic factors and psychological adjustment in advanced cancer patients. *Psychomatic Medicine, 35,* 464–471.

Davis, K., & Rowland, D. (1986). *Medicare policy: New directions for health and long-term care.* Baltimore: Johns Hopkins University Press.

Davis, K., Anderson, G., Schramm, C., Renn, S., & Steinberg, E. (1986). Rising health care costs: 1950–1985. In *Health care cost containment through provider payment reform: Lessons from the past and options for the future* (Chap. 4). Unpublished manuscript, Johns Hopkins University School of Hygiene and Public Health.

de Shazer, S. (1985). *Keys to solution in brief therapy.* New York: W. W. Norton, Inc.

de Tocqueville, A. (1848). *Democracy in America.*

Deford, F. (1983). *Alex: The life of a child.* New York: Viking Press.

DeJong, G. (1979). *The movement for independent living: Origins, ideology and implications for disability research.* East Lansing, MI: University Centre for International Rehabilitation, Michigan State University.

Derogatis, L. R., Abeloff, M. D., Melisartos, N. (1979). Psychological coping mechanisms and survival time in metastatic breast cancer. *Journal of the American Medical Association, 242,* 1504–1508.

Des Jardins, C. (1980a). *How to get services by being assertive.* Chicago: Coordinating Council for Handicapped Children.

Des Jardins, C. (1980b). *How to organize an effective parent/advocacy group and move bureaucracies.* Chicago: Coordinating Council for Handicapped Children.

Desonia, R., & King, K. (1985). *State programs of assistance for the medically indigent.* Washington, DC: Intergovernmental Health Policy Project, George Washington University.

Doherty, W. J. (1986). A missionary at work: A family therapist in a family medicine department. *Family Therapy Networkers, 10,* 65–68.

Doherty, W. J. (in press). Challenges in collaboration: Research and clinical issues. In C. R. Ramsey (Ed.), *The science of family medicine.* New York: Guilford Press.

Doherty, W. J., & Baird, M. A. (1983). *Family therapy and family medicine: Toward the primary care of families.* New York: Guilford Press.

Doherty, W. J., & Baird, M. A. (1987). *Family-centered medical care: A clinical casework.* New York: Guilford Press.

Doherty, W. J., & Burge, S. K. (1987). Attending to the context of family treatment: Pitfalls and prospects. *Journal of Marital and Family Therapy, 13,* 37–47.

Doherty, W. J., & Campbell, T. (in press). *Families and health.* Newbury Park, CA: Sage.

Dohrenwend, B. S. & Dohrenwend, B. P. (Eds.) (1981). *Stressful life events and their contexts.* New York: Prodist.

Doty, P. (1986). Family care of the elderly: The role of public policy. *Milbank Memorial Quarterly, 64*(1), 34–75.

Dovenmuehle, R. H., & Verwoerdt, A. (1963). Factors of length and severity of illness and frequency at hospitalization. *Journal of Gerntology, 18,* 260–266.

Drotar, D. (1981). Psychological perspectives in chronic childhood illness. *Journal of Pediatric Psychology, 6,* 211–228.

Drotar, D., Baskiewicz, A., Irvin, N. et al. (1975). The adaptation of parents to the birth of an infant with a congenital malformation: A hypothetical model. *Pediatrics, 56*(5), 710–717.

Drotar, D., Doershuk, C. F., Boat, T. F., Stern, R. C., Matthews, L., & Boyers, W. (1981). Psychosocial functioning of children with cystic fibrosis. *Pediatrics, 67,* 338–343.

Dushenko, T. W. (1981). Cystic fibrosis: A medical overview and critique of the psychological literature. *Social Science in Medicine, 15B,* 43–56.

Duvall, E. (1977). *Marriage and family development* (5th ed.). Philadelphia: Lippincott.

Edgar, E., & Hayden, A. H. (1984–1985). Who are the children special education should serve and how many children are there? *Journal of Special Education, 18,* 523–539.

Edelman, M. (1980). *Portrait of inequality: Black and white children in America.* Washington, DC: Children's Defense Fund.

Eheart, B. K., & Ciccone, J. (1982). Special needs of low-income mothers of developmentally delayed children. *American Journal of Mental Deficiency, 87,* 26–33.

Elliott, G. R., & Eisdorfer, C. (1982). *Stress and human health: Analysis and implications of research.* New York: Springer.

Ellwood, P. M., Donoghue, P. O., McClure, W., Holley, R., Carlson, R. & Hoagberg, E. (1973). *Assuring the quality of health care.* Minneapolis: InterStudy.

Engel, G. H. (1977). The need for a new medical model: A challenge for biomedicine. *Science, 196,* 129–136.

Engel, G. H. (1980). The clinical application of the biopsychosocial model. *American Journal of Psychiatry, 137,* 535–544.

Enthoven, A. (1980). *Health plan: The only practical solution to the soaring cost of medical care.* Reading, MA: Addison-Wesley.

Epstein, M. H., & Cullinan, D. (1984). Behavior problems of mildly handicapped and normal adolescents. *Journal of Clinical Child Psychology, 13,* 33–37.

Epstein, N. B., Bishop, D. S., & Levin, S. (1978). McMaster model of family functioning. *Journal of Marriage and Family Counseling, 4,* 19–31.

Erikson, E. H. (1963). *Childhood and society* (2nd ed.). New York: Norton.

Estes, C. J. (1982). *Fiscal crisis: Impact on aging services.* San Francisco, CA: Aging Health Center, University of California.

Etzwiler, D. D., & Sines, L. K. (1962). Juvenile diabetes and its management: Family, social and academic implications. *Journal of American Medical Association, 181,* 304–308.

Evans, R. G. (1984). *Strained mercy: The economics of Canadian health care.* Toronto: Butterworths.

Exton-Smith, A. N., & Overstall, P. W. (1979). *Geriatrics.* Baltimore, MD: University Park Press.

Fairfield, B. (1983). Workshops for siblings and parents. *Sibling information network newsletter, 2,* p. 5.

Farber, B. (1959). Effects of a severely mentally retarded child on family integration [Monograph]. *Social Research in Child Development, 24,* 1–112.

Farran, D., Haskin, R., & Gallagher, J. (1980). Poverty and mental retardation: A search for explanations. In J. Gallagher (Ed.), *New directions for exceptional children.* San Francisco: Jossey-Bass.

Featherstone, H. (1980). *A difference in the family.* New York: Basic Books.

Feder, J., Hadley, J., & Mullner, R. (1984). Falling through the cracks: Poverty, insurance coverage and hospital's care to the poor, 1980 and 1982. *Working Paper* (No. 3179-08). Washington, DC: Urban Institute.

Feetham, S. L., & Humenick, S. S. (1982). The Feetham Family Functioning Survey. In S. Humenick (Ed.), *An analysis of current assessment strategies in the health care of young children and childbearing families* (pp. 259–268). New York: Apapleton-Century-Crofts.

Feigon, J. (1981). A sibling group program. *Sibling information network newsletter, 1,* p. 2.

Feldman, W. S., Manella, K. J., & Varni, J. W. (1983). A behavioural parent training programme for single mothers of physically handicapped children. *Child: Care, Health and Development, 9,* 157–168.

Fengler, A. P., & Goodrich, N. (1979). Wives of elderly disabled men: The hidden patients. *The Gerontologist, 23,* 175–183.

Ferrari, M. (1984). Chronic illness: Psychosocial effects on siblings-I. Chronically ill boys. *Journal of Child Psychology and Psychiatry, 25*(3), 459–476.

Ferrari, M., Matthews, W. S., & Barabas, G. (1983). The family and the child with epilepsy. *Family Process, 22,* 53–59.

Figley, C. R., & McCubbin, H. I. (Eds.). (1983). *Stress and the family: Vol. II. Coping with catastrophe.* New York: Brunner/Mazel.

Firth, H. (1982). The effectiveness of parent workshops in a mental handicap service. *Child: Care, Health and Development, 8,* 77–91.

Foster, M., & Berger, M. (1985). Research with families with handicapped children: A multilevel systemic perspective. In L. L'Abate (Ed.), *The handbook of family psychology and therapy* (Vol. II, pp. 741–780). Homewood, IL: Dorsey Press.

Framo, J. (1976). Family of origin as therapeutic resource for adults in marital and family therapy. *Family Process, 15,* 193–210.

Frey, J. (1984). A family systems approach to illness-maintaining behaviors in chronically ill adolescents. *Family Process, 23,* 251–260.

Friedman, P. R. (1979). *Legal rights of mentally disabled persons.* New York: Practicing Law Institute.

Friedrich, W. N. (1979). Predictors of the coping behavior of mothers of handicapped children. *Journal of Consulting and Clinical Psychology, 47,* 1140–1141.

Frydman, M. I. (1980). Perception of illness severity and psychiatric symptoms in parents of chronically ill children. *Journal of Psychosomatic Research, 24,* 361–369.

Fuchs, V. R. (1986a). *The health economy.* Cambridge: Harvard University Press.

Fuchs, V. R. (1986b). Has cost-containment gone too far? *Milbank Memorial Quarterly, 64*(3), 479–488.

Funkenstein, H. H., Hicks, R., Dysken, M. W., & Davis, J. (1981). Drug treatment of cognitive impairment in Alzheimer's disease and the late life dementias. In N. E.

Miller & G. D. Cohen (Eds.), *Clinical aspects of Alzheimer's disease and senile dementia.* New York: Raven Press.

Gabel, J., Ermann, D., Rice, T., & deLissovoy, G. (1986). The emergency and future of PPOS. *Journal of Health Politics, Policy and Law, 11*(2), 305–322.

Gallagher, J. J., Beckman, P., & Cross, A. H. (1983). Families of handicapped children: Sources of stress and its amelioration. *Exceptional Children, 50,* 10–19.

Garbarino, J. (1983). Social support networks: Rx for the helping professions. In J. K. Whittaker & J. Garbarino & Associates (Eds.), *Social support networks: Informal helping in the human services.* New York: Aldine.

Gargiulo, R. M. (1985). *Working with parents of exceptional children: A guide for professionals.* Boston: Houghton Mifflin.

Gartner, A., & Reissman, F. (1984). Afterword. In A. Gartner & F. Reissman (Eds.), *The self-help revolution.* New York: Human Sciences Press.

Gath, A. (1973). The school-age siblings of mongol children. *British Journal of Psychiatry, 123,* 161.

Gath, A., Smith, M. A., & Baum, J. D. (1980). Emotional, behavioral and educational disorders in diabetic children. *Archives of Disorder of Children, 55,* 371–275.

George, L. (1986). Caregiver Burden: Conflict between norms of reciprocity and solidarity. In K. Pillemer & R. Wolf (Eds.), *Elder abuse–conflict in the family.* Dover, MA: Auburn House.

George, L. K., & Gwyther, L. P. (1986). Caregiver well-being: A multidimensional examination of family caregivers of demented adults. *The Gerontologist, 26,* 253–259.

German, M. L., & Maisto, A. A. (1982). The relationship of a perceived family support system to the institutional placement of mentally retarded children. *Education and Training of the Mentally Retarded, 17,* 17–23.

Giblin, P., Sprenkle, D. H., & Sheehan, R. (1985). Enrichment outcome research: A meta-analysis of premarital, marital and family interventions. *Journal of Marital and Family Therapy, 11,* 257–271.

Gilbert, N. (1983). Dilemmas of family policy. In *Capitalism and the welfare state: Dilemmas of social benevolence* (pp. 91–116). New Haven: Yale University Press.

Gilbert, N., & Specht, H. (1974). The basis of social allocations. In *Dimensions of social welfare policy* (pp. 54–80). Englewood Cliffs, NJ: Prentice-Hall.

Gilfix, M. (1984). Legal strategies for patient and family. *Generations, 9,* 46–48.

Gilgoff, I. S., & Dietrich, S. L. (1985). Neuromuscular diseases. In H. Hobbs & J. M. Perrin (Eds.), *Issues in the care of children with chronic illness* (pp. 183–195). San Francisco: Jossey-Bass.

Gilligan, C. (1982). *In a different voice.* Cambridge: Harvard University Press.

Ginsburg, P. G. (1983). Market oriented options in medicare and medicaid. In J. M. Meyer (Ed.), *Market reforms in health care* (pp. 103–118). Washington, DC: American Enterprise Institute for Public Policy Research.

Ginsburg, P. G., & Hackbarth, G. M. (1986). Alternative delivery systems and medicare. *Health Affairs, 5*(5), 7–22.

Glenn, M. L. (1987a). A treatment failure. In W. J. Doherty & M. A. Baird (Eds.), *Family-centered medical care: A clinical casebook.* New York: Guilford Press.

Glenn, M. L. (1987b). *Collaboration in medical care.* New York: Brunner/Mazel.

Glenn, M. L., Atkins, L., & Singer, R. (1984). Integrating a family therapist into a family medicine practice. *Family Systems Medicine, 2,* 137–145.

Glidden, L. M. (1986). Families who adopt mentally retarded children: Who, why, and what happens. In J. J. Gallagher & P. M. Vietze (Eds.), *Families of handicapped persons: Research, programs, and policy issues* (pp. 67–77). Baltimore: Brookes.

Goldberg, S., Marcovitch, S., MacGregor, D., & Lojkasek, M. (1986). Family responses to developmentally delayed preschoolers: Etiology and the father's role. *American Journal of Mental Deficiency, 90,* 610–617.

Goldfarb, A. I. (1967). Geriatric psychiatry. In A. M. Freeman & H. I. Kaplan (Eds.), *Comprehensive textbook of psychiatry.* Baltimore: Williams & Wilkins.

Goldsmith, J. (1981). *Can hospitals survive? The new competitive health care market.* Homewood, IL: Dow Jones–Irwin.

Goldsmith, J. (1984). Death of a paradigm: The challenge of competition. *Health Affairs,* (Fall), 5–19.

Goodin, R. (1985). *Protecting the vulnerable: A reanalysis of our social responsibilities.* Chicago: University of Chicago Press.

Goodman, C., Brown, D., Goodman, S., & Buffton, W. (1984). Independent living for learning disabled adults: An overview. In W. M. Cruickshank & J. M. Kliebhan (Eds.), *Early adolescence to early adulthood: Best of the Association for Children and Adults with Learning Disabilities* (Vol. 5, pp. 19–23). Syracuse, NY: Syracuse University Press.

Gortmaker, S. L., & Sappenfield, W. (1984). Chronic childhood disorders: Prevalence and impact. *Pediatrics Clinics of North America, 31,* 3–18.

Gottlieb, B. H. (1983). Social support as a focus for integrative research in psychology. *American Psychologist, 38,* 278–287.

Grad, J., & Sainsbury, P. (1963). Mental illness and the family. *Lancet, 1,* 544–547.

Graham, R. (1983). The United States health care system. In R. E. Rakel (Ed.), *Textbook of family practice.* Philadelphia: W. B. Saunders.

Grave, G. D. (1976). The impact of chronic childhood illnes on sibling development. In G. D. Grave & I. B. Pless (Eds.), *Chronic childhood illness: Assessment of Outcome* (DHEW Publication No. NIH 76-877, pp. 225–232).

Greenberg, J. N., & Leutz, W. N. (1985, January). *The social health maintenance organization and its role in reforming the long-term care system.* Paper presented at the Conference on Long-Term Care Financing and Delivery Systems: Exploring Some Alternatives. Health Care Financing Administration (HCFA), Washington, DC.

Greenberg, J. N., Leutz, W., & Wallack, S. S. (1984). The social health maintenance organization: A vertically integrated, prepaid care system for the elderly. *Healthcare Financial Management,* (October), 76–86.

Grey, M. J., Genel, M., & A Tamborlane, W. V. (1980). Psychosocial adjustment of latency-age diabetics: Determinants and relationship to control. *Pediatrics, 65,* 69–73.

Grinnell, R. M., Kyte, N. S., & Bostwick, G. J. (1981). Environmental modification. In A. N. Maluccio, *Promoting competence in clients.* New York: Free Press.

Grossman, H. J. (1983). *Classification in mental retardation.* Washington, DC: American Association on Mental Deficiency.

Groves, L., Lazarus, L. W., Newton, N., Frankel, R., Gutmann, D. L., & Ripeckyj, A. (1984). Brief psychotherapy with spouses of patients with Alzheimer's disease: Relief of the psychological burden. In L. W. Lazarus (Ed.), *Clinical approaches to psychotherapy with elderly.* Washington, DC: American Psychiatric Press.

Gurland, B., Dean, L., Craw, P., & Golden, R. (1980). The epidemiology of depression and delirium in the elderly: The use of multiple indicators of these conditions. In

J. O. Cole & J. E. Barret (Eds.), *Psychopathology in the aged*. New York: Raven Press.

Gwyther, L. P. (1985). Family therapy with older adults. *Generations, 10,* 42–45.

Hackett, T. P., Cassem, N. H., & Wishnie, H. A. (1968). The coronary-care unit: An appraisal of its psychologic hazards. *New England Journal of Medicine, 279,* 1365–1370.

Haley, J. (1976). *Problem solving therapy*. San Francisco: Jossey-Bass.

Halpern, P. L. (1985). Respite care and family functioning in families with retarded children. *Health and Social Work, 10,* 138–150.

Hambrecht, M. (1983). Inappropriate helping behavior and its impact on the identified patient. *Psychotherapy: Theory, Research, and Practice, 20,* 494–502.

Hamburg, B. A., Lipsett, L. F., Inoff, G. E., & Drash, A. L. (Eds.). (1980). *Behavioral and psychological issues in diabetes* (NIH Publication No. 80-1993). Washington, DC: U.S. Government Printing Office.

Hammill, D. D., Leigh, J. E., McNutt, G., & Larson, S. C. (1981). A new definition of learning disabilities. *Learning Disability Quarterly, 4,* 336–342.

Hansen, C. L., & Henggeler, S. W. (1984). Metabolic control in adolescents with diabetes: An examination of systemic variables. *Family Systems Medicine, 2,* 5–16.

Hansen, D., & Johnson V. (1979). Rethinking family stress theory: Definitional aspects. In W. Burr, R. Hill, I. Nye, I. Reiss (Eds.), *Contemporary theories of the family* (Vol. 1). New York: Free Press.

Harder, W. P., Gornick, J. C., & Burt, M. R. (1986). Adult day care: Substitute or supplement? *Milbank Memorial Quarterly, 64*(3), 414–441.

Hartford, M., & Parsons, R. (1982). Groups with relatives of dependent older adults. *The Gerontologist, 22,* 175–183.

Hauber, F. A., Bruininks, R. H., Hill, B. K., Lakin, C., Scheerenberger, R. C., & White, C. C. (1984). National census of residential facilities: A 1982 profile of facilities and residences. *American Journal of Mental Deficiency, 89,* 236–245.

Hauser, S. T., Jacobsen, A. M., Wertlieb, D., Weiss-Perry, B., Follansbee, D., Wolfsdorf, J., Herskowitz, R., Houlihan, J., & Rajapark, D. (1986). Children with recently diagnosed diabetes: Interactions within their families. *Health Psychology, 5*(3), 273–296.

Hauser, S. T., Jacobson, A. M., Wertlieb, D., Wolfsdorf, J., Hershkovitz, R., Vieyra, M. A., & Orleans, J. (in press). Family contexts of self-esteem and illness adjustment in diabetic and acutely ill children. In C. Ramsey (Ed.), *The science of family medicine*. New York: Guilford Press.

Havighurst, C. (1986). The changing locus of decision-making in the health care sector. *Journal of Health Politics, Policy and Law, 11*(4), 697–735.

Hayter, L. (1982). Helping families of patients with Alzheimer's disease. *Journal of gerontological nursing, 8,* 81–86.

Health Insurance Association of America. (1984). *A course in group life and health insurance*. Washington, DC: HIAA.

Heiby, E. M. (1982). A self-reinforcement questionnaire. *Behavior Research and Therapy, 20,* 397–401.

Herz, F. (1980). The impact of death and serious illness on the family life cycle. In E. A. Carter & M. McGoldrick (Eds.), *The family life cycle: A framework for family therapy*. New York: Gardner Press.

Hetherington, M. (1984). Stress and coping in children and families. In A. Doyle,

D. Gold & D. Moskowitz (Eds.), *Children in families under stress* (pp. 7–33). San Francisco: Jossey-Bass.

Hill, R. (1949). *Families under stress*. New York: Harper & Row. [Reprinted Westport, CT: Greenwood Press, 1971]

Hill, R. (1958). Social stress on the family. *Social Casework, 39,* 139–150.

Hirst, M. (1985b). Dependency and family care of young adults with disabilities. *Child: Care, Health, and Development, 11,* 241–257.

Hobbs, N., Perrin, J. M., & Ireys, H. T. (1985). *Chronically ill children and their families.* San Francisco: Jossey-Bass.

Hoffman, L. (1980). The life cycle and discontinuous change. In E. A. Carter & M. McGoldrick (Eds.), *The family life cycle: A framework for family therapy.* New York: Gardner Press.

Holland, J. M., & Hattersley, J. (1980). Parent support groups for the families of mentally handicapped children. *Child: Care, Health and Development, 6,* 165–173.

Holmes, D. M. (1986). The person and diabetes in psychosocial context. *Diabetes Care, 9*(2), 194–206.

Horan, P. F., Gwynn, C., & Renzi, D. (1986). Insulin-dependent diabetes mellitus and child abuse: Is there a relationship? *Diabetes Care, 9*(3), 302–307.

Hornby, G., & Singh, N. N. (1983). Group training for parents of mentally retarded children: A review and methodological analysis of behavioural studies. *Child: Care, Health and Development, 9,* 199–213.

Horowitz, A., & Shindelman, L. (1983). Social and economic incentives for family caregivers. *Health Care Financing Review, 5*(2), 25–33.

Hsia, Y. E., Hirschorn, K., Silverberg, R., & Godmilow, L. (Eds.). (1979). *Counseling in genetics.* New York: Alan R. Liss.

Huberty, T. J., Koller, J. R., & Ten Brink, T. D. (1980). Adaptive behavior in the definition of mental retardation. *Exceptional Children, 46,* 256–261.

Hull, K. (1979). *The rights of physically handicapped people.* New York: Avon Books.

Hurley, R. L. (1969). *Poverty and mental retardation: A causal relationship.* New York: Vintage Books.

Hyman, M. (1975). Social and psychological factors affecting disability among ambulatory patients. *Journal of Chronic Diseases, 28,* 199–216.

Hymovich, D. P., & Baker, C. D. (1985). The needs, concerns and coping of parents of children with cycstic fibrosis. *Family Relations, 34,* 91–97.

ICF, Inc. (1985, January). Private financing of long-term care: Current methods and resources—Phase I. *Final report submitted to the Office of the Assistant Secretary of Planning and Evaluation, Department of Health and Human Services.* Washington, DC: ICF, Inc.

Ilfeld, F. W., Jr. (1982). Marital stressors, coping styles, and symptoms of depression. In L. Goldberger & S. Breznitz (Eds.), *Handbook of stress: Theoretical and clinical aspects.* New York: Free Press.

Intagliata, J., & Doyle, N. (1984). Enhancing social support for parents of developmentally disabled children: Training in interpersonal problem solving skills. *Mental Retardation, 22,* 4–11.

Ireys, H. R., & Burr, C. K. (1984). Apart and a part: Family issues for young adults with chronic illness and disability. In M. G. Eisenberg, L. C. Sutkin, & M. A. Jansen (Eds.), *Chronic illness and disability through the life span: Effects on self and family.* New York: Springer Publishing.

Ireys, H. T., Hauck, R. J. P., & Perrin, J. M. (1985). Variability among state crippled children's service programs: Pluralism thrives. *American Journal of Public Health,* *75*(4), 375–381.

Jarvik, L., & Kumar, V. (1984a). Update on diagnosis—a complex problem. *Generations, 9,* 7–9.

Jarvik, L., & Kumar, V. (1984b). Update on treatment—most approaches still prove disappointing. *Generations, 9,* 10–11.

Jeger, A. M., & Slotnick, R. S. (1982). Streams of behavioral-ecology. In A. M. Jeger & R. S. Slotnick (Eds.). *Community mental health and behavioral-ecology: A handbook of theory, research and practice.* New York: Plenum Press.

Jessop, D. J., & Stein, R.E.K. (1985). Uncertainty and its relation to the psychological and social correlates of chronic illness in children. *Social Science in Medicine, 20*(10), 993–999.

Johnson, C. L. (1983). Dyadic family relations and social support. *The Gerontologist, 22,* 394–398.

Johnson, P. J. (1983). Divorced mother's management of responsibilities: Conflicts between employment and child care. *Journal of Family Issues, 4,* 83–103.

Johnson, S. B. (1980). Psychosocial factors in juvenile diabetes: A review. *Journal of Behavioral Medicine, 3,* 95–116.

Jones, M. (1985). *Homecare for the chronically ill or disabled child.* New York: Harper & Row.

Jones, W., & Walkover, M. (1984). *Pharmacy 2000: The chronic disease management center of the future.* San Francisco: The Healthcare, Organization and Management Group, Inc.

Kamerman, S.B., & Kahn, A.J. (1978). *Family policy: Government and family in fourteen countries.* New York: Columbia University Press.

Kamerman, S. B., & Kahn, A. J. (1976). *Social services in the United States: Policies and programs.* Philadelphia: Temple University Press.

Kamerman, S. B., & Kahn, A. J. (1983). Child support: Some international developments. In J. Cassety (Ed.), *The parental child-support obligation.* Lexington, MA: D. C. Heath.

Kane, R. L., & Kane, R. A. (1981). The extent and nature of public responsibility for long-term care. In J. Meltzer, F. Farrow, & F. Richman (Eds.), *Policy options in long-term care* (pp. 78–117). Chicago: University of Chicago Press.

Kaplan, D. M. (1968). Observations on crisis theory and practice. *Social Casework, 49,* 151–155.

Kart, C. S. (1985). *The realities of aging: An introduction to gerontology.* Newton, MA: Allyn & Bacon.

Kasl, S. V. (1982). Social and psychological factors affecting the course of disease: An epidemiological perspective. In D. Mechanic (Ed.), *Handbook of health, health care and the health profession.* New York: Free Press.

Katzman, R. (1976). The prevalence and malignancy of Alzheimer's disease—a major killer. *Archives of Neurology, 33,* 217–218.

Katzman, R. (1986). Alzheimer's disease. *New England Journal of Medicine, 314,* 964–973.

Kazak, A. E., & Marvin,. R. S. (1984). Differences, difficulties, and adaptaion: Stress and social networks in families with a handicapped child. *Family Relations, 33,* 66–77.

Kimmich, M. (1985). *America's children, who cares? Growing needs and declining assistance in the Reagan era.* Washingon, DC: Urban Institute Press.

Kirkham, M. A., Schilling, R. F., Norelius, K., & Schinke, S. P. (1986). Developing coping styles and social support networks: An intervention outcome study with mothers of handicapped children. *Child: Care, Health, and Development, 12,* 313–323.

Kirkham, M. K., Schinke, S. P., Schilling, R. F., Meltzer, N. J., & Norelius, K. L. (1986). Cognitive-behavioral skills, social supports, and child abuse potential among mothers of handicapped children. *Journal of Family Violence, 1,* 235–245.

Kirsch, L. J., & Robertson, P. (1985, March). *A preliminary reconnaissance of long-term care insurance: Report to Commissioner Peter Hiam. Commonwealth of Massachusetts.* Boston: Consumer Health Advocates.

Klaus, M. H., & Kennell, J. H. (Eds.). (1982). *Parent-infant bonding.* St. Louis: Mosby.

Kleinman, A. M. (1975). Explanatory models in health care relationships. In *Health of the family.* National Council for International Health Symposium, Washington, DC.

Kluborsky, L., & Spence, D. P. (1978). Quantitative research on psychoanalytic therapy. In S. L. Garfield & A. E. Bergin (Eds.), *Handbood of psychotherapy and behavior change: An empirical analysis.* New York: John Wiley.

Kluckhohn, F. R. (1960). Variations in the basic values of family systems. In N. W. Bell & E. F. Vogel (Eds.), *A modern introduction to the family* (pp. 304–315). Glencoe, IL: Free Press.

Klusa, Y., Habbick, B. F., & Abernathy, T. J. (1983). Diabetes in children: Family responses and control. *Psychosomatics, 24*(4), 367–372.

Knickman, J. R., & McCall, N. (1986). A prepaid managed approach to long-term care. *Health Affairs, 5*(5), 91–104.

Koch, R., & Dobson, J. C. (1976). The multidisciplinary team: A comprehensive program for diagnosis and treatment of the retarded. In R. Koch & J. C. Dobson (Eds.), *The mentally retarded child and his family: A multidisciplinary handbook* (rev. ed.). New York: Brunner/Mazel.

Kornblatt, E. S., & Heinrich, J. (1985). Needs and coping abilities in families of children with developmental disabilities. *Mental Retardation, 23,* 13–19.

Koski, M., & Kumento, A. (1977). The interrelationship between diabetic control and family life. In Z. Laron (Ed.), *Pediatric and adolescent endocrinology. Volume 3: Psychological aspects of balance of diabetes in juveniles* (pp. 41–45). New York: Karger.

Kramer, R. (1981). *Voluntary organizations in the welfare state.* Berkeley: University of California Press.

Krause-Eheart, B. (1981, April). *Special needs of low-income mothers of developmentally delayed children.* Paper presented at the National Conference of the Society for Research in Child Development, Boston, MA.

Lamm, S. S., Fisch, M. L., & McDonagh, D. (1982). *Learning disabilities explained: The Lamm Institute's guide to diagnosis, remediation, and help for your learning-disabled child.* Garden City, NY: Doubleday.

Langewell, K., & Moore, S. F. (1982). *A synthesis of research on competition in the financing and delivery of health services* (DHHS Publication No. PHS 83-3327). Washington, DC: U.S. Government Printing Office.

Lansky, S. G., Cairns, N. U., Hassanein, R., Wehr, J., & Lowman, J. T. (1978). Childhood cancer: Parental discord and divorce. *Pediatrics, 62,* 184–188.

Lavigne, J. V., & Ryan, M. (1979). Psychologic adjustment of siblings of children with chronic illness. *Pediatrics, 63,* 616–627.

Lazarus, R. S., & Folkman, S. (1984). *Stress, appraisal, and coping.* New York: Springer.

Lee, P. R., & Estes, C. L. (1983). New federalism and health policy. *Annals of the American Academy of Political and Social Science, 468,* 88–101.

Lefcourt, H. M. (1982). *Locus of control* (2nd ed.). Hillsdale, NJ: Lawrence Erlbaum.

Leinhardt, G., Pullay, A., & Bikel, W. (1981). *Unabled but still entitled: Toward more effective remediation.* Unpublished paper. Learning Research and Development Center, University of Pittsburgh.

Leutz, W. (1986). Long-term care for the elderly: Public dreams and private realities. *Inquiry, 23*(Summer), 140–375.

Levenson, H. (1973). Multidimensional locus of control in psychiatric patients. *Journal of Consulting and Clinical Psychology, 41,* 397–404.

Levenson, H. (1974). Activism and powerful others: Distinctions within the concept of internal-external control. *Journal of Pesonality Assessment, 38,* 377–383.

Levenson, H. (1975). Multidimensional locus of control in prison inmates. *Journal of Applied Social Psychology, 5,* 342–347.

Levine, S., & Ebert, R. R. (1983). *An exploratory study: Stress, coping and the role of social supports in families of handicapped children.* Final report to the William T. Grant Foundation.

Levinson, D. J. (1978). *The seasons of a man's life.* New York: Knopf.

Levinson, D. J. (1986). A conception of adult development. *American Psychologist, 41*(1), 3–13.

Levy, R. L. (1983). Social support and compliance: A selective review and critique of treatment integrity and outcome measurement. *Social Science and Medicine, 17,* 1329–1338.

Lewis, J. H., Beavers, W. R., Gossett, J. T., & Phillips, V. A. (1977). *No single thread: Psychological health in family systems.* New York: Brunner/Mazel.

Lezak, M. D. (1978). Living with the characterologically altered brain-injured patient. *Journal of Clinical Psychiatry, 39,* 592–599.

Lindeman, D., & Wood, J. (1985). *Home health care: Adaptations to the federal and state cost-containment environment.* San Francisco: Aging Health Policy Center, University of California, San Francisco.

Litman, T. J. (1974). The family as a basic unit in health and medical care. A social behavioral overview. *Social Science and Medicine, 8,* 495–519.

Liu, M., Manton, K., & Liu, M. (1985). Home care expenses for the disabled elderly. *Health Care Financing Review, 7*(2), 51–58.

Lopata, H. Z. (1973). *Widowhood in an American city.* Cambridge, MA: Schenkman.

Lorion, R. P. (1983). Evaluating preventive interventions: Guidelines for the serious social change agent. In R. D. Felner, L. A. Jason, J. N. Moritsugu, & S. S. Farber (Eds.), *Preventive psychology: Theory, research and practice.* New York: Pergamon.

Love, H. (1973). *The mentally retarded child and his family.* Springfield, IL: Charles C. Thomas.

Luborsky, L., & Spence, D. (1978). Quantitative research on psychoanalytic theory. In S. Garfield & A. Bergin (Eds.), *Handbook of psychotherapy and behavior.* New York: John Wiley & Sons.

Lynch, E. W. (1981). The social worker as part of an interdisciplinary team. In M. U. Dickerson (Ed.), *Social work practice with the mentally retarded.* New York: Free Press.

MacKinnon, C. E., Brody, G. H., & Stoneman, Z. (1982). The effects of divorce and maternal employment on the home environments of preschool children. *Child Development, 53,* 1392–1399.

Mace, N. L., & Rabins, P. V. (1981). *The 36-hour day. A family guide to caring for people with Alzheimer's disease, related dementing illnesses and memory loss in later life.* Baltimore: Johns Hopkins University.

Mace, N. L., & Rabins, P. V. (1984). Day care and dementia. *Generations, 9,* 41–44.

Magrab, P. B. (1985). Psychosocial development of chronically ill children. In N. Hobbs & J. Perrin (Eds.), *Issues in the care of children with chronic illness* (pp. 698–716). San Francisco: Jossey-Bass.

Marcus, G. R. (1980). *Gaps in employee benefit protection: A legislative response from the states* (Report No. 188 EPW). Washington, DC: Congressional Research Service, Education and Public Welfare Division.

Marmor, T. R., Schlesinger, M., & Smithey, R. (1986). A new look at non-profits: Health care policy in a competitive age. *Yale Journal on Regulation, 3*(2), 313–350.

Marrero, D. G., Jacobs, S. V., & Orr, D. P. (1981). The influence of social support on adolescent diabetic metabolic control. *Diabetes 31*(2), 12A.

Martini, L., & MacTurk, R. H. (1985). Issues in the enumeration of handicapping conditions in the United States. *Mental Retardation, 23,* 182–185.

Massie, R. K. (1985). The constant shadow. Reflections of the life of a chronically ill child. In N. Hobbs & J. Perrin (Eds.), *Issues in the care of children with chronic illness* (pp. 13–23). San Francisco: Jossey-Bass.

Masters, J. C., Cerreto, M. C., & Mendlowitz, D. R. (1983). The role of the family in coping with childhood chronic illness. In T. G. Burish & L. A. Bradley (Eds.), *Coping with chronic disease: Research and applications.* New York: Academic Press.

Mattsson, A. (1972). Long-term physical illness in childhood: A challenge to psychosocial adaptation. *Pediatrics, 50*(5), 801–811.

Matus, I., & Bush, D. (1979). Asthma attack frequency in a pediatric population. *Psychosomatic Medicine, 41,* 629–636.

McAnarney, E. D., Pless, I. B., Satterwhite, B., & Friedman, S. B. (1974). Psychological problems of children with chronic juvenile arthritis. *Pediatrics, 53,* 523–528.

McCann, J. (1986). Family oriented interventions in Alzheimer's care. *American Journal of Alzheimer's Care and Related Disorders, 1,* 16–21.

McCubbin, H., McCubbin, M., Patterson, J., Cauble, A., Wilson, L., & Warwick, W. (1983). CHIP—Coping health inventory for parents: An assessment of parental coping patterns in the care of the chronically ill child. *Journal of Marriage and the Family, 45,* 359–370.

McCubbin, H. I. (1979). Integrating coping behavior in family stress theory. *Journal of Marriage and the Family, 41,* 237–244.

McCubbin, H. I., & Figley, C. R. (1983). *Stress and the family. Volume 1: Coping with normative transitions.* New York: Brunner/Mazel.

McCubbin, H. I., & Patterson, J. (1983a). The family stress process: The double ABCX model of family adjustment and adaptation. In H. McCubbin, M. Sussman, & J. Patterson (Eds.), *Advances and developments in family stress theory and research* (pp. 7–37). New York: Haworth.

McCubbin, H. I., & Patterson, J. (1983b). Family stress and adaptation to crises: A double ABCX model of family behavior. In D. Olson & B. Miller (Eds.). *Family studies review yearbook* (pp. 87–106). Beverly Hills, CA: Sage.

McCubbin, H. I., Joy, C. B., Cauble, A. E., Comeau, J. E., Patterson, J. M., & Needle, R. H. (1980). Family stress and coping: A decade review. *Journal of Marriage and the Family, 42,* 855–871.

McCubbin, H. I., Nevin, R. S., Cauble, A. E., Larsen, A., Comeau, J. K., & Patterson, J. M. (1982). Family coping with chronic illness: The case of cerebral palsy. In H. I. McCubbin, A. E. Cauble, & J. M. Patterson (Eds.), *Family stress, coping, and social support* (pp. 169–188). Springfield, IL: Charles C. Thomas.

McCubbin, H. I., Olson, D., & Larsen, A. (1981). *F-COPES—Family crisis oreinted personal evaluation scales.* St. Paul, MN: Family Social Science, University of Minnesota.

McElgunn, B. (1984). Background on the Canadian ACLD definition adopted by CACLD, October 18, 1981. In W. M. Cruickshank & J. M. Kliebhan (Eds.), *Early adolescence to early adulthood: Best of the Association for Children and Adults with Learning Disabilities* (Vol. 5, pp. 19–23). Syracuse, NY: Syracuse University Press.

McGoldrick, M., & Gerson, R. (1985). *Genograms in family assessment.* New York: Norton Press.

McGoldrick, M., & Walsh, F. (1983). A systemic view of family history and loss. In M. Aronson & L. Wolberg (Eds.), *Group and family therapy 1983.* New York: Brunner/Mazel.

McGoldrick, M., Pearce, J. K., & Giordano, J. (1982). *Ethnicity and family therapy.* New York: Guilford Press.

McGowan, B. G. (1983). Historical evolution of child welfare services: An examination of the sources of current problems and dilemmas. In B. G. McGowan and W. Meezan (Eds.), *Child welfare: Current dilemmas, future directions.* Itasca, IL: F. E. Peacock.

Mechanic, D. (1978). *Medical sociology* (2nd ed.). New York: Free Press.

Medicare: Twenty years later. (1985, July 22). *Medicine and Health Perspectives.*

Medicine and Health Perspectives. (1985). Medicare: Twenty Years Later. K. Glenn (Ed.). Newsletter, July 22. Washington, D.C.: McGraw-Hill.

Meiners, M. R. (1984, January), *The state of the art in long-term care insurance.* Paper presented at the Conference on Long-Term Care Financing and Delivery Systems: Exploring Some Alternatives. Washington, DC: Health Care Financing Administration (HCFA).

Menolasceno, F. (1977). A crisis model for helping parents to cope more effectively. In F. Menolascino (Ed.), *Challenges in mental retardation.* New York: Human Sciences Press.

Meyer, D. J., Vadasy, P. F., & Fewell, R. R. (1985a). *Sibshops: A handbook for implementing workshops for siblings of children with special needs.* Seattle: University of Washington Press.

Meyer, D. J., Vadasy, P. F., & Fewell, R. R. (1985b). *Living with a brother or sister with special needs.* Seattle: University of Washington Press.

Mink, I. T., Nihira, K., & Meyers, C. E. (1983). Taxonomy of family life styles: I. Homes with TMR children. *American Journal of Mental Deficiency, 87,* 484–497.

Minuchin, S. (1974). *Families and family therapy.* Cambridge, MA: Harvard University Press.

Minuchin, S., Baker, L., Rosman, B., Liebman, R., Milman, L., & Todd, T. (1975). A conceptual model of psychosomatic illness in children: Family organization and family therapy. *Archives of General Psychiatry, 32,* 1031–1038.

Minuchin, S., Rosman, B. L., & Baker, L. (1978). *Psychosomatic families.* Cambridge, MA: Harvard University Press.

Mitchell, C. M., Davidson, W. S., Chodakowski, J. A., & McVeigh, J. (1985). Intervention orientation: Quantification of "person-blame" versus "situation-blame" intervention philosophies. *American Journal of Community Psychology, 13,* 543–552.

Moldofsky, H., & Chester, W. J. (1970). Pain and mood patterns in patients with rheumatoid arthritis: A prospective study. *Psychosomatic Medicine, 32,* 309–318.

Monk, A. (1983). *Resolving grievances in the nursing home: A study of the ombudsman program.* New York: Columbia University Press.

Moos, R. H. (Ed.). (1984). *Coping with physical illness. 2: New perspectives.* New York: Plenum Press.

Moroney, R. M. (1976). *The family and the state: Considerations for social policy.* London: Longman.

Moroney, R. M. (1983). Families, care of the handicapped and public policy. *Home Health Care Services Quarterly, 3*(3/4), 188–212.

Morris, R. (1982). Caring for vulnerable family members: Alternative policy options. *Home Health Services Quarterly, 3*(3/4), 244–263.

Morris, R. (1985). The future challenge to the past: The case of the American Welfare State. *Journal of Social Policy, 13*(4), 383–416.

Moynihan, P. (1986). *Family and nation.* San Diego, CA: Harcourt Brace Jovanovich.

Murphy, A. M., Pueschel, S., Duffy, T., & Brady, E. (1976). Meeting with brothers and sisters of children with Down's syndrome. *Children Today, 6,* 20–23.

Murphy, M. A. (1982). The family with a handicapped child: A review of the literature. *Developmental and Behavioral Pediatrics, 3*(2), 73–82.

Myers, G. J., & Millsap, M. (1985). Spina bifida. In N. Hobbs & J. M. Perrin (Eds.), *Issues in the care of chronic children with chronic illness* (pp. 214–235). San Francisco: Jossey-Bass.

Myllyluoma, J., & Soldo, B. J. (1983). *Family caregivers to the elderly: Who are they?* Paper presented at the 33rd annual meeting of the Gerontological Society, San Diego, CA.

National Association of Insurance Commissioners (1986, December). *Long-term care insurance: An industry perspective on market development and consumer protection.* Kansas City: National Association of Insurance Commissioners.

National Center for Education Statistics (1985). *The school-aged handicapped* (Contract No. 300-83-0198). Washington, DC: U.S. Department of Education.

National Conference on Social Welfare (1985). *The report of the Committee on Economic Security of 1935 and other basis documents related to the development of the Social Security Act.* Washington, DC: Project on the Federal Social Role.

Neugarten, B. (1976). Adapation and the life cycle. *The Counseling Psychologist, 6*(1), 16–20.

Newacheck, P., Halfon, N., & Budetti, P. (1986). Prevalence of activity limiting chronic conditions among children based on household interviews. *Journal of Chronic Disease, 39*(3), 63–71.

Newbrough, J. R., Simpkins, C. G., & Mauer, M. A. (1985). A family development approach to studying factors in the management and control of childhood diabetes. *Diabetes Care, 8*(1), 83–92.

Nihira, K., Mink, I. T., & Meyers, C. E. (1985). Home environment and development of slow-learning adolescents: Reciprocal relations. *Developmental Psychology, 21,* 784–794.

O'Neill, J. (1965). Siblings of the retarded: II. Individual counseling. *Children, 12,* 226–229.

Olson, D., Sprenkle, D. H., & Russell, C. S. (1979). Circumplex model of marital and family systems I: Cohesion and adaptability dimensions, family types, and clinical applications. *Family Proces, 18,* 3–28.

Olson, D. H., McCubbin, H. I., Barnes, H., Larsen, A., Muxen, M., & Wilson, M. (1983). *Families: What makes them work.* Beverly Hills: Sage.

Olson, D. H., McCubbin, H. I., Barnes, H., Larsen, A., Muxen, M., & Wilson, M. (1982). *Family inventories.* (Available from Family Social Science, 290 McNeal Hall, University of Minnesota, St. Paul, MN 55108).

Olson, D. H., Sprenkle, D. H., & Russell, C. S. (1979). Circumplex model of marital and family systems I: Cohesion and adaptability dimensions, family types, and clinical applications. *Family Process, 18,* 3–28.

Orr, D. P., Golden, M. P., Myers, G., & Marrero, D. G. (1984). Characteristics of adolescents with poorly controlled diabetes referred to a tertiary care center. *Diabetes Care, 6*(2), 170–175.

Parents Educating Parents (1985). *Project PEP (Parents Educating Parents) parents' tool kit.* Renton, WA: Author. (Available from Project PEP, 1025 South Third Street, Renton, WA 98055.)

Parloff, M. B., Waskow, I. E., & Wolfe, B. E. (1978). Research on therapist variables in relation to process and outcome. In S. L. Garfield & A. E. Bergin (Eds.), *Handbook of psychotherapy and behavior change: An empirical analysis.* New York: John Wiley.

Parsons, T., & Bales, R. F. (1955). *Family socialization and interaction process.* Glencoe, IL: Free Press.

Patricelli, P. (1986). Musings of a blind man—Reflections on the health care industry. *Health Affairs, 5*(5), 128–134.

Patterson, J. (1985). Critical factors affecting family compliance with home treatment for children with cystic fibrosis. *Family Relations, 34,* 79–89.

Patterson, J. (in press). A family stress model: The family adjustment and adaptation response. In C. Ramsey (Ed.), *The science of family medicine.* New York: Guilford.

Patterson, J. (in press). Families experienceing stress: The family adjustment and adaptation response model. *Family Systems Medicine.*

Patterson, J., & McCubbin, H. (1985). *Family predictors of health changes in a child with cystic fibrosis.* Paper presented at annual meeting of North American Primary Care Research Group, Seattle, WA.

Patterson, J., & McCubbin, H. (1983a). Family stress and coping with chronic illness. In C. Figley & H. McCubbin (Eds.), *Stress and the fmaily: Volume 2. Coping with catastrophe* (pp. 21–38). New York: Brunner/Mazel.

Patterson, J., & McCubbin, H. (1983b). The impact of family life events and changes on the health of a chronically ill child. *Family Relations, 32,* 255–264.

Paul, N., & Grosser, G. (1965). Operational mourning and its role in conjoint family therapy. *Community Mental Health Journal, 1,* 339–345.

Penn, P. (1983). Coalitions and binding interactions in families with chronic illness. *Family Systems Medicine, 1*(2), 16–25.

Perrin, E. C., & Gerrity, P. S. (1984). Development of children with a chronic illness. *Pediatric Clinics of North America, 31,* 19–31.

Perrin, J. M. (1985). Introduction. In N. Hobbs & J. Perrin (Eds.), *Issues in the care of children with chronic illness* (pp. 1–10). San Francisco: Jossey-Bass.

Pfeiffer, E. (1977). *Behavior and adaptation in late life*. Boston: Little, Brown.

Phipps, P. M. (1982). The merging categories: Appropriate education or administration convenience? *Journal of Learning Disabilities, 15,* 153–154.

Piaget, J. (1952). *The origins of intelligence in children*. New York: International Universities Press.

Pizzo, P. (1983). Slouching towards Bethlehen: American federal policy perspectives towards children. In E. F. Zigler, S. L. Kagan, & E. Klugman (Eds.), *Children, families and government: perspectives on American social policy* (pp. 10–32). Cambridge: Cambridge University Press.

Platt, G., Spivack, J., & Swift, M. (1973). Problem-solving therapy with maladjusted groups. *Research and Evaluation Report,* Hahnemann Medical College and Hospital, Philadelphia, PA.

Pless, I. B., & Perrin, J. M. (1985). Issues common to a variety of illnesses. In N. Hobbs & J. M. Perrin (Eds.), *Issues in the care of children with chronic illness* (pp. 41–60). San Francisco: Jossey-Bass.

Polloway, E. A., Epstein, M. H., & Cullinan, D. (1985). Prevalence of behavior problems among educable mentally retarded students. *Education and Training of the Mentally Retarded, 20,* 3–13.

Polloway, E. A., Smith, J. D. (1983). Changes in mild mental retardation: Population, programs, and perspectives. *Exceptional Children, 50,* 149–159.

Poulshock, S. W., & Deimling, G. T. (1984). Families caring for elders in residence: Issues in the measurement of burden. *Journal of Gerontology, 39,* 230–239.

Powell, T. H., & Ogle, P. A. (1985). *Brothers and sisters—A special part of exceptional families*. Baltimore: Brookes.

Power, P. W. (1985). Family coping behaviors in chronic illness: A rehabilitation perspective. *Rehabilitation Literature, 16,* 78–83.

Power, P. W., & Orto, A.E.D. (1980). *Role of the family in the rehabilitation of the physically disabled*. Baltimore, MD: University Park Press.

President's Commission for the Study of Ethical Problems in Medicine and Biomedical and Behavioral Research (1983). *Securing access to care: The ethical implications of differences in the availability of health services: Vol. 1. Report.* Washington, DC: U.S. Government Printing Office.

Prieto-Bayard, M., & Baker, B. L. (1986). Parent training for Spanish-speaking families with a retarded child. *Journal of Community Psychology, 14,* 134–143.

Ptacek, L. P., Sommers, P. A., Graves, J., Lukowicz, P., Keena, E., Haglund, J., & Nycz, G. R. (1982). Respite care for families of children with severe handicaps: An evaluation study of parent statisfaction. *Journal of Community Psychology, 10,* 222–227.

Quarm, D. (1984). Sexual inequality: The high cost of leaving parenting to women. In K. M. Borman, D. Quarm, & S. Gideonse (Eds.), *Women in the workplace: Effects on families*. Norwood, NJ: Ablex.

Quine, L., & Pahl, J. (1985). Examining the causes of stress in families with severely mentally handicapped children. *British Journal of Social Work, 15,* 501–517.

Quine, L., & Pahl, J. (1986). First diagnosis of severe mental handicap: Characteristics of unsatisfactory encounters between doctors and parents. *Social Science and Medicine, 22,* 53–62.

Rabins, P. V., Mace, H. L., & Lucas, M. J. (1982). Impact of dementia on the family. *Journal of the American Medical Association, 248,* 333–335.

Ramey, C. T., Mills, P., Campbell, F. A., & O'Brien, C. (1975). Infant's home environments: A comparison of high-risk families and families from the general population. *American Journal of Mental Deficiency, 80,* 40–42.

Ransom, R. C. (1981). The rise of family medicine: New roles for behavioral science. *Marriage and Family Review, 4,* 31–72.

Reed, E. W., & Reed, S. C. (1965). *Mental retardation: A family study.* Philadelphia: W. B. Saunders.

Reiss, D. (1981). *The family's construction of reality.* Cambridge: Harvard University Press.

Rice, D., & Estes, C. (1984). Health of the elderly: Policy issues and challenges. *Health Affairs,* (Winter), 25–49.

Ritchie, K. (1980). Research note: Interaction in the families of epileptic children. *Journal of Child Psychology and Psychiatry, 22,* 65–71.

Roberts, J. (1984). Families with infants and young children who have special needs. In J. C. Hansen (Ed.), *Families with handicapped members* (pp. 1–17). Rockville, MD: Aspen Systems Corporation.

Robinson, E. A., Eyberg, S. M., & Ross, A. W. (1980). The standardization of an inventory of child conduct problem behaviors. *Journal of Clinical Child Psychology, 9,* 22–29.

Robinson, N. M., & Robinson, H. B. (1976). *The mentally retarded child: A psychological approach* (2nd ed.). New York: McGraw-Hill.

Roesel, R., & Lawlis, G. F. (1983). Divorce in families of genetically handicapped/mentally retarded individuals. *American Journal of Family Therapy, 11*(1), 45–50.

Rolland, J. S. (1984). Toward a psychosocial typology of chronic and life-threatening illness. *Family Systems Medicine, 2*(3), 245–263.

Rolland, J. S. (1987). Family systems and chronic illness: A typological model. *Journal of Psychotherapy and the Family, 3*(3), 143–168.

Rose, E., & Hardman, M. L. (1981). The abused mentally retarded child. *Education and Training of the Mentally Retarded, 16,* 114–118.

Rossi, A. S. (1985). *Gender and the life course.* New York: Aldine.

Roth, W. (1982). Poverty and the handicapped child. *Children and Youth Services Review, 4,* 67–75.

Rubin, A. (1985). Practice effectiveness: More grounds for optimism. *Social Work, 30,* 469–476.

Rubin, A., & Conway, P. G. (1985). Standards for determining the magnitude of relationships in social work research. *Social Work Research and Abstracts, 21,* 34–39.

Rucquoi, J. R. (1983). Genetic counselling and prenatal genetic evaluation. *Medicine of North America, 36,* 3359–3363.

Sabbeth, B. (1984). Understanding the impact of chronic childhood illness on families. *Pediatric Clinics of North America, 31*(1), 47–57.

Sabbeth, B. F., & Leventhal, J. M. (1984). Marital adjustment to chronic childhood illness: A critique of the literature. *Pediatrics, 73*(6), 762–768.

Sargent, J., & Baker, L. (1983). The sick child: Family complications. *Developmental and Behavioral Pediatrics, 4*(1), 50–56.

Sargent, J., Rosman, B., Baker, L., Nogueira, J., & Stanley, C. (1985). Family interaction and diabetic control. *Diabetes, 34,* 77A.

Satir, V. (1983). Conjoint family therapy (3rd ed.). Palo Alto, CA: Science and Behavior Books.

Satterwhite, B. B. (1978). Impact of chronic illness on child and family: An overview based on five surveys with implications for management. *International Journal of Rehabilitation Research, 1,* 7–17.

Savas, E. S. (1982). *Privatizing the public sector: How to shrink government.* Chatham: Chatham House Publishers, Inc.

Schaffer, H. R. (1964). The too cohesive family: AS form of group pathology. *International Journal of Social Psychiatry, 10,* 266–275.

Schalock, R. L., & Lilley, M. A. (1986). Placement from community-based mental retardation programs: How well do clients do after 8 to 10 years? *American Journal of Mental Deficiency, 90,* 669–676.

Schild, S. (1971). The family of the retarded child. In R. Koch (Ed.), *The mentally retarded child and his family: A multidisciplinary approach.* New York: Brunner/Mazel.

Schilling, R. F. (1987). Limitations of social support. *Social Service Review, 61,* 19–31.

Schilling, R. F., & Schinke, S. P. (1984a). Maltreatment and mental retardation. In J. M. Berg (Ed.), *Perspectives and progress in mental retardation* (Vol. I, pp. 11–22). Baltimore: University Park Press.

Schilling, R. F., & Schinke, S. P. (1984b). Personal coping and social support for parents of handicapped children. *Children and Youth Services Review, 6,* 195–206.

Schilling, R. F., Gilchrist, L. D., & Schinke, S. P. (1984). Coping and social support in families of developmentally disabled children. *Family Relations, 33,* 47–54.

Schilling, R. F., Kirkham, M. A., Snow, W. H., & Schinke, S. P. (1986). Single mothers with handicapped children: Different from their married counterparts? *Family Relations, 35,* 69–77.

Schilling, R. F., Schinke, S. P., & Kirkham, M. A. (1985). Coping with a handicapped child: Differences between mothers and fathers. *Social Science and Medicine, 21,* 857–863.

Schinke, S. P., Blythe, B. J., Schilling, R. F., & Barth, R. P. (1981). Neglect of mentally retarded persons. *Education and Training of the Mentally Retarded, 16,* 299–303.

Schinke, S. P., Gilchrist, L. D., & Blythe, B. J. (1980). Role of communication in the prevention of teenage pregnancy. *Health and Social Work, 5,* 54–59.

Schinke, S. P., Schilling, R. F., Barth, R. P., Gilchrist, L. D., & Maxwell, J. S. (1986). Stress-management intervention to prevent family violence. *Journal of Family Violence, 1,* 13–26.

Schlenker, R. E., & Shanks, N. H. (1983). The private sector and competition in health care markets. *Journal of Health Politics, Policy and Law, 8*(3), 598–606.

Schmale, A. H., & Iker, H. (1971). Hopelessness as a predictor of cervical cancer. *Social Science Medicine, 5,* 95–100.

Schmidt, G., Bonjean, M. J., Widem, A., Schefft, B., & Steele, D. (1986). *Brief psychotherapy for caregivers of demented relatives: Comparison of two therapeutic strategies.* Paper presented at the 39th annual scientific meeting of the Gerontological Society, Chicago, IL.

Schorr, A. (1986). *Common decency.* New Haven: Yale University Press.

Schreiber, M., & Feeley, M. (1965). Siblings of the retarded: I. A guided group experience. *Children, 12,* 221–229.

Schultz, R., & Rau, M. T. (1985). Social support through the life course. In S. Cohen, & S. L. Syme (Eds.), *Social support and health* (pp. 129–149). Orlando, FL: Academic Press.

Schultze, C. (1977). *The public use of private interest.* Washington, DC: Brookings Institution.

Seelback, W. C. (1978). Correlates of aged parents' filial responsibility expectations and realization. *Family Coordinator, 27,* 341–350.

Seltzer, G. B. (1983). Systems of classification. In J. L. Matson & J. A. Mulick (Eds.), *Handbook of mental retardation* (pp. 143–155). New York: Pergamon Press.

Selvini-Palazolli, M., Boscolo, L., Cecchin, G., & Prata, G. (1980). The problem of the referring person. *Journal of Marital and Family Therapy, 6,* 3–9.

Shapiro, J. (1983). Family reactions and coping strategies in response to the physically ill or handicapped child: A review. *Social Science in Medicine, 17*(14), 913–931.

Sherman, B. R., & Cocozza, J. J. (1984). Stress in families of the developmentally disabled: A literature review of factors affecting the decision to seek out-of-home placement. *Family Relations, 33,* 95–103.

Shock, N. W. (1961). Physiological aspects of aging in man. *Annual Review of Physiology, 23,* 97–122.

Shortell, M. S., Morrison, E. M., Hughes, S. L., Friedman, B., Coverdill, J., & Berg, L. (1986). Hospital ownership and non-traditional services. *Health Affairs, 5*(4), 97–111.

Shouval, R., Ber, R., & Galatzer, A. (1982). Family social climate and the health status and social adaptation of diabetic youth. *Pediatric Adolescent Endocrinology, 10,* 89–93.

Silverman, P., & Smith, D. (1984). "Helping" in mutual help groups for the physically disabled. In A. Gartner & F. Reissman (Eds.), *The self-help revolution.* New York: Human Sciences Press.

Simeonsson, R. J., & Bailey, D. B. (1986). Siblings of handicapped children. In J. J. Gallagher & P. M. Vietze (Eds.), *Families of handicapped persons: Research, programs, and policy issues* (pp. 67–77). Baltimore: Brookes.

Simmons, R. J., Corey, M., Cowen, L., Keenan, N., Robertson, J., & Levison, H. (1985). Emotional adjustment of early adolescents with cystic fibrosis. *Psychosomatic Medicine, 47*(2), 111–121.

Simonds, J., Goldstein, D., Walker, B., & Rawlings, S. (1981). The relationship between psychological factors and blood glucose regulation in insulin-dependent diabetic adolescents. *Diabetes Care, 4*(6), 610–615.

Simonton, C. O., Mathews-Simonton, S., Sparks, T. F. (1980). Psychological intervention in the treatment of cancer. *Psychosomatics, 21*(3), 226–233.

Sinclair, E. (1983). Education assessment. In J. L. Matson & J. A. Mulick (Eds.), *Handbook of mental retardation* (pp. 245–255). New York: Pergamon Press.

Skrtic, T. M., Summers, J. A., Brotherson, M. J., & Turnbull, A. P. (1984). Severely handicapped children and their brothers and sisters. In J. Blacher (Ed.), *Severely handicapped young children and their families.* New York: Academic.

Slater, S. B., Sussman, M. B., & Stroud, M. W. (1970). Participation in household activities as a prognostic factor for rehabilitation. *Archives of Physical Medicine and Rehabilitation, 51* 605–611.

Smith, G. (1986). A patient's view of cystic fibrosis. *Journal of Adolescent Health Care, 7,* 134–138.

Soldo, B. (1980). America's elderly in the 1980's. *Population Bulletin, 35* (November).

Solnit, A. J., & Stark, M. H. (1961). Mourning and the birth of a defective child. *Psychoanalytic Study of Child, 16,* 523–537.

Somers, A. (1986). The changing demand for health services: A historical perspective and some thoughts for the future. *Inquiry, 23* (Winter), 395–492.

Sourkes, B. M. (1982) *The deepening shade: Psychological aspects of long-term illness.* Pittsburgh: University of Pittsburgh Press.

Starr, P. (1986). Health care for the poor: The past twenty years. In S. Danziger & D. Weinberg (Eds.), *Fighting poverty: What works and what doesn't*. Cambridge: Harvard University Press.

Stein, R.E.K, & Jessop, D. J. (1984). Does pediatric home care make a difference for children with chronic illness? Findings from a pediatric ambulatory care treatment study. *Pediatrics, 73*(6), 845–853.

Steinberg, F. U. (1976). *Cowdry's the care of the geriatric patient*. St. Louis, MO: C. V. Mosby.

Steiner, P. A., & Needleman, J. (1981). *Cost-containment in long-term care: Options and issues in state program design* (Contract No. 233-79-3-18). Washington, DC: National Center for Health Services Research, Statistics and Technology.

Steinhauer, P. D., Mushin, D. N., & Rae-Grant, Q. (1974). Psychological aspects of chronic illness. *Pediatrics Clinics of North America, 21*, 825–840.

Steinhausen, H., Borner, S., & Koepp, P. (1977). The personality of juvenile diabetics. In Z. Laron (Ed.), *Pediatric adolescent endocrinology* (Vol. 3, pp. 1–7). Basel: Karger.

Stewart, J. C. (1978). *Counseling parents of exceptional children*. Columbus, OH: Charles E. Merrill.

Stone, R. (1985). *Recent developments in respite care services for caregivers of the impaired elderly* (Policy Paper No. 17). San Francisco: University of California, Aging Health Policy Center.

Stone, R., Cafferata, G. L., & Sangl, J. (1986). *Caregivers of the frail elderly: A national profile*. Rockville, MD: National Center for Health Services Research, Publications and Information Branch.

Strauss, A. L. (1975). *Chronic illness and the quality of life*. St. Louis: Mosby.

Strauss, A. L., Corbin, J., Fagerhaugh, S., Glaser, B., Maines, D., Suczek, B., & Wiener, C. (1984). *Chronic illness and the quality of life* (2nd ed.). St. Louis: C. V. Mosby.

Strunk, R. C., Mrazek, D. A., Wolfson-Fuhrmann, G. S., & Labrecque, J. F. (1985). Physiologic and psychological characteristics associated with deaths due to asthma in childhood. *Journal of American Medical Association, 254*(9), 1193–1198.

Summers, J. A. (1981). The definition of developmental disabilities: A concept in transition. *Mental Retardation, 19*, 259–265.

Suran, B. G., & Rizzo, J. V. (1979). *Special children: An integrative approach*. Glenview, IL: Scott Foresman.

Sussman, M. B., & Slater, S. B. (1971). Reappraisal of urban kin networks: Empirical evidence. *The Annals, 396*, 40.

Sutkin, L. C. (1984). Introduction. In M. G. Eisenberg, L. C. Sutkin, & M. A. Jansen (Eds.), *Chronic illness and disability through the life span* (pp. 1–19). New York: Springer.

Swanson, D. W., & Maruta, J. (1980). The family's viewpoint of chronic pain. *Pain, 8*, 163–166.

Swoap, D. B. (1984). Beyond DRG's: Shifting the risk to providers. *Health Affairs, 3*(4), 117–121.

Tavormina, J. B., Boll, T. J., Dunn, N. J., Luscomb, R. L., & Taylor, J. R. (1981). Psychological effects on parents of raising a physically handicapped child. *Journal of Abnormal Child Psychology, 9*(1), 121–131.

Tavormina, J. B., Kastner, L. S., Slater, P. M., & Watt, S. L. (1976). Chronically ill children: A psychologically and emotionally deviant population. *Journal of Abnormal Child Psychology, 4*(2), 99–109.

Telzrow, C. F., & Hartlage, L. C. (1984). A neuropsychological model for vocational planning for learning disabled students. In W. M. Cruickshank & J. M. Kliebhan (Eds.), *Early adolescence to early adulthood: Best of the Association for Children and Adults with Learning Disabilities* (Vol. 5, pp. 19–23). Syracuse, NY: Syracuse.

Terkelson, K. (1980). Toward a theory of the family life cycle. In E. Carter & M. McGoldrick (Eds.), *The family life cycle*. New York: Gardner Press.

Thompson, L. W., Dis, G. C., Obrist, W. D., & Heuman, A. (1976). Effects of hyperbaric oxygen on behavioral and physiological measures in elderly demented patients. *Journal of Gerontology, 31*, 23–28.

Titmuss, R. M. (1974). *Social policy: An introduction*. New York: Pantheon Books.

Tobin, S., & Kulys, R. (1980). The family and services. In C. Eisdorfer (Ed.), *Annual review of gerontology and geriatrics* (Vol. 1). New York: Springer.

Toseland, R. W., & Rivas, R. F. (1984). *An introduction to group work practice*. New York: Macmillan.

Toseland, R. W., Denico, A., & Owen, M. L. (1984). Alzheimer's disease and related disorders: Assessment and intervention. *Health and Social Work, 9*, 212–226.

Townsend, J. (1986). Hospitals and their communities: A report on three case studies. In B. Gray (Ed.), *For-profit enterprise in health care* (pp. 458–473). Washington, DC: National Academy Press.

Traunstein, D. M. (1984). From mutual-aid self-help to professional service. *Social Casework, 65*, 622–627.

Travelers Insurance Company (1985). Survey shows many traveler's employees caring for relatives or friends. *News Summary, 12* (December).

Travis, G. (1976). *Chronic illness in children*. Stanford, CA: Stanford University Press.

Trevino, F. (1979). Siblings of handicapped children: Identifying those at risk. *Social Casework, 60*, 488–492.

Troll, L. E. (1971). The family of later life: A decade review. *Journal of Marriage and the Family, 33*, 263–290.

Tucker, J. A. (1980). Ethnic proportions in classes for the learning disabled: Issues in nonbiased assessment. *Journal of Special Education, 14*, 93–105.

Turk, J. (1964). Impact of cystic fibrosis on family functioning. *Pediatrics, 34*, 67–71.

Turnbull, A. P., Summers, J. A., & Brotherson, M. J. (1986). Family life cycle: Theoretical and empirical implications and future directions for families with mentally retarded members. In J. J. Gallagher & P. M. Vietze (Eds.), *Families of handicapped persons* (pp. 45–65). Baltimore: Brookes.

Tusink, J., & Mahler, S. (1984). Helping families cope with Alzheimer's disease. *Hospital and Community Psychiatry, 35*, 152–156.

Tymchuk, A. J. (1983). Interventions with parents of the mentally retarded. In J. L. Matson & J. A. Mulick (Eds.), *Handbook of mental retardation*. New York: Pergamon.

U.S. Bureau of the Census (1984). *Statistical abstract of the United States* (p. 144). Washington, DC: U.S. Government Printing Office.

U.S. Office of Special Education and Rehabilitative Services (1982). Assistance to states for education of handicapped children (P.L. 94–142 Regulations). *U.S. Code for Federal Regulations* (Part 300, pp. 781–857). Washington, DC: U.S. Department of Education.

Uhlenberg, P. (1980). Death and the family. *Journal of Family History, 5*(19), 313–320.

Ungerson, C. (1983). Why do women care? In J. Finch & D. Groves (Eds.), *A labour of love: Women, work and caring*. Boston: Routledge & Kegan Paul.

United States Bureau of Labor Statistics (1984). *Employment and earnings (January): Table 3*. Washington, DC: U.S. Government Printing Office.

United States Congressional Budget Office (1985, March). *An analysis of selected deficit reduction options affecting the elderly and disabled* (staff working paper).

United States Department of Education (1980). *Summary of existing legislation relating to the handicapped* (Publication No. E-80-22014). Washington, DC: U.S. Government Printing Office.

Vance, J., Fazan, L., & Satterwhite, B. (1980). Effects of nephrotic syndrome on the family: A controlled study. *Pediatrics, 65*, 948–956.

Venters, M. (1981). Familial coping with chronic and severe childhood illness: The case of cystic fibrosis. *Social Science and Medicine, 15A*, 289–297.

Verwoerdt, A. (1981). Individual psychotherapy in senile dementia. In N. Miller & G. Cohen (Eds.), *Clinical aspects of Alzheimer's disease and senile dementia*. New York: Raven Press.

Vietze, P. M., & Coates, D. L. (1986). Research with families of handicapped persons: Lessons from the past, plans for the future. In J. J. Gallagher & P. M. Vietze (Eds.), *Families of handicapped persons: Research, programs, and policy issues* (pp. 67–77). Baltimore: Brookes.

Viney, L. L., & Westbrook, M. T. (1981). Psychosocial reactions to chronic illness related disability as a function of its severity and type. *Journal of Psychosomatic Research, 25*(6), 513–523.

Voysey, M. (1972). Impression management by parents with disabled children. *Journal of Health and Social Behavior, 13*, 80–89.

Waldo, D., & Lazenby, H. (1984). Demographic characteristics and health care use expenditures by the aged in the United States: 1977–1984. *Health Care Financing Review, 6*(1), 1–29.

Walker, G. (1983). The pact: The caretaker-parent/ill-child coalition in families with chronic illness. *Family Systems Medicine, 1*(4), 6–30.

Wallston, B. S., Alagna, S. W., DeVellis, B. M., & DeVellis, R. F. (1983). Social support and physical health. *Health Psychology, 2*, 367–391.

Wallston, B. S., Wallston, K. A., Kaplan, G. D., & Maides, S. A. (1976). Development and validation of the health locus of control (HLC) scale. *Journal of Consulting and Clinical Psychology, 44*, 580–585.

Wallston, K. A., & Wallston, B. S. (1978). Development of the multidimensional health locus of control (MHLC) scales. *Health Education Monographs, 6*(2), 160–170.

Wang, H. A., & Whanger, Z. (1971). Brain impairment and longevity. In E. Palmer & F. C. Jeffers (Eds.), *Prediction of life span*. Lexington, MA: D.C. Heath.

Ware, L., & Carper, M. (1982). Living with Alzheimer's disease patients: Family stresses and coping mechanisms. *Psychotherapy: Theory, Research, and Practice, 19*, 472–481.

Washington Cofo Memo. (1986). December, VI, 4. Newsletter of the Coalition of Family Organizations. (Available from National Council on Family Relations, 1910 W. County Road B., St. Paul MN 55113.)

Wasserman, G. A., Allen, R., & Solomon, C. R. (1985a). At-risk toddlers and their mothers: The special case of physical handicap. *Child Development, 56*, 73–83.

Wasserman, G. A., Allen, R., & Solomon, C. R. (1985b). The behavioral development of physically handicapped children in the second year. *Developmental and Behavioral Pediatrics, 6*, 27–31.

Watzlawick, P., Weakland, J., & Fisch, R. (1974). *Change: Principles of problem formation and problem-resolution*. New York: Norton.

Weiss, H. M. (1983). Personal communication.

Weiss, S. M., Herd, J. A., & Fox, B. H. (Eds.). (1981). *Perspectives on behavioral medicine*. New York: Academic Press.

Weissert, W. (1983, July). *Size and characteristics of the non-institutional long-term care population*. Report prepared for the United States Department of Health and Human Services, Washington, DC.

Welford, A. (1980). Sensory, perceptual, and motor processes in older adults. In J. E. Birren & R. B. Sloane (Eds.), *Handbook of mental health and aging*. Englewood Cliffs, NJ: Prentice-Hall.

White House Conference on Families. (1980). *Listening to America's families: Action for the 80's. Summary of the Report to the President, Congress and Families of the Nation*. Washington, DC: U.S. Government Printing Office.

White, K., Kolman, M.L.W.P., Polin, G., & Winter, R. J. (1984). Unstable diabetes and unstable families: A psychosocial evaluation of diabetic children with recurrent ketoacidosis. *Pediatrics, 73*(6), 749–755.

Whitt, J. K. (1984). Children's adaptation to chronic illness and handicapping conditions. In M. G. Eisenberg, L. C. Sutkin, & M. A. Jansen (Eds.), *Chronic illness and disability through the life span* (pp. 69–102). New York: Springer.

Whittaker, J. K. (1974). *Social treatment: An approach to interpersonal helping*. Chicago: Aldine.

Whittaker, J. K. (1979). *Caring for troubled children*. San Francisco: Jossey-Bass.

Whittaker, J. K. (1983). Social support networks in child welfare. In J. K. Whittaker, J. Garbarino & Associates (Eds.), *Social support networks: Informal helping in the human services* (pp. 167–187). New York: Aldine.

Wikler, L. (1981). Chronic stresses of families of mentally retarded children. *Family Relations, 30*(2), 281–288.

Wikler, L. (1986). Periodic stress of families of older mentally retarded children: An exploratory study. *American Journal of Mental Deficiency, 90*, 703–706.

Wikler, L., Wasow, M., & Hatfield, E. (1981). Chronic sorrow revisited: Parent vs. professional depiction of the adjustment of parents of mentally retarded children. *American Journal of Orthopsychiatry, 51*(1), 63–70.

Wilensky, G. (1985). Access to care: Where are holes in the net? The plight of the uninsured. *Health Matrix, 3*(3), 8–10.

Wilensky, H. L., & Lebeaux, C. N. (1965). *Industrial society and social welfare*. New York: Free Press.

Williamson, P. S. (1985). Consequences for the family in chronic illness. *Journal of Family Practice, 21*(1), 23–32.

Wills, T. A. (1983). Social comparison in coping and help-seeking. *New Directions in Helping, 2*, 109–141.

Winik, L., Zetlin, A., & Kaufman, S. Z. (1985). Adult mildly retarded persons and their parents: The relationship between involvement and adjustment. *Applied Research in Mental Retardation, 6*, 409–419.

Wishner, W. J., & O'Brien, M. D. (1978). Diabetes and the family. *Medical Clinics of North America, 62*, 849–856.

Wolff, C. T., Friedman, S. B., Hofer, M. A., & Mason, J. W. (1964). Relationship between psychological defenses and mean urinary 17-hydroxy corticosteriod excretion rate. I. A predictive study of parents of fatally ill children. *Psychosomatic Medicine, 26*, 576–591.

Wolinsky, M. A. (1985). Consultation: A treatment model for aging and their families. *Social Casework, 66,* 540–546.

Wright, J. C., Mersheimer, W., Miller, D., & Rotman, D. (1976). *Cancer.* In F. U. Steinberg (Ed.), *Cowdry's the care of the geriatric patient.* St. Louis, MO: C. V. Mosby.

Wynne, L. C., McDaniel, S. H., & Weber, T. T. (1986). *Systems consultation: A new perspective for family therapy.* New York: Guilford Press.

Yoder, S. J. (1986). Profits and health care: An introduction to the issues. In B. Gray (Ed.), *For-profit enterprise in health care* (pp. 3–25). Washington, DC: National Academy Press.

Zarit, S. H., Reever, K. E., & Bach-Peterson, J. (1980). Relatives of the impaired elderly: Correlates of feelings of burden. *The Gerontologist, 20,* 649–655.

Zarit, S. H., & Zarit, J. M. (1982). Families under stress: Interventions for caregivers of senile dementia patients. *Psychotherapy: Theory, Research, and Practice, 19,* 461–471.

Zarit, S. H., Orr, N. K., & Zarit, J. M. (1985). *The hidden victims of Alzheimer's disease: Families under stress.* New York: University Press.

Zarit, S. H., Todd, P. A., & Zarit, J. M. (1986). Subjective burden of husband and wife caregivers: A longitudinal study. *The Gerontologist, 26,* 260–266.

Zborowski, M. (1969). *People in pain.* San Francisco: Jossey-Bass.

Zetlin, A. G., & Turner, J. L. (1985). Transition from adolescence to adulthood: Perspectives of mentally retarded individuals and their families. *American Journal of Mental Deficiency, 89,* 570–579.

Zigler, E., Balla, D., & Hodapp, R. (1984). On the definition and classification of mental retardation. *American Journal of Mental Deficiency, 89,* 215–230.

Zimmerman, S. (1982). Confusions and contradictions in family policy developments: Applications of a model. *Family Relations, 31,* 445–455.

Zimmerman, S. L. (1984). The Mental Retardation Family Subsidy Program: Its effects on families with a mentally handicapped child. *Family Relations, 33,* 105–118.

Zlatich, D., Kenny, T. J., Sila, U., & Huang, S. (1982). Parent-child life events: Relation to treatment in asthma. *Developmental and Behavioral Pediatrics, 3*(2), 69–72.

Zucman, E. (1982). *Childhood disability in the family.* New York: International Exchange of Information in Rehabilitation, World Rehabilitation Fund, Inc.

Zung, W.W.K., & Green, R. L., Jr. (1973). Detection of affective disorders in the aged. In C. Eisdorfer & W. E. Fann (Eds.), *Psychopharmacology and aging.* New York: Plenum Press.

Index

About the Editors and Authors

James Blackburn is Associate Professor at the School of Social Welfare and Senior Research Scientist at the Urban Research Center, University of Wisconsin-Milwaukee. He has a master's degree in social work and a Ph.D. in life-span human development from the University of Wisconsin-Madison. Dr. Blackburn's major research focus has been on cognitive and intellectual functioning in the elderly, and he has taught courses in life-span human development, family development, research methods, and gerontology.

Marilyn J. Bonjean, Ed.D., a clinical member and approved supervisor of the American Association for Marriage and Family Therapy, is in private practice at the Brief Family Therapy Center, Milwaukee, and is Director of Social Services at Marian Catholic Home, a 350-bed, long-term care facility. She teaches gerontology and family therapy at the University of Wisconsin-Milwaukee and has been a speaker and consultant for community programs for the elderly. Her publications for children of the aging include *Something for the Family, Making Visits Count,* and *In Support of Caregivers.* Her current research interest is the evaluation of techniques used in psychotherapy with older adults and their families.

Pauline Boss, Ph.D., is a professor in the Department of Family Social Science at the University of Minnesota and Director of the department's Marital and Family Therapy Program. Since receiving her doctorate in child development and family studies from the University of Wisconsin-Madison in 1975, Dr. Boss has conducted research on family stress and has been published in the areas of family stress management, ethics, and gender issues. The author of *Handbook on Marriage and the Family* and *Family Stress Management,* Dr. Boss's professional affiliations include the National Council on Family Relations, the American Family Therapy Association, the American Association of Marriage and Family Therapists, and the Groves Conference on Marriage and the Family.

Wayne Caron, M.A., is a Ph.D. student in the Department of Family Social Science, University of Minnesota, and a research assistant for Dr. Pauline Boss's family research project at the Alzheimer's Disease Clinical Research Center at the Minnesota Veterans Administration Medical Center. He has experience as a therapist and researcher working in the areas of divorce, family violence, marital relations, and aging.

Catherine S. Chilman, Professor Emeritus and part-time instructor at the School of Social Welfare, University of Wisconsin-Milwaukee, has her M.A. in social work from the University of Chicago and Ph.D. in psychology from Syracuse University. Her work experience includes direct service, administration, teaching, and research in the field of the family. Among other organizations, Dr. Chilman has served on the National Council on Family Relations, the Council on Social Work Education, the International Conference of Social Work, the American Psychological Association, and the Groves Conference on Marriage and the Family, of which she has been President. Her books include *Growing Up Poor, Your Child 6–12,* and *Adolescent Sexuality in a Changing American Society: Social and Psychological Perspectives for the Human Services Professions.*

Fred M. Cox is Dean and Professor of Social Work at the University of Wisconsin-Milwaukee School of Social Welfare. He earned the M.S.W. degree from the University of California in 1954 and the D.S.W. from the University of California at Berkeley in 1968. From 1954 through 1957 he was employed as a social worker with the Family Service Bureau in Oakland, California. His specialties are social welfare policy and community organization practice. He is principal editor of two works, *Strategies of Community Organization,* now in its fourth edition, and *Tactics and Techniques of Community Practice,* now in its second edition. He served as Secretary-Treasurer of the National Association of Deans and Directors of Schools of Social Work between 1985 and 1987 and was recently reelected to the Board of Directors of the Council on Social Work Education.

William J. Doherty is currently an Associate Professor in the Department of Family Social Science at the University of Minnesota. He has a Ph.D. in family studies from the University of Connecticut and has been a faculty member at the University of Iowa's Department of Family Practice and the University of Oklahoma's Department of Family Medicine. He has worked as both a therapist and a researcher in the area of families and health. His books include *Family Therapy and Family Medicine* (with Macaran Baird), *Family-Centered Medical Care: A Clinical Casebook* (with Macaran Baird), *Family Medicine: The Maturing of a Discipline* (with Charles Christianson and Marvin Sussman), and *Families and Health* (with Thomas Campbell).

Joan Horbal graduated summa cum laude from the University of Minnesota with a Bachelor of Arts degree in psychology and is currently a research interviewer with Dr. Pauline Boss's family research project at the Alzheimer's Disease Clinical Research Center at the Minnesota Veterans Administration Medical Center. She has experience in conducting family interaction research and served as a project coordinator for a study of outcomes in the treatment of depression.

Maura A. Kirkham is currently a doctoral candidate in social welfare at the University of Washington, where she received her M.S.W. in 1983. She has worked in the field of child welfare as a practitioner, researcher, and program evaluator and most recently directed several research projects designed to develop and evaluate interventions aimed at reducing stress, improving coping, and enhancing social networks in families with handicapped children.

Elam W. Nunnally is a family life educator who is a codesigner of the (Minnesota) Couple Communication Program. He is also a marriage and family therapist who assisted in the development of solution-focused brief therapy at the Brief Family Therapy Center in Milwaukee, where he has his practice. He is Associate Professor in the School of Social Welfare, University of Wisconsin-Milwaukee, where he teaches marriage and family therapy, family development, and courses in parenting and parent education. During his summers he teaches Couple Communication and brief therapy in Scandinavia. He coauthored *Alive and Aware, Talking Together, Straight Talk,* and articles on communication and brief therapy.

Joan M. Patterson, Assistant Professor at the University of Oklahoma Health Sciences Center in the Department of Family Medicine, has her M.A. and Ph.D. in family social science from the University of Minnesota. She is the Director of the Chronic Illness Center for Families, teaches family systems theory and intervention for medical practice, does family counseling, and directs several research projects, including a three-year study examining family adaptation after coronary angioplasty or bypass surgery. Her current research interests include family adaptation both to chronic illness and to normative life-cycle transitions, the biomedical impact of family stress, and family perceptions as they affect health and illness.

John S. Rolland, M.D., is currently Founder and Medical Director of the Center for Illness in Families in New Haven, Connecticut, and Assistant Professor in Psychiatry at the Yale University School of Medicine. He is also on the teaching faculty of the Family Institute of

Westchester in Mount Vernon, New York. Dr. Rolland has his M.D. degree from the University of Michigan and his residency training in community psychiatry from Yale, and he has been a fellow at the Institute for Social and Policy Studies at Yale. He has developed a subspecialty in the application of family systems theory to clinical practice with families facing chronic or life-threatening medical illnesses and has written extensively on this subject.

Robert F. Schilling, Assistant Professor at Columbia University School of Social Work, received his M.S. in social work from the University of Wisconsin-Madison and his Ph.D. in social welfare from the University of Washington. Before beginning his career in research and academia, he was a direct practitioner in child welfare and developmental disability settings. Dr. Schilling has conducted federally funded research on child maltreatment, social support, and families with disabled children; he has a particular interest in preventing social and health problems among disadvantaged populations.

Steven Paul Schinke, Professor at Columbia University School of Social Work, earned master's and Ph.D. degrees in social work at the University of Wisconsin-Madison. He has received numerous federal and private grants to test strategies to prevent adolescent pregnancy and drug abuse. Author, coauthor, and editor of three books, Dr. Schinke has published extensively in professional journals. His research interests focus on the application of skills-training approaches in preventing health problems among adolescents.

Margaret Walkover is an independent consultant in health policy research. She received a B.A. in social welfare from the University of California at Berkeley and a master's degree in public health from the Yale University School of Medicine. Her past experience includes management consulting in strategic planning for multihospital systems. In addition, she has served as a consultant to the Non-Profit Sector Project at the Urban Institute in Washington, D.C. Ms. Walkover is currently the health care editor of the *Yale Journal on Regulation*. Her academic and professional interests include the theory of public and private health insurance, welfare state policy and politics, and research in the design, implementation, and financing of health care delivery systems.

Carolyn Kott Washburne, who received her M.S.W. in community organization from the University of Pennsylvania School of Social Work, worked as a social worker for 15 years. She is now a freelance writer and editor and teaches English part-time at the University of Wisconsin-Milwaukee.